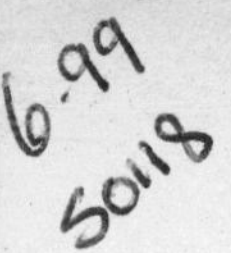

ben osborne

Ben Osborne writes about clubs and dance music for the *Guardian* and has contributed to the *Independent on Sunday* and numerous magazines including *i-D* and *Sky*. He has presented a dance music radio show on Xfm in London, and lives in Camden.

The A–Z of Club Culture

Twenty Years of Losing It

BEN OSBORNE

SCEPTRE

First published in 1999 by Hodder and Stoughton
A division of Hodder Headline PLC
A Sceptre Paperback

10 9 8 7 6 5 4 3 2 1

A CIP catalogue record for this book is
available from the British Library

ISBN 0 340 72824 8

Typeset by Palimpsest Book Production Limited,
Polmont, Stirlingshire
Printed and bound in Great Britain by
Clays Ltd, St Ives PLC, Bungay, Suffolk

Hodder and Stoughton
A division of Hodder Headline PLC
338 Euston Road
London NW1 3BH

For Ella, with all my love.

acknowledgements

Club culture has many narratives and this is only one account. Any mistakes or inaccuracies are entirely my own. I am indebted to many people and I've undoubtedly missed some – my apologies and thanks to anyone who's been omitted here.

I would first like to express my gratitude to friends who gave me information and helped me trace people. Several pints are on the way. Special thanks, too, are due to Clare James for being so patient and to Gary Crowley, Kirk Field, Mike Robinson and Dave Hill for filling in gaps and providing a book full of contacts and anecdotes.

The following have also been a considerable help in supplying facts and fables: Arthur Baker; Dave Beer; James Brown; Matthew Collins; Tom Whitwell and Viv Craske at Ministry; Mr C (a.k.a. Richard West); DJ Cam; Catrin Jones and Mau; Spiral Tribe; Richard at *Jockey Slut*; Mike Chadwick; Deep Dish (what Ali and Sharam don't know about Home Office bureaucracy isn't worth knowing); Eric and Gary at Potential Development; Tony Marcus; Andrea Daschner; Jeremy Case at *Sky* magazine; Ashley Beedle; Mimi Freestyle; DJ Harvey; Tina Jackson; Rupert Brewer (a.k.a. DJ Rupe); Matt Brown and the Sancho Panza sound system; Dina Cohen; Pete Herbert and the Atlas records boys; Ian and Woolfie at Appearing; Clare Craven and all at FFI; Emily at Main Source; Lorna (Bass Baby) and Alessandra at Italian Job; Simon 'FAZE Action' Lee; Dom Phillips and all at *Mixmag*; Maurice O'Hara; Marshall Jefferson; Richard Thair; Ali Friend, Hannah Poole and Sam Wollaston at the *Guardian* (who helped develop the original idea); Kevin Saunderson; Junior Sanchez; Roger Sanchez; DJ Sneak; James Snodgrass; Ricky Gervais; Dave, Sev, Jules and Billie at Nuphonic Records; Clare Sturgess, Frazer Lewry, Joe Chislet, Millie G, Ernesto Elule, Ginger Mick (Pelirocco) and Jane, DJ Ritu, David Sandhu, Jan Schmidt and all from April Records; Pete and Katrina Lawrence; Paul Gilmore; Gary Crossing; Justin Robertson; Justin Only Child and Luke Una Bomber; Mark Elliot; Tom Kihl; Gilles Peterson; Olaf Furnis; Tarba Gill; Isabelle at Concrete; Bob and Amon Dog; Mike Chadwick; Guy 'Gondwanna' Morely; John Dasilva; Mark Rae; Howie at Grande Central; Nicky Trulocke; George Power; Nicky Holloway; Nick Coleman; Jen McConachie; Corado and everyone who shared the good times.

My thanks also to *Mixmag* and *i-D* for allowing me to trawl their archives, use their photocopiers and generally be a pain around the office, and also to *DJ*, *Muzik*, *The Face* and *Jockey Slut* magazines.

There is a wealth of books on club culture but the following deserve a special mention: Matthew Collin's excellent *Altered State*; Jane Bussmann's highly amusing *Once In A Lifetime*, Colin Larkin's *The Guinness Who's Who of Rap, Dance and Techno* (a highly comprehensive work) and his *Virgin Encyclopedia of Popular Music.* Sue Tilley's biography of Leigh Bowery captures the man and his era, while Phil Johnson's *Straight Outa Bristol* and Martin James' *State Of Bass* are thorough accounts of the Bristol sound and the story of jungle. I hope *The A-Z of Club Culture* proves as enjoyable.

Finally a special thanks to my editor, Sarah Such, for guiding and inspiring me, and her worthy assistant Mary Wessel.

Ben Osborne

contents

a

A Guy Called Gerald A former collaborator with the Hit Squad and 808 State, with whom he penned 'Pacific', Gerald Simpson left the band and went on to produce his classic, 'Voodoo Ray'. The single peaked at number 12 in 1989 and had great influence prefiguring the musical development of dance in the early nineties.

An early pioneer of UK house, techno and drum 'n' bass, he started DJing in a youth club in the mid-eighties. A deal with CBS allowed him to start his own record label, Subscape, and he later formed Juicebox Records, named after his Juicebox collaboration with MC Tunes in 1992. His albums include 1988's *Hot Lemonade*, 1990's *Automanikk* and 1995's *Black Secret Technology*.

A Man Called Adam Formed around the nucleus of north London scene people Steve Jones and Sally Rogers, A Man Called Adam began life as a ten-piece Latin jazz outfit, performing at their own series of one-off parties in Soho in the mid-1980s.

As they progressed towards the close of the decade they successfully straddled house and acid jazz music, producing themic tracks such as 'APB' and 'Earthly Powers' for the Acid Jazz label in 1988, before signing on to Big Life. Their biggest hit came with 'Barefoot In The Head', while their combination of cool house tempos, jazz arrangements and Latin edge continued to mark them out as Ibiza favourites. Back in the UK they continued working in a jazz house vein, forming their own label and releasing their album, *Duende*, in summer 1998.

A Tribe Called Quest Formed in Manhattan by Q-Tip, Ali Shaheed Muhammad and Phife while they were still at school, A Tribe Called Quest started life as part of the Native Tongues collective – their new name was given them by Afrika Baby Bam from the Jungle Brothers. Debuting with 'Description Of A Fool' in August 1989, they found international success with 'Bonita Appelbum' in 1990, while Q-Tip appeared on Deee-Lite's smash hit, 'Groove Is In The Heart', in the same year. Riding on the crest of the jazz hip hop crossover of the early nineties, they scored again with the seminal 'Can I Kick It?' in 1991. As part of the Native Tongues they were influential in popularising the Africentricity movement, which sought to promote African awareness among black US citizens.

Although their third album, 1993's *Midnight Marauders*, made pointed references to the rise of gangsta rap, their positive sound was being eclipsed by gangsta rap by the mid-nineties. This didn't stop them being awarded Group of the Year by *The Source* magazine in 1994 – much to the outrage of Tupac, who reportedly threw them off stage.

'Aceeed!' Yelled by people in smiley T-shirts across the dance floors of 1987-8, aceeed! became the calling card of acid house and heralded the birth of the dance revolution that still grips us more than ten years later.

The music combined regular, four-four dance beats with squelchy electronic noises created by the Roland 303 – an instrument originally created as a guitarist's companion.

The term was used alongside other phrases that were invented to describe the feeling of taking 'E', such as 'Loved up' and 'On-one'. Acid should not to be confused with sixties slang for LSD, which is exactly what journalists did at the time.

Acid House According to urban mythology the acid house sound was invented when Chicago producer Marshall Jefferson and his younger protégé DJ Pierre were playing around on a Roland 303, under the influence of drugs and drink in 1986. Suddenly the machine started producing a weird squelching noise and, accidentally, the sound that was to shape the future of club culture was invented.

Alternatively there's the legend about the familiar acid squelches being discovered when Pierre's battery for his 303 went flat. Both are good stories, but then again so are the *Iliad* and the *Odyssey*.

Then there's the version that has DJ Pierre and his sidekick Spanky installing their new 303 in 1986 and trying to work out to how use it. Accidentally they stumbled across the acid bleeps as they tried to clear the sounds that were already programmed into the unit. While Pierre fiddled, Spanky played a break beat he'd already programmed. The result was recorded and passed on to Ron Hardy, who slipped it into his DJ sets. Soon Hardy's new sound was being referred to as his acid tracks.

Meanwhile Marshall Jefferson tells a story about a tune called 'I've Lost Control', which he produced for Ron Hardy's DJ set in 1985, using a 303 to create squelching noises. A couple of years later Jefferson was contacted by DJ Pierre, who asked him to produce a track he'd written using a 303. From there Phuture, the original acid house outfit, was formed.

Whereas Jefferson had used the 303 on 'I've Lost Control' to create more sparse effects, Pierre was overdriving his 303's modulation across whole tracks. The result, 'Acid Trax', was an immediate dance-floor hit in Chicago, but its lasting legacy was secured across the Atlantic in the UK.

Here the arrival of the acid sound coincided with the youth explosion around ecstasy culture and the Balearic scene. Although the acid title originally had no reference to drugs, the media in the UK quickly, and wrongly, associated the drug-induced mayhem of acid house parties with LSD and popularised the acid house tag to describe the scene taking off at clubs such as Shoom.

The association with sixties psychedelia was further cemented by the re-introduction of hippie icons (the smiley face), clothes (baggy T-shirts and long hair) and slogans ('turn on', 'tune in', 'drop out').

Acid Jazz An attitude rather than a genre of music and no relation to acid house, acid jazz has its distant roots in the jazz funk scene of the seventies and in bands such as the Meters and Funk Inc. It grew out of the mid-eighties London soul, hip hop, sound system and rare groove scene, epitomised by Norman Jay's Shake and Finger Pop parties and his legendary nights at the Bass Clef (now The Blue Note). The term acid jazz was popularised by DJ Gilles Peterson and Chris Bangs, who wanted to create a jazz scene that captured the energy of acid house.

Although acid house and acid jazz became increasingly divided with the onset of rave, the early days saw a large amount of crossover as Shoomers filed to Peterson's Sunday afternoon sessions at The Belvedere. Most of the punters, after all, came from the same roots. *Acid Jazz And Other Illicit Grooves* compilation albums further popularised the music.

The crowning glory came with the Sunday afternoon Dingwalls sessions Talkin' Loud And Saying Something, where bands such as the Brand New Heavies, Galliano and the Jazz Renegades played live sets between DJs Gilles Peterson and Patrick Forge. The Sunday session finally came to a close when the venue closed for redevelopment.

In its purest form bands such as the Brand New Heavies rose to stardom. The music however evolved with Galliano, Ronnie Jordan and others adding hip hop and with labels such as Mo Wax pushing musical boundaries into trip hop, beat music and drum 'n' bass.

Jazz heads pioneered much of the music that currently dominates clubs up and down the country. They're also responsible for convincing a generation of recordbag-carrying boys that Cat Weasel-style goatees look cool.

Acid Teds The first Balearic/Acid events at Shoom and the Ibiza Reunion Project were, as the name implies, cosy affairs where the Ibiza set of '87 relived the excitement of the previous summer.

As word spread about Shoom, mates let on to mates, who in turn let more people in on the secret. Soon old Shoomers were complaining the vibe had been ruined and their club hijacked by people who didn't understand it.

Jenni Rampling found herself policing the door and, flying in the face of the relaxed, loved up attitude the club espoused, began enforcing a strict door policy. The Balearic set hit back. Adopting the lingo of *The End* fanzine, which used 'ted' to describe the terminally uncool, the new arrivals in their copied acid house clothing were denounced as acid teds.

Who first coined the term is a matter for conspiracy theorists, but *Boy's Own* fanzine famously came up with the slogan 'Better dead than an acid ted', which kind of caught the mood.

Adrenaline Started by DJ Tony Wilson in October 1988, the Friday night Adrenaline was the first acid house club to be launched in the East End. Attracting custom from the harder edges of London, including football-terrace boot boys and East End gangs, their previously violent tendencies were tamed by ecstasy – a trend that was repeated across the country and showed up in official figures on football hooliganism.

Adrenaline consisted of a new breed of ravers who had little connection with the Balearic scene, which had started the acid house ball rolling.

Africa Centre A community centre-cum-club, the Africa Centre became the essential club of the mid- to late eighties. Here the two-step heroes Soul II Soul killed the tempo and united a collective of DJs and MCs who inspired the dance floor to wiggle, gyrate and sweat it out beneath the impossibly narrow balcony and drapes.

A small unpretentious club, it burst at the seams with a sussed, black music-orientated dance crowd. Here the Bristol and London scenes merged as Nellee Hooper, formerly of The Wild Bunch, joined with Soul II Soul's Jazzie B and Philip Harvey.

Having lost favour at the end of the decade, the venue became home to the long-running P-Funk and B-boy night, Funkin' Pussy, in 1994.

Afro Funk and Afro Beat One of the main driving forces behind world music in the UK, Afro funk combines US soul and funk themes with African tribal percussion rhythms and jilting rhythm guitar licks.

Among Afro funk artists a Nigerian pan-Africanist called Fela Kuti, who died of AIDS in August 1997, was undisputed king.

A larger than life and fiercely political character, with an equally large appetite for women, his songs could last for over an hour. Locked down in a churning groove, he would spike the riff with sermons on African social issues, such as greed and corruption, around which his jazz horn sections and a battalion of singers would stab and blast funky refrains.

His European influences derived from his musical training at London's Trinity College of Music, where he formed his first band. Returning to Nigeria, by the mid-seventies his band, Africa 70, were stars throughout Africa and he opened a night-club, The Shrine, in Lagos.

As Fela's reputation for pro-civil liberties and anti-government agitation grew, he started a commune, the Kalakuta Republic, which was promptly stormed by 1,000 government troops and raised to the ground. His response was to form his own political party, Movement of the People.

Other Afro funk artists of note include Benin's Angelique Kidjo, King Sunny Ade, Rai singer Cheb Khaled and Youssou N'dour.

Aga-Doo-Doo-Doo, Push Pineapple . . . If this phrase means anything to you, you've clearly been going to the wrong nights.

Alfredo Godfather of the Balearic sound, Alfredo was born in Argentina where he worked as a journalist before fleeing and settling in Ibiza. Securing his first DJ gig at a bar called Bebop in 1982, when the manager asked him to run the bar, Alfredo discovered how to work the mixer and became hooked.

In 1984 he became resident DJ at Amnesia, where his girlfriend suggested he continued to play music while the staff were counting the night's takings after the club had closed. His DJ sets developed into legendary, seven-hour marathons and soon the club's opening hours were revolving around him opening at 3 a.m. and then not closing until mid-morning.

His Amnesia residency finally came to an end in 1990, by which time his style was being imitated all over the world.

The Aloof Formed in London in 1990 by Dean Thatcher and Jagz Kooner, who were drinking mates, London club heads and general over-indulgers, The Aloof sprang out of Thatcher's desire to develop beyond his DJ skills by making tunes.

Using Kooner's garden shed to produce their first record, the techno/house hybrid 'Never Get Out The Boat', they soon found favour, selling all 1,000 copies of the limited run and ending up on Pete Tong's radio play list. Deciding to get serious, they enlisted keyboardist Gary Burns, while Ricky Barrow, an old connection of Thatcher's, was invited to sing.

Taking a break in 1993, they re-emerged on Flaw, Thatcher and Richard Thair's underground label. Thair, a drummer and main man behind Sweatmouth, was roped into the band, which, rebelling against the predominantly cheesy house sound of the time, evolved into a dub/techno/rock outfit and honed their skills as a live band. Their debut album, *Cover The Crime*, secured them a major record deal with East West, for whom they also recorded their second album, *Sinking*. Thair went on to form the live downbeat techno band Red Snapper with Ali Friend and David Ayers.

Ambient A broad term used by devotees to describe almost any music that evokes an atmosphere, Ambient has its roots in Brian Eno's experimental moody soundscapes.

Legend has it Eno drew his inspiration while lying in a hospital bed in the seventies. A radio was playing almost inaudibly and being too ill to adjust the volume he was forced to absorb soft nudging music. Marrying this experience with the work of the composer Erik Satie, he evolved a new musical genre. In general the sound is emotional and embracing, using sweeping chords, electronic and sampled sound effects in place of obvious rhythm structures, tunes or vocals.

Ambient first appeared on the house scene in 1988 with Alex Paterson's Ambient Lounge at the Land Of Oz. By 1991 the house scene had begun experimenting in earnest with mood-swinging vibes to heighten the senses during DJ sets and journalists such as Kirk Field applied the ambient tag to the new chill-out sound. Clubbers would drift into the surround sound of the ambient room and be taken on a voyage as the drugs melted into the music.

Paterson, who had formed the Orb with Jimmy Cauty, began collaborating with Steve Hillage, Miquette Giraudy, Andy Falconer, Thrash, Youth and others. After Cauty split, Paterson and Thrash released the Orb's 'Adventures Beyond The Ultraworld', establishing the band at the forefront of the ambient movement. Meanwhile, in 1990, Cauty had released *Space*, a highly sought-after Ambient album, while his JAM project, KLF, continued to exploit ambient attitude. Ambient also extended its influence into the dark sounds of jungle, with DJs such as Goldie sampling David Byrne, of Talking Heads, and Eno's 'My Life In The Bush Of Ghosts'.

If you're still confused, use this simple rule: if it makes your spine tingle, has you staring blankly at a wall or has dolphin samples, classify it as ambient. Devotees of ambient quite happily include anything from 808 State's *Pacific* to Mike Oldfield's *Tubular Bells* in the category – and so should you.

Amsterdam (where the pills come from) A long-time favourite hangout because of its liberal attitude on sex, sexuality and drugs (not only because smoking cannabis is legal but also because of the enlightened attitude to testing ecstasy in clubs), Amsterdam has secured a unique status in European club culture. This small friendly city is famous for its coffee shops and clubs that allow people to smoke spliff, although legends about copious quantities of ecstasy being quaffed tended to exaggerate reality.

In the nineties it became the capital city of gabber, where on gabber party nights up to 10,000 punters gathered to nash and writhe to the 200 b.p.m. frenzy. Usually held in large industrial spaces, the dance floors were bombarded with lasers and strobes, while video walls depicted gory macabre images. A mostly male activity, the dance floor exploded with energy as shaven-headed young men in boiler suits kicked, jumped and twisted to the beats. On nights when there wasn't a large gabber rave, the small Amnesia club in the red light district would heave with sweat drenched bodies.

In common with the rest of Europe, house music came to dominate the regular venues such as Roxy, Escape, De Mazzo, Paradiso, Melkweg the gay iT and April's Exit, with after parties taking over when clubs close at 6 a.m.

The city's notorious squat parties petered out in the late nineties, although the infamous Silo and Vrieshuis Amerika continued to maintain the DIY vibe.

Amyl House A short-lived and messy term for the early Big Beat scene, dreamed up by music journalists who weren't ready for a new form of dance music that wasn't fuelled by ecstasy and house music. Generally the term refers to fast, break-beat-orientated house that uses furious Roland 303-style bleeps and squelches with rough guitar edges.

Aphex Twin Born Richard D. James, the son of a Cornish tin miner, Aphex Twin began making music as a teenager.

His first releases came with 'Aphex Twin' EP and 'Analogue Bubblebath' on Mighty Force Records in 1991. Success followed with 'Didgeridoo', on R&S, in 1992.

His early records locked him securely into the UK techno scene, although he protests that his roots are far more mainstream. Releasing his 1992 album, *Selected Ambient Works 85-92* and 1993's *Surfing On Sine Waves*, both as Polygon Window on Warp Records, he rode the crest of the ambient wave.

He moved permanently to Warp Records at the end of 1993. Meanwhile, his recording antics were matched by a DJ career that saw him lining up sanding paper and food mixers on the turntable in place of records – which makes you wonder about his culinary and DIY skills.

His reputation as a remixer also led him to work for a plethora of artists. Noted for his business acumen, Aphex Twin formed his record label, Rephlex, releasing tracks by unlikely stable mates from techno and loungecore backgrounds.

Asian Underground Rising from the clash of musical influences over British Asian youths, who had grown up listening to traditional music such as Bollywood film scores and Bangra with their parents and Western music with their friends, the Asian Underground emerged as a fresh new dance music genre in the mid-nineties.

Its forerunners can be traced to artists such as Ravi Shankar and Shakti, as well as crossover fusion artists such as Bill Laswell. In the eighties, Asian sound systems such as Joi, Osmani and State Of Bengal emerged in the Brick Lane area of London, holding one-off events predominantly among the Bengali community. By the nineties the scene's first record label, Nation, had set the fuse, which was soon to be lit by the Outcaste label and finally explode with the arrival of Talvin Singh. The Asian scene had attracted media attention in the mid-eighties, largely because their events were held during the day so thousands of Asian teenagers were bunking off school – but these were mainly one-off events.

The first monthly club dedicated to the scene, the mixed-gay Shakti night, opened its doors in January 1989. Blending Asian music with handbag-house and gay club anthems, the club night was soon followed in June by Asia at the Paradise in Islington, London. Here Shakti's resident DJ Ritu would spin Asian vibes alongside Declan Buckley's Latin sets and John Tyler's African music. When Buckley left he was replaced by David McAlmont, who became notorious for singing along to his records and later became a pop star as half of McAlmont and Butler.

With the Asian underground taking off in the gay scene it was only a matter of time before it crossed over into straight clubs. This it did when Bombay Jungle opened at The Wag in 1993. The night was an immediate success, proving there was a demand for Asian dance music. Meanwhile DJ Ritu split with Shakti and established her seminal Kali nights, while Talvin Singh followed with his legendary Anokha club at The Blue Note, leading the UK's dance floors through a blend of tabla- and sitar-based grooves.

Artists such as Asian Dub Foundation, Fun Da Mental, Earthtribe, Badmarsh and Sri, Nitin Sahwney, Black Star Liner and Corner Shop finally began to achieve the recognition that had alluded them. The Asian underground had gone overground.

Athletico The first post-house super-club, Athletico started in the Midlands, where it established itself as the shape of things to come.

Alex Sparrow, Kirsty McAra and Simon Fathead started Athletico in 1994 in Birmingham before opening a monthly outing in London's Blue Note venue in 1995 and in the process helped to transform The Blue Note into the hippest night spot of the late nineties.

Moving to the Sanctuary, their own mega-venue in Birmingham, they formed a record label and added an additional short-lived night in London at The End in 1997.

Although they probably wouldn't welcome the description, they were instrumental in popularising Big Beat (or Electronica to our American cousins) and relaunching eclectic music policies in clubs up and down the country. Their nights were a much-needed antidote to the precious glamour scene of the mid-nineties, capturing a new mood of alcohol-fuelled messiness on the dance floor – making for a staggeringly good night out.

Juan Atkins One of the Detroit techno legends, Juan Atkins, and his younger school chums Kevin Saunderson and Derrick May, married European electronic music influences to electro and Chicago house, to develop the techno sound in the mid-eighties.

All three techno gurus had been to the same school, Bellville High. The most electro influenced of the three, Atkins had previously been part of the Cyberton, with Richard Davis (a.k.a. 3070), who were best known in the UK for their 'Techno City' release in 1984. Atkins introduced Saunderson and May to European electronic bands such as Kraftwerk, while the latter two turned Atkins on to Chicago and New York dance beats.

Soon Atkins was recording as Model 500, Juan and Magic Juan. Tracks such as 'Night Drive Thru Babylon', 'No UFOs', 'Ocean To Ocean', 'The Chase' and 'Electronic' became classics, but as techno took off in Europe in the early nineties, Atkins became a recluse before finally reopening his Metroplex label in 1992 as part of Mad Mike Banks' Submerge complex.

In 1998 Model 500 were almost brought back to life to play Tribal Gathering. After much anticipation, their appearance was thwarted when Universe were forced to cancel the festival. It would have been their second-ever performance.

Atlas Records Atlas grew out of Sarah's Jazz and Soul record store on Berwick Street, where Pete Herbert supplied the cream of London's leftfield scene.

Herbert and Simon Lee built the shop's reputation, eventually getting their own room in the basement, which led to the shop featuring in the Bucketheads video for the their dance hit, 'The Bomb'. Building on their success, Herbert left to form his own shop, while Simon Lee formed FAZE Action.

Atlas Records, based in Soho's Archer Street, soon became a Mecca for DJs of all persuasions, although most notably of the downbeat and leftfield variety. The shop was soon supplying in-the-know DJs from across the board of dance music.

Autechre Formed in 1987 by the Manchester-based duo of Sean Booth (from Rochdale) and Rob Brown (from Torquay), having been introduced by a mutual friend, Autechre grew out of a love of electro and hip hop.

Progressing through acid house and the harder-edged sounds of Renegade Sound Wave and Meat Beat Manifesto, they released their first record, MYSLB's 'Cavity Job' in 1991. But it wasn't until they moved to Warp Records in 1992 and released 'The Egg' and 'Crystel' for the Artificial Intelligence compilation, that they began turning heads.

The release of 1993's 'Incunabula' on Warp Records saw them join the advanced guard of the leftfield UK techno scene. The follow up, 1994's 'Amber', saw them take electronic music into a new subtle form, while 'Tri Repetae', released in 1995, was greeted with acclaim.

Lest we forget:

Adeva
Adonis
Dave Angel
Arrested Development
Astralwerks

Best we forget:

Abba Tribute Bands
Acid trips (bad)
Avin' it large . . . and other corporate clichés

b

Back to Basics An absurdly popular name, a legion of clubs promoters have dubbed themselves Back to Basics. Some have taken the name and tried to re-install the original funk and soul groove of the seventies and eighties. Others, such as a night at The Borderline in 1990 featuring Nicky Holloway, Paul Oakenfold, Pete Tong and Danny Rampling, used it to recreate the Balearic house vibe in the face of rave adversity. Usually, however, the name is associated with a night in Leeds. Organised by Dave Beer, Back to Basics began in the early years of the Leeds club scene.

Beer, a regular Hacienda and Blackburn rave devotee and general 'lunatic', became frustrated with travelling across the Pennines and decided to kick the Leeds night life. In 1992 he opened the doors of Basics at the now-defunct Music Factory. Around 80 people, mostly friends, swarmed in. DJ Ralph Lawson and Beer himself took over the decks. The lack of quantity was more than made up for by trademark extravagant behaviour of the punters. In subsequent weeks the crowd sized doubled on each night as word spread, until Back to Basics joined the new wave of super-clubs, such as Cream, attracting thousands from all over the north of England.

In 1994 the club moved to The Pleasure Rooms where it stayed until 1997. In 1998 Back to Basics took a three-month residency in the back room of Gatecrasher in Sheffield, before starting a new night, called Basics, with DJs Ralph Lawson and James Holroyd.

Beer recalls the early days being utter madness before the popularity of house turned the scene into a corporate enterprise. Beer's reputation for barmy behaviour has remained in tact, despite the success of his ventures. Going into production, the Basics crew remixed stars such David Bowie and Chrissie Hynde, and appeared on Soma Records while also setting up their own label.

Baggy and Bandannas Possibly the most unattractive period of club fashion, alongside the fly-away collar and wide lapels of high-camp disco, Baggy started innocently with the holiday-wear simplicity of acid house. Soon everyone was floating around in tent-sized trousers, T-shirts that would be loose on Chancellor Kohl and wearing bandannas, which for a while gave them instant street-cred – or instant acid ted, depending on your view of these things. The garb was accompanied by a bug-eyed stare and much arm-waving and finger-twisting – to give the impression of being on ecstasy.

Then everyone started taking ecstasy and realised Class A drugs and dancing made them thin. As the beer guts dropped off, so did the T-shirts and pretty soon the sorry baggy episode was forgotten about – except for the early nineties skate-wear obsession with baggy trousers. This was followed by the late nineties skate-wear obsession with baggy trousers, with chains, which was followed by . . . a rather baggy yawn.

Arthur Baker Baker's long voyage into music started in Boston, Massachusetts where he worked in a record store when he was 13 years old – mainly to obtain promotional copies and supply his passion for music. Having started from a progressive rock background, he heard 'Papa Was A Rolling Stone', by The Temptations in the early seventies and thought 'What the fuck are they doing here?'

Whereas rock music had been orientated around bands, here was a form of music that was orientated around the producer. Gripped, he began listening to WILD radio in Boston and searching for any black music he could find, such as the Jackson 5, The OJs, The Spinners, anything on Motown and Al Green. Desperately wanting to imitate the sounds coming out of Philadelphia records, despite having no background in the music industry, he managed to blag some studio time.

Having moved to university, the 18-year-old Baker bought himself two turntables and began DJing at college parties. From here he began playing in clubs in Amherst, Massachusetts and in 1973 was introduced to the New York club scene by Puerto Rican friends. This was the pre-12in record era of Buttermilk and Walter Gibbon's night at Galaxy 21, later to be followed by the opening of The Paradise Garage and The Loft, when the New York dance scene took off in earnest.

Moving into production for Emergency Records, his first track, Heart of Stone's 'Losing You', was only released in Canada. After working on Northend and Michelle Wallace's 'Happy Days', he moved to New York in 1979 where he became interested in the nascent rap culture and recorded a rap tune, 'Rap-O-Clap-O', with Joe Bataan for London Records (which went bust before the track was released).

Having worked on a medley with Glory called 'Can You Guess What Groove This Is?', he hooked up with Tom Silverman's Tommy Boy Records and recorded 'Jazzy Sensation' with Afrika Bambaataa and Shep Pettibone. His partnership with Bambaataa led to the two collaborating on the seminal electro release, 'Planet Rock'.

Starting his own record label, Streetwise, he could now concentrate on his love of club culture, progressing through a range of dance music styles and producing Wally Jump Junior's 'Tighten Up', Jack E Makossa's 'The Opera House' and Criminal Orchestra Element's 'Put The Needle On The Record'. By now his international reputation also saw him being called in to work with non-dance super stars such as Bob Dylan and Bruce Springsteen.

Balearic Dating from the late eighties, Balearic is not so much a sound as an attitude, with DJs slipping between different musical styles. It originated in Ibiza, where DJs such as Alfredo and Jose Padilla reigned supreme as the original Balearic Gods.

The Balearic scene in the UK, promoted by DJs such as Paul Oakenfold, Danny Rampling and Nicky Holloway, soon ran aground as acid house swept into rave and hardcore music. It was revived in the early nineties by DJs and promoters orbiting around *Boy's Own*, and figures such as Charlie Chester brought together a national network of eclectic DJs.

Interest was again rekindled by the emergence of the new London- and Glasgow-based eclectic disco-house movement, which has attracted silly names such as New Med from music journalists.

While the new movement still involves some of the old names, many of the DJs who play the stuff, reject the New Med label and say they're too young to know what Balearic means.

Balls An early eighties alternative to warehouse parties and clubs, balls fitted into the 'can't-pay, won't-pay' attitude of the time, with young punters spending most of the night inventing elaborate schemes to gate-crash events. The more expensive the better – hence the attraction of Sloane Ranger balls. Once inside, clubbers, dressed in their ragamuffin garb, would stand out a mile among the ball gowns and black tie suits.

Soon warehouse parties were masquerading as balls in order to secure late licenses. In an odd twist, dodgy promoters began charging gullible rich kids a fortune to go to their run-of-the-mill, one-off events in night-clubs.

Promoters made a fortune holding balls – attracting custom by printing a fictitious ball committee, made up of the movers and shakers in the London scene, on the back of the ticket. Naturally, the movers and shakers knew nothing about the events, but the promoters had tapped a rich vein and some made it their life's work, conning the parents of public school kids to fork out wads of cash for apparently respectable events. I guess they deserved each other.

Pre-Club Bars Between 1988 and 1992, the founders of the ecstasy generation dropped their old habits of downing endless spirits and pints of lager, opting instead for pills, Lucozade and bottled water. The effects showed in official figures, with alcohol consumption nose-diving while drug offences soared. By the mid-nineties the rave industry was said to be worth £2 billion a year.

Reaction from the brewing industry, desperate to win back custom, was inevitable. Meanwhile the growth and violence of the drugs gangs started to worry local authorities and the police, who decided that increasing the availability of alcohol, and promoting it as an alternative to drug use was in their interests, even if alcohol was in fact more likely to promote unorganised violence between drinkers than the loved-up effects of ecstasy. By the mid-nineties there was a marked shift in attitude towards granting later licenses and a growth among landlords who deliberately sought to attract club-goers into their establishments.

In some ways the introduction of pre-club bars inevitably followed European culture. The Italian, Spanish and Balearic habits of staying in bars until two or four in morning and then heading off to a club suited post-acid house club culture far better than the traditional English pub and 11 p.m. closing. Another factor was that by the mid-nineties, many who had burned from Friday night to Monday morning in the early days had matured into more laid-back pursuits. The interest in music was still there, but nights that finished the following afternoon, became harder to handle.

By the early 1990s, pre-club bars with DJs and designer drinks, had begun to spring up in Manchester. Establishments such as Dry 201 and Manto led the way for Ten, Atlas, Barca, Prague V, Metz and Velvet. The city has now become a Mecca of drinking establishments and a bar crawl in the area around Canal Street would have the most hardened drinker paralytic within 50 metres, although this has done little to ease the violence.

In London, bars such as Riki Tik and The Medicine Bar were joined by The Dog Star, The Junction, Bar Vinyl, The Brick Layers, Fridge Bar and Freedom all offering club experiences in pub settings.

The pattern was repeated around the country with Baa Bar in Liverpool, Luna in Leeds, Skid Row in Brighton, Mud Dock in Bristol and The Medicine Bar mark II in Birmingham, to name a few.

Musically pre-club bars have given DJs the chance to air styles and genres that were too adventurous or leftfield to secure a night in the restrictive club venues. Just as pubs acted as outlets for emerging dance music in the 1980s, bars are cutting the ground in the nineties.

In tandem to the development of bars, club venues were also redesigned to promote alcohol sales. Whereas clubs at one time emphasised the dance floor, a new breed of club sacrificed dance space for imposing bar areas. The epicentre of clubbing reverted to alcohol, making it easier to reach for a refill than find room to shake your booty. Other established clubs, such as The Fridge, The End and Heavenly Juke Box, moved to soak up the profits of bar culture by opening bars adjacent to their venue.

Pissed up punters, happily lobbed their money into the pockets of the brewing industry and the status quo was resumed.

Watch out for *The A-Z of Pubbing*.

Basement Jaxx A band-cum-club night and record label (Atlantic Jaxx), Basement Jaxx was formed by Felix Burton and Simon Ratcliff after they met at one of Ratcliff's Thames boat parties in 1994. Both were lovers of deep US sounds – Burton being a passionate house enthusiast and a former regular at Gilles Peterson's Talkin' Loud And Saying Something acid jazz sessions, while Ratcliff was a raw funk enthusiast.

Forming their record label at the end of the year, they issued their first 12in record releases, with their debut EP – a crossbreed of US rhythms and harder London sounds – being greeted with critical acclaim. The following year they released 'Samba Magic', which was immediately snapped up by Virgin.

A resolutely self-sufficient duo, they built their DJ reputation through their Brixton, London-based club night. Originally held in the George IV pub before moving briefly to The Brix, their rise coincided with the rejuvenation of the previously run-down Brixton area and the re-emergence of disco house.

Their sound, a cacophony of mutant disco licks married to the vocals of Corrina Joseph and Ronnie Richards, maintained the energy of their DJ sets, which often had Joseph and Richards singing live.

Earning a significant international reputation, US DJs such as Roger Sanchez, Van Heldon, Masters At Work and DJ Sneak all count themselves as admirers. A compilation of Atlantic Jaxx tracks was released in 1997, followed by the Basement Jaxx's first album in 1998.

La Beat Route The pinnacle of early to mid-eighties clubbing, La Beat Route in Soho opened as a New Romantics club in 1981 during the period when early hip hop and other black music was starting to seep on to London's dance floors. Soon La Beat Route was being cited as the place to go to hear US 12in imports slipped in among the latest from Spandau Ballet. Resident DJ Steve Lewis gradually replaced the New Romantics' records with a set built almost entirely from early funky, NYC grooves and rap. The club's membership rocketed and trend-setters from the fashion communities of London, who had been divided into soul boys and rockabilly, united under the new groove.

A new look emerged, first adopting an easy jump into the Zoot suit cool of Kid Creole and then progressing into the club's own look. Hard Times, as the look came to be known, reacted against the yuppie chic of the eighties, emphasising downbeat cheapness, ripped 501 jeans, battered leather flying jackets, fifties flat top hair and funky head wear – a look that would sadly be popularised by Bros in the late eighties.

This was the age of strict door policies and half of going out was whether you would get in or not. Even regulars would be turned away on a whim by the doorman, Oliver O'Donnell. Everyone approached their night out with the apprehension of being socially humiliated in front of their friends and, worse, fashionable strangers. Smirking at rejects was a central London sport, even though this could frequently backfire when it came to the smirkers' turn to blag their way in. For young lovers, door policies were a nightmare as one half of a recently formed couple found themselves relegated from being super stud to super dud and left to wander central London alone.

Ashley Beedle It was in his early teens that Ashley Beedle first ventured into Gulliver's, on Down Street in Mayfair, in the late seventies. Inspired he began frequenting Crackers, a Soho venue where garage-guru Paul Trouble Anderson would hold sway over the dance floor.

His first introduction to the possibilities of mixing records came at a Caster Soul weekender, when he saw Froggy mixing two copies of Brothers Johnson's 'Stomp'. Bought decks by his dad when he was 15 years old, he began organising house parties with his mate Rob Mello.

With the arrival of the eighties, Beedle went to early hip hop nights, such as The Language Lab in London, and The Dug Out in Bristol, before hearing Norman Jay and Derek B at Blackmarket at The Wag. In 1983 he hooked up with Stan Lee and Dean Zepharian's rare groove and hip hop Shock sound system. Starting as a box boy, he served his apprenticeship, before being promoted to record selector and finally being allowed to DJ. This led to sound clashes with outfits such as Soul II Soul, before landing the back room in the legendary Rip club on Clink Street, London in 1988. By this time Shock were playing pure house.

At the end of the eighties Beedle began producing his own music. His first release came out on Jack Tracks, for whom he released 'Give Me Your Love'. One of the earliest British garage tunes, it was produced by Marshall Jefferson and Byron Stingly. Taken under the wing of Phil Perry, whom he met at Queens, the Sunday camp Balearic club, Perry gave Beedle his first solo slot, enabling him to play alongside Andrew Weatherall and Charlie Chester. This put Beedle in touch with the *Boy's Own* group, through which he released 'Where Were You?', under the moniker of Black Science Orchestra, and he was booked by Mick Robinson to headline the Cheeky Half parties. Through *Boy's Own* he also met Rocky and Diesel and was asked to collaborate with them on their X-Press 2 project.

He went on produce records under a stream of aliases, such as Ballistic Brothers, Delta House of Funk, Black Science Orchestra and Black Jazz Chronicles, whilst his DJ career progressed to securing a short-lived residency at Cream in the late nineties.

Joey Beltram Creator of the 1991 club classic 'Energy Flash' when he was a tender 17 year old, Joey Beltram hails from New York but produces music that clearly reveals Detroit techno influences.

Picked up by Belgian techno label, R&S, 'Energy Flash's' deep, hypnotic bass and whispering 'ecstasy' sample immediately stood out against the lightweight piano tunes of European house in the early nineties and the lack of subtlety in the UK's hardcore scene.

Beltram already had pedigree, having started DJing in Queens when he was a precocious 12 year old. By the age of 16, he had released records under the alias Code 6 and Lost Entity, on New York's deeply underground Nu Groove label. His first records were originally intended to increase his DJ bookings but they led to a string of releases under various aliases, such as Final Exposure, Program 2 and Disorder.

His influences are eclectic and under his own name Beltram released a trance-inspired EP, 'Odyssey Nine', and the seminal 'Calibre' EP, on Warp Records.

The Belvedere The legendary Sunday chill in Richmond, Surrey. The Belvedere would have DJs such as Gilles Peterson entertaining scene heads and the Shoom posse as they drifted through last night's comedown.

Sadly the musical unity of the early years was short-lived, as the Shoom originals watched their scene being invaded by acid teds and the Ramplings closed the doors on late arrivals. The jazz heads took off in their own direction.

Leah Betts At her eighteenth birthday party, on 12 November 1995, Leah Betts, after vomiting repeatedly and going into violent convulsions, collapsed into a coma on the bathroom floor of her parents' home near Basildon, Essex. Her coma lasted a week and by the time she died the tabloid press had had a field day. Her normality – she had been an apparently clean-living, home-counties girl – provided a powerful message. If Leah Betts was taking Class A drugs, then so were all our sons and daughters.

Anti-drugs posters using her image were printed and reporters were dispatched to find the 'murderers' who supplied her with the drug. Her stepfather (a retired police officer) and mother (a voluntary anti-drugs worker) became ready spokespersons for the media war on drugs.

If nothing else, the very normality of Leah Betts' life led to suggestions that greater education on safe use and quality control would be more practical than attempting to stop a nation from pill popping.

Regular users consoled themselves with the verdict that she had drunk too much water avoiding the uncomfortable fact that whatever the case, ecstasy had in some way contributed to her death.

Big Beat Growing out of trip hop, Balearic and the 'anything goes' attitude of jazz heads, big beat borrows sped-up hip hop and break beats, rock guitars, funk and dub bass lines, punk posturing and acidic techno bleeps and squelches. Its rise can be charted from the Dust Brothers' clubs Naked Under Leather in Manchester and the Sunday Social in the Albany Pub in London's Great Portland Street in 1993. Intended to be a chill-out session it became a table dancing (no, not that sort), arms in the air affair.

For legal reasons the Dust Brothers changed their name to become the Chemical Brothers and their 'Leave Home' single remains a big beat classic. Other classics include Monkey Mafia's 'Work Mi Body', Dylan Rhymes' 'Naked and Ashamed' and The Headrillaz's 'Space Fuck'.

House and techno purists complain the music is a sop to guitar-loving indie fans who don't understand dance music, while big beat fans are usually too drunk and speedy to come up with a sensible reply.

The Big Chill Launched in 1994 by Pete Lawrence, former Cooking and Pure Bliss Records head honcho and Club Together promoter, The Big Chill was formed in response to overkill on the rave scene. In place of the full-on mayhem, it introduced downbeat events where people from different backgrounds could meet and exchange ideas. Linking up with Stewart Warren-Hill of Hextatic Visuals, they moved into Union Chapel in Islington for a series of Sunday sessions. The club became a cinematic and musical collage, reversing the norms of clubbing by devoting the main room to laid-back ambient sounds, while the side rooms pumped out up-beat dance genres.

After years of pill-popping hedonism at clubs – where people's conversation was limited to what drugs they'd taken – The Big

Chill brought socialising back to centre stage. Full-on clubbers, coming down from a weekend of excess, would mingle with musos and older punters.

The Big Chill held the Black Mountains Gala, their first outdoor event, in August 1995. Illegally organised, it relied on word of mouth to spread the news. Alerted by the unusually heavy traffic cruising up isolated mountain roads, the police turned up on the first evening, Criminal Justice Act in hand.

Their arrival had been anticipated and instead of finding a rave they were greeted by a well-behaved crowd, sitting in a big top watching circus acts. Hard-pressed to classify the event as a rave they left and their departure was immediately followed by a storming three-hour DJ set by Global Communication.

The follow-up, planned to take place in Norfolk in 1996, was organised within the law. It easily gained approval from the local police and council until an article appeared in the *NME* saying Twisted Scientist and Kid Loop were playing at the biggest dance event of the year. Soon the local press were running stories on 'a mystery rave' and in desperation the organisers postponed and looked for an alternative venue.

A phone call out of the blue invited them to a site in Hingham, where an apparently smooth application became unhinged after a solitary local resident voiced opposition, starting a campaign called RAGE (Residents Against Gala Event). The ensuing local scrap proved to be irresistible for the media and to protect themselves The Big Chill launched their own propaganda initiative, CALM (Chillers Against Local Misinformation). Eventually a license was granted, although the council attached a rigorous list of 200 demands and obligations.

The resulting débâcle had council officials zealously applying volume restrictions to the sound systems and refusing to allow music to be played after 12 p.m., a ruse that prompted two punters to dress up as officials telling the systems to start up again at 1 a.m.

The moral of the story? Obviously every dance promoter has organised within the law ever since.

Big Life Formed during the rise of acid house in 1987, Big Life quickly picked up on commercial dance. Singles such as 'Yazz' and Coldcut's 'Doctorin' The House' and Yazz's 'The Only Way Is Up' became anthems, with the latter staying at number one for eight weeks in 1988. Their stable also included an eclectic range, from The Soup Dragons, through to the Orb, Naughty By Nature and De La Soul, who each in their way defined the era.

Birmingham Famed for its handbag-house scene, the English Midlands capital of Birmingham has also gained a reputation for techno clubs such as Atomic Jam and House Of God. Venues such as The Que club, a cavernous dance arena with a capacity of 2,000, the Sanctuary (home of House Of God and Athletico), Wolverhampton's Canal club and the Custard Factory complex of bars and restaurants, provided Birmingham with a new lease of life from the mid-nineties.

Club nights such as Wobble, Crunch, Scott Bond and Andy Cleeton's Republica, Decadance, Miss Moneypenny's, Sundissential and the long-running Lovesexy, ensured a hungry dance media presence loyally plugged the city, while they did their best to ignore the motorways tearing through the city's heart.

Black Market In summer 1984 a Lancashire lad called Rene Galston hooked up with Billy McIntosh and started a new Friday night at The Wag club called Black Market.

Playing deep funky grooves, hip hop and, later, emerging Chicago house, Black Market became legendary, introducing London to hard-edged black dance music.

Drawing a packed crowd of young and fashionable kids, soul boys and MA 1 jacketed youths, the walls and windows of The Wag dripped with condensation as punters managed to eke out enough space to dance. Meanwhile the queues would throb and twist down Wardour Street, Soho, fighting to get in.

The cream of London's DJs would pour down there to catch the rare grooves of seminal players such as Horace Carter-Allen and Steve Jervier and the early Chicago house sets of Derek Boland. At the end of 1997, Black Market opened a sister club night in New York.

By summer 1998 they had moved into what was to become one of the most famous of Soho's many dance specialist record shops. A host of DJs, producers and record-label managers have at one time worked behind the counter of Dave Piccioni's Black Market record store.

Kept alive by its progressive attitude, Black Market started selling house music, ragga and jungle while others were shaking their heads dismissively, saying there was no future in it.

Blackburn Raves Starting in the heyday of Manchester's Summers of Love of 1988-90, the Blackburn raves provided post-Hacienda entertainment after the two o'clock curfew, becoming a focus for the northern scene.

In contrast with the high production light displays and sets of the south-east's raves, Blackburn's were low-key affairs. In place of state-of-the-art sound systems and VJs, there were low-budget sound systems and DJ-operated strobes.

As local dialect has it, the Blackburn raves weren't quite as pretty as the Manchester or southern scenes, but they had a pumping, vibrant, DIY energy to them. In the absence of meaningful lighting, head-lamps hats became the clothing of choice, enabling punters to skin up in dingy corners.

Springing up in disused warehouses and industrial complexes, they sometimes accidentally set up in working industrial sites. One venue turned out to be a functioning meat factory, providing the ravers with ready-made Lancashire sausages to shower the police with when they raided it.

Blagging As long as there have been guest lists and door policies, punters have practised, honed and refined the art of blagging their way into clubs for nothing, or at least found ways of paying less.

In the early eighties, when many of the younger punters literally didn't have the cash to pay, combing the architecture of a venue to find an unguarded back entrance, open window or vulnerable skylight was part of the weekend ritual. As the scene progressed, more direct ways of ensuring cheap entry were perfected. At some clubs, such as Taboo, punters would have to elaborate complex stories just for the privilege of paying the full entry fee.

Reeling off connections (all false, naturally) with Boy George, Leigh Bowery or some other scene personality might have been enough to get you past the security staff, but the introduction of door whores, who controlled the guest list, and the sheer volume of people trying the same tricks, demanded greater enterprise. Pretending to be someone else became a popular activity, especially when the growth of dance and style magazines meant there was a vast pool of club journalists to imitate on Saturday night. Soon journalists would be starting their club nights overhearing complete strangers claiming to be them. One individual printed a load of bogus *Face* business cards. When he lost them they were duly returned to *The Face*, who naturally printed his mugshot in their next edition – somewhat blowing his cover.

The down side of blagging is that it's deeply infectious and the more people that do it the harder it becomes to pull off. But, like shoplifting and gambling, it has a highly addictive adrenaline buzz to it. It also has honour – a true blagger would rather end up on their own with a kebab than pay. It's a matter of principle.

Bogart's In the dance-starved and anti-establishment period of the early eighties, when lazers, light shows and swish clubbing were somewhere lower than pants, central Londoners would travel as far afield as south Harrow to search out small pubs that were on the scene.

Bogart's, a pub where Gary Crowley, a young Capital Radio DJ, played soul and dance grooves, attracted regulars from places such as the Dirt Box and Flim Flam, as well as a local suburban crowd.

In place of the later exodus to raves, these were innocent naïve pleasures. The nights were fuelled by speed and the odd snort of poppers, washed down with copious amounts of lager and the obligatory spliffs. This was the aftermath of punk and the glam of new romance, a period of new optimism when people stopped going out to watch bands or other dressed-up punters pout. Instead they migrated to scene pubs and the dance floor. In place of passive observation, people had started interacting. The roots of club culture were being formed.

Bournemouth Weekenders During the mid- to late eighties, Bournemouth weekenders and the infamous Rockley Sands parties were organised by promoters such as Nicky Holloway and featured DJs such as Chris Bangs, Johnny Walker, Gilles Peterson, Phil Perry and Danny Rampling, spinning dance music of all flavours but mostly soul and jazz funk.

In the pre-ecstasy days, the punters would wolf down speed and alcohol but by the summer of 1988 a split emerged in the scene. The DJs and punters who had been to Ibiza for summer 1987 had been converted to Balearic beats. Waves of punters alternated between the bar and the dance floor as acid house pundits raved to the Balearic DJs and deserted the floor to the earlier sounds, while soul boys and girls continued to groove to the funky beats.

It was a division that set the trend and gave birth to acid jazz and acid house. The Rockley Sands events came to a halt and Nicky Holloway began organising The Trip, his acid house night, at the Astoria in central London. In fact the split was nothing like as wide as subsequent punters made out. Gilles Peterson, the guru of the new jazz scene, was even heard screaming 'Aceeed!' in one of his radio sets in 1988. His tongue however may well have been planted firmly in his cheek.

Meanwhile the Bournemouth authorities introduced early licenses for clubs, killing the action at 1 a.m. Clubs such as Glasshoppers kept the faith by packing in the punters earlier in the evening, while DJ Lewis Copeland spun Crystal Waters, FBI Project and Italian house piano-led anthems. It was here that Simon Lee (FAZE Action), Pete Herbert (Atlas Records) and Andy Williams (Fuzz Against Junk) first ventured on to the turntables at a night called Remix.

Boy George Long-term club personality, occasional pop star and regular DJ, Boy George's association with dance music started in the late seventies. A regular Blitz club member and cloakroom attendant, he secured his first DJ residency in 1981 when he went behind the decks with Jeremy Healy at Phillip Sallon's Planets club. Healy and 17-year-old Boy George had been booked because they had large record collections, not because they knew what they were doing. In the event they played whatever they wanted, including tunes from the *Sound of Music*. Later forming

Culture Club, their first single, 'White Boy', was a testimony to club music.

Throughout his career as lead singer of Culture Club, Boy George would be seen regularly at London's happening club nights. Frequently spotted in the early days of the Camden Palace, in 1983 he sang for more than his supper in one of the back passages of the Palace. Surrounded by a frightening clutch of skinheads, he pacified them with a rendition of Culture Club's first hit single, 'I Didn't Mean To Hurt You', which had just charted.

Throughout the eighties Boy George was an essential face on the scene at clubs such as Taboo and on into the house scene. Visiting New York in 1985 he went to clubs such as the Paradise Garage and the Palladium, where he was introduced to ecstasy and, like many DJs, he first came across house in Ibiza.

In 1988 he teamed up with Jeremy Healy and penned a house protest song, 'No Clause 28'. This laid the foundations for More Protein, which was formed to release 'Everything Begins With An E' by E Zee, before recording an album under a pseudonym, Jesus Loves You.

Following the footsteps of Jeremy Healy, Boy George went from being a pop star to becoming a star DJ, putting his years of club experience to use behind the turntables.

Boy's Own Created in 1986 in the lead up to the first Summer of Love by Terry Farley, Andrew Weatherall, Steve Mayes and Cymon Eckles, the *Boy's Own* fanzine soon became a bible for the acid house and Balearic scene. Inspired by Peter Hooton and The Farm's Liverpool-based magazine *The End*, *Boy's Own* combined football, music, booze, drugs and humour – as well as a dose of Mayes' off-the-wall politics.

After acid house took off in 1988, Weatherall started DJing at Shoom while the fanzine started organising the infamous *Boy's*

Own parties, making it a conduit for DJs such as Charlie Chester, Ashley Beedle, Steve Hall, Rocky, Diesel and Ginger Mick Robinson.

Weatherall and Farley gained notoriety after Weatherall remixed Primal Scream's 'Loaded' and Farley reworked The Farm's 'Stepping Stone' – both crediting their work to *Boy's Own* and inspiring the move towards a record label.

Deliberately steering clear of the by-now corrupt rave scene of the early nineties, the *Boy's Own* parties sprang into the national headlines when one was organised in Northamptonshire on HM the Queen's property, spawning headlines along the lines of 'Ravers Hold Acid Party On Royal Land'.

As the musical side of the operation flourished the emphasis of the organisation changed direction, dropping the fanzine in favour of launching a record label, financed by London Records with Farley and Weatherall at the helm. Having already attracted a group of notable DJs and producers to the *Boy's Own* gang, these contacts were now utilised to provide the label's output, with the first release, Bocca Junior's 'Raise 63 Steps To Heaven', coming out in August 1990. By 1992 the label had fallen apart and Weatherall departed to form Sabres of Paradise and become a master of leftfield remixes. Farley pursued his career as a house DJ, while another *Boy's Own* veteran, Steve Hall, launched a new label called Junior Boy's Own. Although the first label had failed to find a significant market, its offspring launched the musical careers of seminal outfits such as the Chemical Brothers, Underworld and the Black Science Orchestra.

B.P.M. The abbreviation of beats per minute, b.p.m. was originally only important to DJs but became increasingly crucial as different genres of dance music were defined by the speed at which they were recorded.

Back in the mid- to late eighties DJs would faithfully recite a mantra which held that dance music was usable only if it came in at between 80 and 120 b.p.m. As house took hold and DJs pitched the music increasingly upward, the market fell off the bottom end and 120 b.p.m. began to sound decidedly slow. By the turn of the decade the news that Belgian producers were experimenting with tempos of 150 b.p.m. had train spotters itching their pants with speculation. Now it all seems rather boring.

By this time b.p.m. was so firmly etched into the culture that it wasn't long before magazines, such as *DJ*, were recording a track's b.p.m. in their reviews. DJ's could now select their set by only buying records at the same b.p.m., thereby minimising mixing difficulties and maximising boredom for the punters. And since DJ turntables allow for pitch variation, this meant that a record collection consisting only of 130 b.p.m. records didn't have to be played at that tempo.

As Deep Dish, US deep house producers laconically point out, the fetish for labelling genres of dance music disguises the fact that the difference between, say, tech house and techno can be easily explained by the speed the DJ plays the records. For tech house you simply slap Red Planet on your turntable and pitch it down by minus eight and for trance, whack it up to plus eight. Cynical, but they've got a point.

Break Beat One of the key innovations to shape modern dance music, break beat has become central to a host of genres and has consequently come to mean different things to different people, depending on what musical source they're taking their definition from.

Break beats were originated by Kool Herc, a Jamaican who moved to New York in 1967 and became a reggae DJ. He soon picked up the urban funk sounds of the Big Apple. Noticing that the dance floor reached its height during bass- and percussion-led funky instrumentals, rather than during vocal sections and cheesy string and horn breaks, he began cutting between short sections of two copies of the same records on two turntables.

He called these rough-and-ready chops between four-to eight-bar section break beats, and notoriously kept the crowd locked in the same thigh-grinding funky groove for hours.

Herc would go to great lengths to disguise the breaks he was using, soaking the labels off his records and refusing to tell rival DJs what tracks he was playing. Nonetheless many of the grooves he cut up have become legendary – most notably the Apache break, which he lifted from the Bongo Bong Band's version of Cliff Richard and The Shadows song, 'Apache'.

As Herc's style took hold, a legion of legendary New York DJs such as Grand Master Flash adopted his style, spinning discs over increasing numbers of turntables (although two remained the standard) and adding their own innovations – transforming the scratch into its own form of rhythmic expression, as they hopped between break beats.

As hip hop grew, it burst over the Atlantic to the UK, where artists such as Soul II Soul took it in a new downbeat direction and, later, the Jungle scene looped break beats into samplers and using new time stretching technology, pitched the music up to a new fast and furious tempo.

Meanwhile a new school of break beat science emerged, adopting the baggy clothing of the skate scene, B-boys delighted in hip hop breaks with deeper sub-bass lines and kick drums, twisted electro and mutated downbeat techno.

Bristol Sound For a long time there was some controversy over whether there was really such a thing as the Bristol Sound. The term has come to be synonymous with downbeat dance music, a fusion of dub reggae and hip hop themes, electronic sequencing, sampling and techno, with a head nod to post-punk UK guitar music.

Whether the artists come from Bristol and whether the Bristol bands actually sound like each other has become less important.

The undisputed grand daddies of the Bristol scene were The Wild Bunch, an early eighties DJ and rap collective who began holding parties at the legendary Dugout night-club in Park Row. Inspired by New York hip hop artists and in particular the movie *Wildstyle*, Nellee Hooper, Milo Johnson, Grant Marshall, Rob Del Naja and Claude Williams began cutting, scratching and breaking their own loops.

Marrying the US sound to West Country concerns, such as the post-punk funk of Pigbag and the ingrained dub reggae sound of Bristol's Caribbean community (On U Sound had involved Bristolians Gary Clail and Mark Stewart), The Wild Bunch soon built a following that included most of the artists who were to shape the Bristol sound.

The Wild Bunch extended their links across the UK, hooking up for sound clashes with the early London-based hip hop night, The Language Lab. By the mid-eighties they were touring internationally and working alongside the Soul II Soul collective, who Nellee Hooper teamed up with after The Wild Bunch's demise.

The Wild Bunch had ignited the Bristol flame, which former members Massive Attack (3D Del Najo, Daddy G and Mushroom) took up in 1988. After working with Neneh Cherry, who did much to popularise the city's music and for whom 3D composed the lyrics for 'Manchild', Massive Attack released their seminal album *Blue Lines* in 1991. Once again Bristol was locked firmly on to the musical map.

Notoriously slow workers, Massive Attack rested on their laurels and Bristol once again took a two-year sojourn, before a white label of Portishead's 'Sour Times' and the release of 'Aftermath' by former Massive Attack collaborator Tricky turned heads back towards the West Country in 1993.

By this time trip hop was beginning to be coined as a genre, and Bristol acts were increasingly thrown into the trip hop pile – a trend that was cemented by Mo Wax releasing their seminal remixes of another Bristol band, Foundation.

The trip hop moniker was to annoy Bristol acts even more than the suggestion there was a Bristol sound.

Bugged Out Started in 1995 and promoted by the Manchester-based *Jockey Slut* dance music magazine, Bugged Out managed to keep the house and techno vibe going in Manchester despite the city's hassles. Opening up at the new Sankeys Soap venue in the northern quarter of the town, Bugged Out avoided being devastated by an IRA bomb that ripped through the city centre. Following Sankeys Soap's closure in 1998, Bugged Out started a monthly residence at Cream in Liverpool. They also returned to their roots with a monthly club at Balearica in Manchester.

LTJ Bukem A prime mover in the drum 'n' bass scene, LTJ Bukem's early singles, '1990s Logical Progression' and 1991's 'Demon's Theme', with their jazz and techno influences and mellow breakdowns, automatically marked out a new direction in the dark scene. Dubbed intelligent jungle, artcore, jazz step and jazz 'n' bass, Bukem's style was to bring a new following to jungle music that had little time for its hardcore roots.

Bukem's musical history began when his adoptive parents sat him down in front of a piano as a child.

He was soon playing the trumpet and drums in bands, but it wasn't until he saw Rapattack that he realised the power of turntables. Forming a Luton-based sound system called Sunrise, his DJ career kicked off, while he regularly visited London to see DJs such as Gilles Peterson and Tim Westwood. By the 1990s he'd discovered raves and the hardcore scene. While being sucked into the atmosphere, he, like many early junglists, avoided ecstasy culture, instead concentrating on the music.

After months of sending demo tapes he secured a slot at Raindance in 1990. His more melodic DJ style sat uncomfortably among the usual banging fare pumped out by other rave DJs, although he soon became an icon for a significant minority.

His 1993 release, 'Music', saw him reworking the familiar Apache break beat through a rolling, deep double bass-driven epic. The effect brought Bukem out of the cold, from being a maverick to the epicentre of the scene. In 1994 he hooked up with Fabio and Kemistry and Storm to open Speed, the night that was to launch him into popular consciousness.

Set in the intimate Mars club, Speed was on one hand a reaction to the cavernous rave scene, and on the other a rejection of the mid-nineties preconception that jungle was synonymous with ragga.

The club's size contributed to the effect of Bukem's swirling, touchy-feelie orchestral sweeps and melodies, which swelled from the more familiar chopped break beats. In its first month the club was empty, but by the fifth week punters were queuing around the block to get in.

Although Speed closed in 1996, Bukem went on to secure a show on Kiss FM, and his popularity soared from the mid-nineties onwards. Meanwhile his Good Looking Record label found a stable following through releases by artists such as Wax Doctor, Peshay, PFM, Aquarius and The Invisible Man.

Lest we forget:

Bandulu

Biology

Bizarre Inc and Playing With Knives
Björk
C.J. Boland

Best we forget:
Black Box
Body Paint

C

Mr C The cheeky chappie of techno, Richard West (aka Mr C), was raised in Camden and built his reputation in the mid-eighties as an MC working on LWR pirate radio with Jasper the Vinyl Junkie and at the Ambassador's club in Euston. He famously worked on a milk round before teaming up with Evil Eddie Richards to release his first record, 'Page 67' by Myster-E (not a drug or page reference) on Baad Records.

Mr C took an MC residency at the Camden Palace, working with Richards and Colin Faver. His first appearance as a DJ came on 2 January 1988, at his birthday party. The manager of the HQ club, a friend of a friend, heard his set and offered him a night. The result, Fantasy, was one of the first acid house parties in London and led to Mr C hooking up with Paul Rip, the promoter and organiser of the infamous Clink Street parties.

The first Rip party was held in April in a basement on Eversholt Street, Euston. Moving to Clink Street, its reputation exploded and by the end of May the venue had queues of 500 outside. Madness ensued with people trying to smash through the doors or climbing up drainpipes to break in.

Soon the Saturday night had extended into a weekend-long party, with A-transmission on Friday, Rip on Saturday and Zoo on Sunday.

At this point Mr C began playing warehouse parties such as the huge Brainstorm, in Wharf Road, King's Cross – an event he describes as one of the greatest parties of his life.

At the beginning of 1989 he set up Voodoo and made an amicable split with Paul Rip. By this time Mr C was recording with The Shaman, a Scottish-based band that relocated to London after their manager visited the Clink Street parties. They invited Mr C to do a rap on 'Move Any Mountain'.

Alongside his commitment to the band he carried on playing at Synergy, organising Release (later called Release the Pressure) warehouse parties with Nathan Coles (now of Wiggle) and setting up a new pirate radio station, Dance FM.

Mr C played most of the major raves such as Sunrise, Energy, Biology and Back to the Future in the late eighties and early nineties, but unlike warehouse jams found them impersonal. He also played Subway, at Maximus.

In 1992 he began organising Harmony, with DJ Unique, and The Main Buzz – small underground affairs, which were probably the first tech house parties.

At the end of December 1992, Mr C started Plink Plonk Records and six months later started the legendary Drop club in Farringdon Road to promote the record label. Concentrating on making the environment as classy an experience as possible, the events cost £7,000 to put on while holding only 500 people, who paid £10 for their tickets.

In 1994 he set up Vapour Space, a tech house night in Gray's Inn Road, and Cyclone, which returned to his warehouse roots. In 1993 he joined forces with Layo to open The End. Mr C's a good, or at least a persistent, geezer.

Camden Palace Opened in 1983 by former Blitz club promoter Steve Strange and partner Rusty Egan, the Camden Palace was built on the former site of the Music Machine, a music hall theatre-cum-punk venue.

One of the first clubs to be dedicated to London's emerging club culture, it opened in a burst of publicity and immediately attracted the cream of the city's various scenes. Decked in plush fabrics, with steep bar prices and stairs dotted with fairy lights, which linked a multitude of bars, the Palace was intended to be a massive pleasure dome for the clubbing élite. Eventually it was too big to maintain a vibe, although for a period in 1983 it was frequented by scene stars such as Boy George and pop stars such as Martin Fry.

Strange and Egan's Tuesday night, Slum It In Style, captured the hard-times style of the period, even though the luxurious venue fitted more with yuppie aspirations.

Among the local Camden Town trendies, Wednesday night, which was dubbed as birthday night, became the essential meeting point. While rap clubs and warehouse parties occupied the weekend, Wednesday at the Palace offered cheap mid-week clubbing. In addition to special offers on the house lager, the Palace started sending six birthday invites to people who had entered their date of birth on the club's mailing form. Since the venue didn't cross-reference their data bank, the same person could write down different dates on each visit, thereby securing at least one birthday a month and six free invites.

The Camden Palace also introduced London clubbers to their first taste of sophisticated dance floor lighting, stopping the music some nights to show off the laser display. It also introduced the idea of live filmed footage, which would be projected on a screen above the dance floor – an idea that became popular again in the nineties with the advent of the Internet, although this allowed footage of dance floors across the world to be linked up.

Usually boring, the film screen grabbed everyone's attention one night when the camera operator discovered a drugged or drunk dancer derobing himself on the dance floor. Having ceremoniously undressed to his underpants, he then discarded them with a flourish, before being shown the door by the bouncers. It must have been a cold walk home.

Although the venue nose-dived in status in the late eighties, it still provided the training ground for DJs and MCs such as Mr C and Kid Batchelor. In the early nineties the venue had a revamp but never quite managed to throw off its image as a teeny bop venue, despite often lining up an awesome collection of DJs.

Derrik Carter One of the leading lights of the second generation of Chicago house, Derrik Carter inspired a plethora of new house DJs to take to the decks. He came to prominence in the mid-nineties with the release of 1994's 'The Sound Patrol' EP on Organico records. His follow-up, 'The Music' EP, included samples from Chaka Kahn's 'Ain't Nobody' on a track called 'An Open Secret', mapping out further sneaky sampling of early disco tunes that would come to represent the new Chicago sound.

Castlemorton Part of the traveller/crusty festival circuit, the spring Avon festival of 1992 became a landmark battleground for the right to party when the police forces of Avon, Gloucestershire and Somerset combined to drive back convoys of travellers. By this time the convoys had started taking evasive action, outwitting the police by converging on ad-hoc meeting points rather than making for a deliberate destination. In the event the travellers found themselves being directed by the police towards Castlemorton – where some 400 of them set up camp.

By Saturday over 50,000 people had converged on the site and the Spiral Tribe, Bedlam, Adrenaline and DIY Sound Systems had set up for a five-day binge. Rather than pile into the event, West Mercia police decided to confine the free festival in one space – Castlemorton Common.

Soon TV coverage had ravers from all over the country flooding into a temporarily autonomous state where all needs were catered for 24 hours a day, from food and drink to drugs and even a swim in the lake.

As good as it was, Castlemorton was the swan song of free festivals, with John Major declaring war at that year's Conservative Party Conference, paving the way for the Criminal Justice Act.

Celebrity DJs As DJs attracted star status, promoters inverted the meaning and began booking stars who didn't know technics from toast to appear behind the decks.

Among the more unlikely stars to take their turn in the DJ box was David Hasslehoff, who is said to have played a set at the Café de Paris. Indie band Pulp's Jarvis Cocker has also been known to line-up tunes, provoking the bizarre spectacle of a crowd of intense on-lookers leaning over the decks so they're practically cheek to cheek – the nearest thing to a Victorian freak show in the late twentieth century.

Meanwhile TV personality Dani Behr, was given a prime-time slot on London's dance radio station Kiss FM.

Champagne House Not so much a reference to music as lifestyle, the Champagne house set consists of professionals who, having graduated through the rave years, cannot put their old habits to bed but have on the way picked up new habits commensurate with their occupational status (and pay packet).

In the early eighties these people would have been huddled in élitist groups, drinking champagne, snorting charlie and being derided as yuppies. Today they're more likely to be staggering around the dance floor spilling bubbly down complete stranger's throats and grinning like imbeciles. After the explosion of speed garage in 1997, people also began to use Champagne house to describe the extravagant displays of wealth of the smartly dressed punters attending clubs such as Absolute and Twice As Nice.

Cheeky Half Growing out of the loose association around the *Boy's Own* fanzine, Mick Robinson's Cheeky Half held a series of nights in the early nineties with Ashley Beedle and Terry Farley headlining.

Taking over venues such as Battersea Film Studios, the events contrasted with the growing glam scene of the period. More casually dressed and staying with the earlier Balearic vibe, the nights attracted people from across the spectrum of the contemporary club scene.

Cheese and Cheesy A general term for naff and kitsch music or instrumental breaks, 'cheesy' is an endearing insult for music that is obvious and often frankly naff.

Coming into popular currency in the early nineties, around the time of handbag house, the emergence of loungecore and the resurgence of jazz funk, it was used to excuse lame lyrics, crap melodies and terrible passages in otherwise funky tunes.

The term can be applied to anything from pop house to Burt Bacharach and Roy Ayers. Generally it recognises that the DJ playing the tune or artist producing it, is fully aware that the music stinks like a hunk of Gorgonzola but has a healthy sense of irony.

Cheesy Quaver A derogatory reference to the hardcore set, cheesy quaver raver was used to describe the legion of boys and girls who turned up to hardcore raves wearing boiler suits, white gloves and gas and paint masks, frantically waving an illuminous light stick, blowing on air horns and jerking their arms and bodies as if they were in the middle of the throws of an epileptic fit. Most cheesy. Most quaver like.

Chemical Brothers Tim Rowlands and Edward Simons met as students in Manchester in 1989, where they became devotees of the Hacienda during the second Summer of Love.

Orbiting around Justin Robertson's Manchester Balearic scene and clubs such as Most Excellent, they started their own night, Naked Under Leather, and adopted the Dust Brothers' moniker as a tribute to the US production team.

Releasing 'Song To The Siren' on Junior Boy's Own Records, they marked out their future territory of break beat driven music that borrowed the sounds of house music and funk and rock attitudes – an eclectic attitude that pointed in the direction of big beat.

Securing remixes of Robertson's 'Lionrock' project, Leftfield's 'Open Up' and Saint Etienne, they moved back south to Simons' native London and in 1994 they teamed up with Jeff Barrett to start their seminal Sunday social nights at the now re-named Albany pub in Great Portland Street. Intended to be a relaxed, anything goes evening, the night was almost instantly rammed with people dancing on tables and queues stretching from upstairs in the pub on to the street and around the corner.

The 'My Mercury Mouth' EP followed and became a classic, while their success also alerted the US Dust Brothers of their existence. A change in name became legally expedient and they relaunched themselves as the Chemical Brothers in 1995, releasing *Exit Planet Dust* and the club classic, 'Leave Home'.

Club and chart success followed, with the release of the *Dig Your Own Hole* album in 1997 and their Heavenly Social nights moving from Smithfield's to Turnmills, where it was renamed Heavenly Juke Box. By 1998 this was staffed by the next generation of DJs, such as Richard Fearless. The Chemicals still make rare appearances there.

Chic Formed around the funk-driven partnership of guitarist Nile Rodgers and bassist Bernard Edwards, who met while playing in the Big Apple Band in 1971, Chic evolved from a series of demos that the duo began recording. Recruiting two vocalists, Norma Jean Wright (who was later replaced by Alfa Anderson) and Luci Martin, as well as drummer Tony Thompson, the band scored an instant hit in 1977 with the disco hit 'Dance, Dance, Dance' (Yowsah, Yowsah, Yowsah).

By 1978 they had released 'Le Freak', which became Atlantic/WEA's biggest-selling single to date. Further hits included 'Good Times', with its classic bass line that was to underpin early hip hop hits such as 1979's 'Rapper's Delight'.

Meanwhile Rodgers and Edwards were called in to give their treatment to other artists' disco classics, such as Diana Ross' 'Upside Down' and Sister Sledge's 'We Are Family', while Rodgers kicked funky licks into David Bowie's early eighties hit, 'Let's Dance'. Attempts to revive the band in the nineties came to a halt after Edwards died in 1996.

Circus An early eighties one-off party organisation, the Circus was run by Patrick Lilley, Annie Le Paz and Jeremy Healey – some of the most influential names in London's New Romantics movement. Like the party organisations that would follow in their wake, such as Westworld and Pushca, Circus would put on events in obscure disused industrial locations, which would be extravagantly decorated in orchestrated themes. Tickets would be deliberately difficult to find, often distributed through telephone lines and relying on word of mouth to spread the information. The crowd dressed in a mixture of hard-times styles and outrageous overhangs from New Romantics lavish dressing.

Clink Street Paul 'Rip' Stone and Lu Vucovic's legendary Clink Street parties began on Saturday night with the legendary Rip parties. Attracting a more working class and racially mixed north London scene than the Balearic brigade at Shoom, the Clink Street parties had soon spread from being one-night affairs to three-day, all-weekenders.

Held in a recording studio complex set in an old prison, the night was perfectly timed, with thousands of punters fighting to get in. Inside ex-football hooligans, streetwise kids, musicians, fashion kids and pop and TV stars rubbed shoulders and got messy. DJs such as Evil Eddie Richards, Kid Bachelor, Mr C, and the Shock sound system would be joined by rappers, MCs and singers, blending house music with reggae-sound system traditions.

Unlike Shoom, which had begun to have a more accommodating attitude towards the press, the Rip parties were hostile to press interference, helping it maintain an underground vibe – sentiments that have stayed with those still involved.

Club Clichés As the club scene has evolved and transformed, it has thrown up its own musical genres, fashion and language. At each stage a new lexicon has emerged.

The more durable terms, such as 'wicked' (meaning brilliant), 'natch' (meaning naturally) and 'wrecked' (meaning out of it), have been adopted as mainstream phrases, while the more obscure are invented and dropped by style setters with breathtaking regularity.

Despite the self-professed egalitarianism of club culture, language defines a set of barriers between those in the know and those who tag along. There are few things more embarrassing for 'try hard' clubbers than being caught out using yesterday's language.

Phrases and words such as 'pukka', 'bubba', 'having it', 'mental' and 'radio rental' drop from everyone's lips for six months and then drop totally out of sight, as if they'd been marked by an agreed sell-by date before they were accepted into currency.

Although it's embarrassing being caught using a dated word, the greater sin lies in using tirelessly repeated club clichés, which quickly mark the user as not only being out of touch but also being the worst of all night creatures – a club bore. Phrases such as 'I was there when . . .' and 'things are not like they used to be' are best left alone unless you happen to be Ron Hardy or Larry Levan, which would be death defying.

Given the competitive nature of testosterone, these phrases tend to be uttered by disgruntled males trying to mark their status of being die-hard clubbers. Female clichés are more likely to come in the form of 'I'm sure I talked to you in the toilets at . . .'. which brings to mind another cliché about the sixties. 'If you can remember, you weren't really there.' If you must utter clichés, try 'I've forgotten where . . .'

Cocaine A long-serving club drug, cocaine was first extracted from the *Erythroxylon coca* bush by the German chemist Albert Niemann in the mid-nineteenth century and was initially used in medicines for its assumed effectiveness against a variety of ailments. It was also used as a local anaesthetic for eye, ear and throat surgery.

Sigmund Freud praised it as a potential cure for depression, alcoholism and morphine addiction. However, it was soon found that cocaine poisoning could be fatal and had a depressant and potentially addictive effect on users. Also, although there is no clear evidence to show that cocaine is physically addictive, users can become psychologically dependent.

In the early 1980s cocaine, which had always been prohibitively expensive, became more readily available in the London club scene, where it became the drug of style among glamorous clubbers and yuppies. While most people stuck to poppers, speed, occasional flutters of ecstasy (when it was available) and alcohol, a significant minority was snorting coke.

After the ecstasy explosion in the late eighties, style leaders again moved back to cocaine to distinguish themselves from the people they saw as mass morons, who were by now knocking back pills like they were smarties.

Throughout the nineties, cocaine gradually became more accessible and increasingly the drug of choice among clubbers, while speed re-emerged as the poor person's option. In the early to mid-nineties, crack, a base form of cocaine that vaporises at low temperatures and can therefore be smoked, began to be used, especially in the ragga/jungle scene. Noted for its concentrated high, it has a corresponding comedown and is more addictive, potentially leading to violent behaviour.

Cock Happy After acid jazz was coined as a term by Chris Bangs and Gilles Peterson, to counter the rise of acid house and create an alternative that had the same energy, Peterson and Bangs organised Cock Happy in Lauderdale House, Highgate.

Cock Happy was acid jazz's answer to raves. Peterson and Bangs would drop fast jazz funk tunes and watch the dance floor spin. It was here that a young rap poet called Rob Galliano appeared on the scene.

Coldcut Matt Black, a biochemist and computer boffin, and Jonathan More, a silversmith and art teacher, met while working behind the counter at Reckless Records in Soho, London. Both had also been DJing at nights such as Flim Flam and found they had a mutual interest in mixing and playing with beats.

They released the first Coldcut record, 'Say Kids What Time Is It?', in January 1987 – one of the first UK tracks to use sampling. Following this with a remix of Eric B and Rakim's 'Paid In Full', Coldcut caught the attention of Big Life Records who used them to remix artists such as Yazz and Lisa Stansfield. Coldcut's first album, *What's That Noise*, went silver, while they continued to notch up a stream of remixes with artists as diverse as James Brown, Elvis Costello, the Orb and Blondie.

In 1994, Coldcut left Big Life and released their *Philosophy* album on Arista, but they soon recoiled from the pressures of producing pop hits for a major label and left to form their own independent label, Ninja Tune/Ntone.

Evolving alongside Coldcut's fascination with break beat, Ninja artists such as DJ Food, Up Bustle and Out, The Herbaliser and Funki Porchini led the way in forming the trip hop and nineties break beat sound. Meanwhile, Coldcut concentrated on their work with the Hextatic VJ outfit, releasing a CD-ROM with them in 1998.

Combat Trousers Club land's ubiquitous choice of legging, combat trousers having been essential festival clobber and favoured crusty gear exploded on to every dance floor in the UK in the mid-nineties. Fitting in with the punk revival ethos of the period, army trousers also had the advantage of being multi-pocketed, allowing space for all your night-club essentials. A supermarket's worth of cigarettes, mobile phones, address books, Rizla papers, multi-packs of chewing gum, illicit drink, toothbrush (in case you got lucky) and, of course, that little something for the weekend could all be stored comfortably in their copious pockets.

At the time of storage this seemed to be distinctly practical, but by half way through a night of drink and drugs Accrington Stanley had more chance of winning the FA Cup than you had of finding anything in your stuffed pockets.

The Committee As jungle grew in 1994, the original DJs and promoters, who had previously felt ownership over the scene, began to see their vibe being grappled away from them by new promoters, MCs and media interest. Cheap imitations began to make it on to radio stations, which in turn reflected on the original artists, tarring them all with the same brush. A division emerged between the ragga-junglists and the original dark-core pioneers.

In one of the club scene's more bizarre and organised moments, the originals got together and formed The Committee to rescue their scene. The idea of Rebel MC, The Committee acted as the mediator between jungle and the media and promoters. Although some of the originals such as Dego McFarlane refused to participate, enough of the big names in drum 'n' bass took part to ensure The Committee had influence.

Focusing on General Levy, who had been made the media image of the scene, they agreed to boycott his 'Incredible' single from all DJ sets and to ostracise any DJ or promoter who supported him. Eventually gaining a stranglehold, The Committee demanded a letter of apology from Levy to be printed in *The Face*, where, in an earlier interview, Levy had claimed to be running jungle.

Levy responded, saying he was but one voice among DJs, pirate radio stations and record shops, trying to further the cause of black music. It wasn't an unconditional surrender but it proved the power of the committee, even if it also alienated some of those who should have been on board.

Computer Games As music technology came to dominate dance floor production sounds, with producers searching for ever more exciting and exclusive electronic sounds – using anything from microwaves to engine noises – the association between computers and nerds became displaced by cyberpunks, techno warriors and dance floor boffins.

Computers became cool. The drift of computer technology from out of the cold of the classroom came at the end of the seventies with the arrival of the now low-tech *Space Invaders*.

Against the backdrop of acts such as Kraftwerk, computer game music began to inform electronic music while, as technology advanced, computer game companies began to commission dance acts to write music for their new products.

The interaction of the club experience had obvious parallels with that of computer games, and by the mid-nineties market researchers had recognised club venues and dance events as valuable outlets for merchandising computer games. Rather than getting stuck at the bar with a geriatric raver banging on about taking a cheeky half and how things aren't as good as they used to be, club kids could now spend their night communicating with vastly more intelligent programs called things like *Grim Reaper – Angel of Armageddon III*.

And people used to worry about computers killing the art of conversation.

Confusion Hosted by Nicky Trax, in its short life Confusion gained a massive reputation. Starting in Bill Stickers on Greek Street, it moved to Shaftsbury's where Keith Franklin played a New Beat version of the Doors' standard 'Hello I Love You', alongside DJs Cisco Ferrera, Colin McBean, MC Pugwash, Paul Trouble Anderson and Ashley Beedle.

Pugwash specialised in picking on people in the crowd, whipping them up and taking the piss.

Carl Cox One of the UK's most prolific DJs, Carl Cox (affectionately known as Coxy) has been known to play up to 14 gigs regularly each week. Leaving school to take a course in electrical engineering, he quit to become a painter and decorator before graduating to become a dance floor legend. His early breaks came at friends' house parties, which led to bookings at weddings and eventually clubs. Hailing from Sutton in Surrey, his initial fame came in the seaside resort of Brighton, where he broke house and particularly acid house music in the late eighties.

By the time Danny Rampling launched Shoom, Cox was renowned enough to play the first night. He went on to do further legendary nights such as Spectrum and Land Of Oz. In 1989 he further increased his status by introducing a third deck to his sets at Sunrise.

Going on to become a champion of hardcore and then techno, he scored a top 30 chart single in 1991 with 'I Want You (For Ever)'. Forming a management company, Ultimate Music Management, he set up his own record labels, Ultimatum Worldwide, Ultimatum Breaks and Ultimatum Trax, before breaking into film in 1998 with an appearance in the club-based feature film *Human Traffic*.

As well as numerous DJ appearances, in the late nineties Cox held a residency, Ultimate BASE, at The End in central London.

Crackers The seminal underground jazz funk, black dance club of the late seventies, this small venue on Wardour Street, Soho had its heyday during George Power's residency there in 1977 and 1978. The club usually took place on Friday afternoons, when young teenagers would bunk off school and flock to Crackers, changing out of or re-arranging their uniforms on route to ensure they'd gain entry.

Once inside they'd rub shoulders with the hard core of the early London dance scene. While Power played underground funk and early disco imports and album tracks, the dance floor would throng, spin and slide. As this was way before the media had clocked what was happening, the dancers had little in the way of role models on which to base their moves so they invented their own techniques by combining jazz dance steps and spins with ballet moves, traditional Indian dance and anything that could be used to fit the beats. In the hands of dancers such as Mohammed, John Brown and Paul Trouble Anderson, an elaborate pattern of dance moves emerged, which still inform dance floors in the UK today.

By the time Power left in 1978, the dancers from his club had become legends on the London dance scene. Power went on to play the Horse Shoe Jazz Funk Double Disco nights, before moving to the Electric Ballroom and helping to launch Kiss FM. He now runs Nice 'n' Ripe record label.

Carl Craig and Planet E One of Detroit's next generation of techno artists, Carl Craig first turned heads with his releases on Derrick May's Transmatt record label under aliases such as Psyche and BFC.

A devotee of European acts such as Kraftwerk and The Human League, he was introduced to techno while supporting May as part of his Rhythim Is Rhythim project. Having recorded 'Strings Of Life '89' with May, he left to form his own label, the seminal Planet E, before moving to England for six months in 1990.

By now a recognised Detroit star, Craig became a prolific artist releasing a wealth of material, most notoriously his Paper Clip People excursions and a collaboration with Mauriza on Mind, both of which were released by Ministry Of Sound in the UK.

Cream The first house super-club, Cream started in the annex of the Academy (now Nation), in Liverpool in October 1992. During a fallow period of Manchester night life it immediately attracted an in-the-know crowd from across the north-west.

Its original 400 following has now swelled to 3,000 plus across the UK. The brainchild of Darren Hughes and James Barton, it has sprawled into an empire employing 100 full- and part-time staff, who oversee a bar, a shop, record releases, a DJ agency – representing (predictably) the cream of UK and USA DJs – and the club itself.

Alongside its regular Liverpool nights, Cream runs monthly events in Dublin, at the P.O.D. club, and in Glasgow's Tunnel club. In 1998 Hughes left the organisation to pursue other projects.

Criminal Justice Act Drafted in the aftermath of the big free festivals, such as Castlemorton, in the early nineties, the Criminal Justice Act 1994 was designed to secure the property rights of landowners, protect the Tory ideal of rural England and curtail the activities of non-conformists such as travellers, political protesters and animal rights activists. Against the wishes of senior police officers and civil rights activists, the CJA introduced the criminalisation of trespassing, removed the right to silence and sought to outlaw playing house music at raves.

The problem was that the Conservative government wanted to outlaw free festivals and raves while preserving the right of the good gentry of the UK to congregate and listen to opera music at festivals such as Glyndebourne. Consequently the CJA for the first time enshrined the word 'rave' in statute, while outlawing music that is 'wholly or partly . . . a succession of repetitive beats.' For the first time in British history the government was attempting to outlaw a youth culture.

In response the anarchic groupings of the free festival movement, which orbited around the Spiral Tribe, met in October 1993 at a launderette in Kensal Rise to initiate the Advance Party. A new force in the UK's political culture, the Advance Party responded to the attack on the right to dance by organising demonstrations that resembled raves rather than political rallies.

In place of the traditional format of marching on Trafalgar Square to hear rousing speeches, Advance Party gatherings danced into rallying points, drowning out such speakers as there were with sound systems, whistles and horns. The protesters danced, weaving around the lions and fountains of the Square and erupted in cheers as slogans and banners were draped across the speaker's platform.

Meanwhile the Freedom Network, a loose alliance of anti-Criminal Justice Act organisations, linked into the Advance Party and other causes of the moment, such as the anti-road building protest at Twyford Down and animal rights protests.

By the time of the third rally against the Bill, held in October 1994, the demonstrations had grown so big the organisers decided to end the march in Hyde Park. The sound systems were out in force, each one surrounded by a throng of writhing bodies. The police were poised to act, which they did as a sound system truck attempted to contravene instructions and enter Hyde Park. The resulting running battle between police and protesters went on well into the evening but did little to halt the Criminal Justice Bill being passed into the statute book on 3 November 1994.

Crusty Significant enough to attract legislation specifically designed to outlaw their activities, crusties were right up there with trade unions and surcharged councillors in attracting the authoritarian wrath of the UK's nineties Conservative government.

The Criminal Justice Act famously targeted open-air events with 'repetitive beats' in a bid to stamp out free raves and convoys of travellers cruising between festivals – obviously intolerable in a liberal society.

Oblivious to the law in general, crusty culture has gone from strength to strength. Heavily involved in single-issue and environmental campaigns such as Reclaim The Streets, they have become a credible political force as well as a musical one.

Mega Dog, a London-based crusty club that won't appreciate the label, held their first legal festival in 1997.

Crusties are notorious for not believing in baths and synthetic inventions such as deodorant and shampoo – hence their name. Instead they prefer growing dreadlocks and tying dogs on pieces of string. They like the countryside and all things natural but live in places such as Hackney and Manchester's Hulme housing estate – until it was knocked down.

They party to psychedelic Goan Trance music and see no contradiction with also being bang into Bob Dylan and traditional English folk music.

Cubase Opening the way for DJs and producers to arrange break beats, drum patterns, keyboard riffs and samples, the appearance of the Cubase sequencer alongside the Notator and Creator versions moved dance music from the preserve of live rhythm sections to one person productions in a thousand DJs' bedrooms.

Whereas dance floor edits, which extended the funkiest and most dance floor-worthy chunks of a song, had previously relied on the DJ cutting live between records or editing on a reel-to-reel tape, sequencers allowed DJs to programme in a sound such as drum pattern and loop it perfectly on a machine.

Sampling other sounds, or programming them on a bass or drum unit, enabled DJs to create totally new tracks without playing a single note. Speeding samples up by recording them on middle C of a keyboard and then playing them an octave up or simply speeding up the b.p.m. of a sequencer, enabled dance music to evolve into hardcore and jungle.

Meanwhile artists such as Soul II Soul used sequencers to take the beats in the opposite direction.

Lest we forget:
C&C Music Factory
Champion Records
Gary Clail
The Cooker
Cowboy Records

Best we forget:
Chewing the same piece of gum for two days
Children's themes as samples
Coming Down
Condoms as fashion accessories
Cult of House classics

Daft Punk Leading the French dance invasion that leapt across the globe in the late nineties, Thomas Bangalter Guy and Manuel de Homem-Christo met while at school in 1987 when they were thirteen years old. Forming Darlin in 1992, they released a track through Duophonic Records. The following year, they came into contact with Scotland's Soma Records and released their first single by Daft Punk called 'New Wave', in 1994. Their following single, 1995's 'Da Funk', became a much sought-after club classic while the duo's live tour of Europe further enhanced their reputation and attracted interest from Virgin Records, who released their debut album, *Homework*, in January 1997.

Dark As jungle emerged out of the hardcore scene it was seen as a sub genre rather than a distinct new form of music. Its use of samples from horror movies, macabre ambient qualities and time-stretched break beats led it to be christened horrorcore, darkcore and, more permanently, dark.

Often related to the economic decline of the early nineties and corresponding angst, dark reflected the pessimism of the period and the rise of the alternative economy. Faced with the prospect of long-term unemployment, an urban underclass developed their own economy, often involving scams from dole-fiddling and drug dealing to theft. Dark was deliberately unsettling. Classics include 4 Hero's 'Mr Kirk's Nightmare' and Metalheadz's 'Terminator'.

DeConstruction and Concrete Founded by partners DJ Mike Pickering, Keith Blackhurst and, later, Pete Hadfield, DeConstruction (a division of BMG) has been responsible for releasing a string of club classics. Balancing somewhere between the commercial face of the scene yet maintaining credibility, they were responsible for releasing *North* in 1988, which is frequently cited as the first house compilation album.

The label became the outlet for Pickering's band, M People, whose pop success alongside acts such as Kylie Minogue, Black Box, N Joi, the Grid, Sasha and K-Klass naturally associated the label with the more commercial and less demanding side of dance.

Acts such as Justin Robertson's Lionrock, who are by turns commercial and leftfield, have given the label a harder edge, while its related labels, Concrete and Heavenly, have associated the family with big beat and more cutting-edge sounds such as Deep Dish's *Junk Science*.

Deee-Lite Formed by husband-and-wife team, Lady Miss Kier and DJ Dimitry Brill, this American/Russian partnership met in New York in 1982 and Deee-Lite became the seminal pop-house act of the early nineties.

Teaming up with Japanese computer expert Towa Towa, they scored a massive hit with 'Groove Is In The Heart', backed with 'What Is Love?'. The single ensured them a place in the annals of dance music, although subsequent releases failed to repeat the success. Kier, nonetheless, became a lasting club fashion icon.

Deep Dish Formed in 1992 by Ali Dubfire Shirazinia and Sharam Tayebi, two Washington-based Iranian DJs who met while DJing at the same party, Deep Dish set out to redefine deep house music.

Inspired by New York and Detroit sounds, they blended the house sound with a myriad of influences from jazz to Led Zeppelin. Turning their production skills to remixes and original tunes, they released under their own Deep Dish and Yoshitoshi labels and for Tribal, as well as remixing tracks for artists such as Joi Cardwell, Ashley Beedle, The Shaman, Janet Jackson, Kristine W, D*Note, the Rolling Stones, Adam F and Sandy B.

Their albums, *Penetrate Deeper* and *Junk Science*, stand out as carefully crafted, house, long players that don't hold back surprises.

Collaborating with other artists, such as Ali's schoolmate Brian 'BT' Transeau, they created an original and crisp, deep house, tribal sound. Continuing to DJ in and around Washington, they attracted the attention of Tribal America and in 1994 launched their subsidiary label, Yoshitoshi, with the release of 'Submarine'.

Not keen on resting on their laurels, they set up a new hip hop label, called Middle East, in 1997 and currently want to record percussionists from their native Iran.

Delirium Frequently cited as one of London's original house nights, Delirium started life at the Astoria Theatre in 1986 and was run by DJs Noel and Morris Watson and by long time DJ, promoter and journalist Nicky Trulocke. A well-known party animal, Trulocke famously spent a night handing out Delirium flyers in an intoxicated state and inadvertently started doshing crisp ten pound notes into the hands of would-be clubbers.

Delirium soon built its reputation by booking the choice acts of the time such as Chuck Brown and breaking seminal house acts such as Frankie Knuckles and Ten City, who they brought to the UK well ahead of the hype.

In fact Delirium had an eclectic music policy but at the time the only other nights playing large sections of house were a few gay clubs such as Jungle and Mark Moore and Colin Faver's The Pyramid.

Delirium came to a sad end after a management buy-out of the Astoria in summer 1987. It folded, but a year later house music had taken over the nation's dance floors.

Detroit The roots of techno can be traced to European bands such as Kraftwerk, Depeche Mode and The Human League, but the home of techno is Detroit in the USA.

Here the often-bland pop of European electronic music was transformed by an experimental electro/hip hop community, who developed their sound alongside the early Chicago house scene. In particular Derrick May, Kevin Saunderson and Juan Atkins used new music technology to create a stripped-down, energetic, urban sound track. A crop of legendary labels sprang up, including Transmat, Metroplex, KMS, Planet E, Red Planet and Underground Resistance.

Techno arrived at the same time as the house explosion, but its hip hop roots give it more varied rhythm patterns, ranging from hard furious beats to funkier arrangements, and allows for greater experimentation. Reflecting the shattered economy of the Motor City, the Detroit sound is often dark, subtle and industrial.

Tony De Vit Considered by many to be the main force behind nu-NRG, Tony De Vit's DJ career took off when he was in his late thirties after being booked to be the resident at Trade.

His career in fact had already reached back 20 years into the gay scene, where he started playing Funkadelic tracks. A gay icon,

De Vit became one of the UK's most popular DJs in both the gay and straight community, although he only quit his day job (as a quality-control manager for a factory producing tiles for the space shuttle) some three-and-a-half years before his death. By that time he was able to command fees of £1,000 a set.

Setting up his first label, Jump Records, he split from the project and set up a new imprint, TDV. Having been one of the most prolific DJs of the mid-nineties, his sudden death, in July 1998, sent shock waves across club land.

Diggin' In The Crates Better than ecstasy and more addictive than heroin, diggin' in the crates managed to keep the jazz faith alive during the era of dodgy pill-popping, 30,000-strong raves and all-out hedonistic having it.

While the rest of the UK's youth were tearing up and down the countryside in pursuit of the next party and being pursued by old plod, the jazz boys and occasionally girls had found their own deviant behaviour. For them there was no better buzz than spending all their waking hours in the dingy back rooms of obscure record shops, digging out ever more obscure records by German jazz bands that no one had heard of 30 years ago, let alone now.

While others were losing their youth in a haze of chemicals, jazz heads lost it in the haze of dimly lit record crates. Snorting dust mites they broke out in cold sweats, lest the geezer with the reversed tweed flat cap going through the crate next to them found a record they were after.

John Digweed Starting his DJ career at the tender age of thirteen, John Digweed played his first gig at The Crypt, a pub-cum-club, in his home town of Hastings in 1984. Honing his skills and taste, he went on to refine long, smooth-running sets that build through funky garage, to hard house.

Becoming a regular DJ at Renaissance parties, a guest star DJ all over the place, he frequently collaborated with Sasha, with whom he released a series of epic house-mix tapes such as 'Northern Exposure' and 'Renaissance: The Mix Collection'.

Dirtbox The only surviving club from London's influential warehouse period of the early eighties, Dirtbox is about 497 years old in club-land terms.

Before night-clubs cottoned on to the new club-going population, sound systems squatted in and transformed disused industrial spaces and offices. To get round legal restrictions, charging on the door and selling alcohol involved elaborate rituals such as holding raffles in which each ticket won a beer. Bars would invisibly transform into tea and biscuit counters at the first sight of a blue uniform.

Older and wiser, Dirtbox has maintained its illegal groove with slick professionalism. Starting at 3 a.m., publicity is held back until the night and regulars seem to know by osmosis where to find it. Watching promoter Phil Dirtbox gathering his punters for a night is the closest you'll get to seeing the Pied Piper in London.

Disco Remembered for permed hair, medallions and flares, Disco was in fact a primary influence on contemporary club music. Labels such as Philadelphia International and Salsoul, which gave us the first 12in single in 1975, transformed dance music. Despite being desperately uncool during the late seventies punk period, the music was re-introduced to the UK via the first and second waves of Rap music – predominantly through the Sugar Hill Gang in 1979 and Grandmaster Flash in 1982.

New York's Paradise Garage club (which gave its name to contemporary garage music) and Chicago's Warehouse (which bestowed its title on house music) were both disco clubs. The music continued to play a strong influence among the original acid house DJs such as Jon Da Silva, who would shamelessly drop Gloria Gaynor's 'I Will Survive' in the middle of his set.

The current UK Nu House movement, spearheaded by FAZE Action, Basement Jaxx, Paper Recordings and Nu Phonic, openly pays homage to its disco roots. The next time you're laughing at 'Earth Wind and Fire', spare a thought for how your children will feel about that video of you flailing your arms in a Lycra top. Long Live Ottowan.

Disco Divas The emergence of garage and house music in the USA and Europe gave a new lease of life to the forgotten heroines of disco – the divas who, like Gloria Gaynor, gave us the now fashionably cheesy dance anthems of the late seventies.

Nowhere was their influence more delightfully felt than in handbag classics. Gwen Guthrie, Sister Sledge, Martha Wash, Jocelyn Brown, P.P. Arnold alongside new artists such as Toni Braxton, Dina Carroll, Billie Ray Martin, Joie Cardwell, Ce Ce Peniston, Rozalla and Ultra Nate were chucked into the mix by house producers and snapped up by record labels such as A&M, WEA and Pulse 8.

Once again people could sing along as they spun on the dance floor. Altogether now . . .

DIY DIY sound system grew out of the anarcho post-punk and hip hop scene and led the way in cementing the crossover between the latter-day hippie/traveller scene and dance music.

Based in Nottingham their name, Do It Yourself, espoused a political ethos and commitment that house events should be run by and for people from the scene – a reaction against the money-making rave mentality of the early nineties. Linking up with a group of travellers in 1990, they began holding free parties in the West Country. Consisting of a free-flowing membership, their most famous members were Harry, Damien, Simon D.K., Emma, Digs and Woosh.

DIY launched during a period of intense police activity in which officers expected to bust parties and confiscate hoards of cash. At DIY parties confused police officers would find nothing but a bunch of DJs who had travelled 200 miles to put on raves for nothing.

DIY became a focus for other seminal sound systems, such as the Spiral Tribe, that formed a backbone for events such as Castlemorton and naturally became a key focus of, and opposition to, the Criminal Justice Act. They turned their hand to recording and released their first album, *Strictly for Groovers*, in 1993.

DJ Courses There are few clearer indications that something's become institutionalised than when it enters the education system as a legitimate subject for study. DJ mixing and scratching, an art that started on the streets of Bronx, has come a long way. Largely as a result of the introduction of National Vocational Qualifications in the UK – a system that recognises educational standards in work-related activities – pupils attending some further education colleges and voluntary educational establishments can now take courses in DJing and receive certificates to prove it.

Soon night-clubs will be demanding proof of qualification before booking DJs and trendy governments will be proposing a National Academy of Dance. Step forward Professor Herc, Dr Flash and Bachelor of Science Bambaataa.

Doorpeople Beyond the unity of the groove, drugs and communal dancing, clubbers are united in an even more binding, shared experience. Everyone has at least one tale about abusive door staff.

Some incidents can be put down to one bad apple. One bouncer used to delight in leading the police to the gutter where his latest victim would be drowning in their own blood.

Among the minor frustrations are the clubs with door policies that deprive punters of their chewing gum, apparently to protect a carpet that turns out be a figment of the management's imagination. Other offences include the slightly more drug-related removal of cigarette papers, which leaves roll-up smokers with a totally useless packet of tobacco. Then there's the job's-worth bouncers, who, given a uniform and milligram of power, turn into a sociological experiment on the parallels between role playing and the behaviour of Nazi concentration camp guards. Closely related, there's the short fuse, who takes his frustrated life out on punters and is never happy going home without having first dusted his fists with a customers' incisors.

Strangely club managers seem to be oblivious to complaints from their paying clientele and don't seem to mind that their club's fame is often preceded by that of their bouncers.

Then again, there are all those clubs that are run by, ahem, security firms.

Dorado/Filter Dorado, an eclectic jazz, funk and club-influenced label, was established by Ollie Buckwell in 1992. Its first release, Monkey Business' 'Funk driven 'Ain't No Fun', came out on a white label and established the label's trademark blue-and-gold or blue-and-silver record sleeve design.

The label soon diversified, releasing dance-related tracks from across the musical spectrum, although its releases always maintained a jazz element – Buckwell deliberately took up the mantel from earlier labels such as Talkin' Loud. Among devotees Dorado releases became supremely collectable. Alongside artists such as Jehlisa Anderson, Sunship and Matt Cooper's Outside, D*Note became the label's flagship act, taking their sound into drum 'n' bass and anywhere else they pleased.

Setting up a second label, Filter, to release their more leftfield dance floor-orientated tracks, Dorado's position at the forefront of intelligent club music was firmly established.

Not surprisingly the head of the new outlet, the long-serving jazz buff and DJ Ross Allen, was soon snapped up by Island to work in their A&R department. Dedicated to staying underground, Dorado and Filter had the major's sniffing around them for years before finally allowing WEA to carry their distribution in Europe in 1988.

Downbeat Growing out of the original London and Bristol-based hip hop scenes, and in reaction to heightening b.p.m. of the house in the early nineties, downbeat has a long heritage.

Containing references to the dub sound systems of the seventies and underground soul and hip hop of the early eighties, Downbeat is the offspring of the two-step scene of east London, where promoters such as Mistri organised nights at Night Grooves in Shoreditch and laid the ground for later sound systems such as Soul II Soul.

Two-step seldom went above 90 b.p.m. but it swung. Soul II Soul took the laid-back funky vibe into warehouse jams, finding common ground with a fashionable London crowd who had grown through hip hop to rare groove and house. Suddenly the vibe was chilled. Via the collaboration of Nellee Hooper, Soul II Soul's first album, *Club Classics*, married the London and Bristol break beat scenes.

By 1990 the original Balearic DJs such as Paul Oakenfold, who had been instrumental in picking the beats up, had switched to bringing them back down again – forming Movement 98 in an attempt to do so.

By 1992 a distinctly new form of downbeat music had emerged which, merging hip hop, dub bass and techno sounds, was soon dubbed trip hop – much to everyone's irritation.

Artists such as Howie B, an ex Soul II Soul member and key innovator in the downbeat/trip hop movement, started releasing deep, underground and uncompromisingly long dub-laced tracks, although he went on to produce the somewhat less underground U2.

Labels such as Mo Wax, Hard Hands, Pork Productions and Ninja Tune reinvented the break beat and hip hop scene, reintroducing and updating turntable technician skills for an audience that had got used to seamless house mixing.

Meanwhile Hextatic used new visual equipment to bring eighties warehouse projections into the nineties. While break beat had found its way back on to the dance floor through jungle, a new variety of downbeat mixes used the same basics to re-invent music forms from techno to jazz, hip hop and house – eventually spawning a revival in B-boy culture as well as big beat.

Dragonfly Records Formed by the ubiquitous, one-time Killing Joke bass guitarist, Youth, Dragonfly records concentrates on underground trance and techno. Youth's devotion to sound is derived from his earlier passion for bass-driven funk, the technological trickery of dub reggae sound systems and tribal rhythms.

After going to Goa and experiencing the all-night parties, where DJs merged techno tracks with didgeridoos, drums and the sounds of nature, Youth returned determined to recreate the throbbing, tripped-out, mesmerising music in the UK.

Dreem Teem Formed in 1996 by UK garage DJs Mikee B, Timmi Magic and DJ Spooney, they released their first single, 'The Theme', in December 1997 on DeConstruction. Having already been a club anthem in summer 1997, 'The Theme' immediately scored national chart success in the UK but just failed to hit the top 30.

Releasing the first speed garage compilation, *The Dreem Teem In Session Volume 1*, on 4 Liberty records, they secured a slot on London's dance music radio station, Kiss 100 and set up their own record label, DJs for Life.

In spring 1998 they launched the first Europe-wide tour of UK garage, which took them to 19 venues in the UK as well as some in Amsterdam, Belgium and France.

Dress Code The fetish of eighties London, dress codes during the yuppie era decided whether you spent the night hanging out with bright young things or were shown the red card and sent home with your tail between your legs and a pizza under your arm.

At first dress code policies tended to opt for dressed up or smarter guises, but the advent of the hard-times look flashed a clear signal as to whether you were in the know or a drongo.

While all clubs that were worth going to operated strict door policies, some such as The Wag and La Beat Route, and later the Mud club and Taboo, were notorious for even turning away regulars on a whim. Being first in queue at ten o'clock, half an hour before the club opened, was no insurance against being rebuffed because the person at the door didn't like your shoes or thought your socks clashed with your T-shirt.

Even clubs such as the cavernous Warehouse, at the Electric Ballroom, would give you the shoulder if they thought you didn't look like a clubber. And to make matters worse, dismissal would often be carried out through a third party. 'Sorry mate, you can come in but your friend? . . .'

Naturally punters soon tired of the attitude, and by the end of the decade this strict sense of style had given way to the anything-goes attitude of acid house. The tolerance was short-lived, as dress codes were introduced up and down the UK in a bid to keep the more violent punters out. This re-emergence was however a far looser assessment of character than the earlier fashion fascism.

The one area of what might be loosely called club culture that has maintained a strict adherence to door policy is the no-trainer venue. Populated by boys in white shirts and no jackets – whatever the weather – and called things like Cinderella's, these clubs play chart music to a female-only dance floor and the night is guaranteed to end with a fight. Luckily these venues tend to advertise their no-trainers policy, ensuring discerning clubbers can avoid them like the plague.

Drill 'n' Bass Applied to a group of UK techno outfits, such as Mike Paradinas' u-Ziq, Aphex Twin, Squarepusher and Plug, drill 'n' bass takes techno's fascination with electronic noises and matches them with the choppy, break beat drum patterns of jungle.

Inspired by early hardcore and the latter-day drum 'n' bass of artists such as LTJ Bukem, Paradinas has come to represent the sound, with his crafted use of melody and cutting drum riffs, although he refers to his music as speed funk.

Drum Club The namesake of the Sunderland club that introduced Balearic beats in 1983, the Drum club – the acid house club that refused to let it lie – opened its doors at the Soundshaft, Heaven, London, in 1992. Two years of pumping acidic house and techno followed until it closed on 30 June 1994, with farewell appearances from Fabio, Justin Robertson, Billy Nasty and others.

Those who had missed the acid revolution the first time around, and those who didn't want to let a trivial thing like time and history get in the way of having a good time, stripped to the waist and sweated until they melted into the speaker stack. The fact it was a mid-weeker only added to the revivalist spirit as the revellers spent the following day at work knocking back revival remedies.

Drum 'n' Bass Originally a generic term used as an alternative to jungle, by the mid-nineties drum 'n' bass had become increasingly associated with new converts to the scene, who were often accused of being white, middle class youths who sought to disassociate jungle from its ragga roots.

In fact the drum 'n' bass strain of jungle developed a more sophisticated musical approach that was in keeping with the eclectic roots of the music and maintained the drive of the drum patterns while adding more subtle, jazz-driven arrangements.

The rise of drum 'n' bass was in many ways a reaction to the domination of jungle by the ragga scene. Many of the original DJs, such as Bukem, Fabio, Rob Haigh's Omni Trio, 4 Hero and Kemistry and Storm, were tiring of the relentless rough-cut, ragga chants and sought to promote a more diverse and melodic style of jungle.

The rise of drum 'n' bass served to popularise the music, give lease to a new crop of artists, such as Reprazent, Adam F and Photek, and trained people's ears for harder sounds such as Jump up.

DTPM Techno for tarts, DTPM started life alongside Trade and FF as the third component of the endless weekends out. Back then the gay weekend would start at Heaven, move to Turnmills, slip back to Heaven, then back to Turnmills, then to Heaven and finally back to Turnmills, until Monday morning. Then throw a sicky.

In the late nineties DTPM was reincarnated at The End, although the days of full-weekend clubbing were just not like they used to be.

Dub Dub evolved out of the instrumental B sides of Jamaican reggae releases on labels such as Trojan, for whom the legendary King Tubby recorded a series of groundbreaking records between the early and mid-seventies. Tubby hit on his formula when he realised his instrumental versions of popular tunes, which twisted into landscapes of reverberating snare drums and booming bass lines, were going down better at sound system parties than the vocal original.

His reputation grew rapidly and his services were soon being used by every influential Jamaican artist. Others were quick to follow, with Lee Scratch Perry introducing dub effects into seminal works, such as 'Police and Thieves', in the mid-seventies. By the end of the decade Dub had evolved into a distinct genre, with sound systems competing to maximise the distinctive bass, reverb, echo and percussion patterns.

In the UK dub found expression in the late punk movement, with John Lydon taking refuge in Jamaica after splitting from the Sex Pistols and numerous punk bands attempting to recreate the dub sound.

Artists such as producer Dennis Bovell, moved from lovers of rock to punk-dub collaborations with The Pop Group and The Slits, before working with acts such as Steel Pulse and poet Linton Kwesi Johnson. Meanwhile Mad Professor and Adrian Sherwood and his On U Sounds label kept dub moving through the eighties.

By 1988 the Nu Groove record label in New York was using dub expressions on New York house and garage tracks. Dub has continued to influence the dance floor, informing UK progressive house artists such as Andrew Weatherall, the bass lines of jungle and sub-bass of late nineties hip hop, trip hop and big beat.

Dub Pistols Far from containing any dub references, DJ Barry Ashworth's Dub Pistols are a firing, openly big beat band. Ashworth, who before becoming a DJ in 1994, promoted clubs and sang with Déjà Vu, is renowned for his manic behaviour. According to him he had to be carried off at the end of his first gig, at RAW, after he head-butted the turntable.

The Dug Out The epicentre of the Bristol scene, and consequently legendary for its influence on what became known as the Bristol sound, The Dug Out was a dingy basement club on Park Row that originally operated as a jazz club.

The Dug Out came into its own in 1982 when a DJ and MC collective, called The Wild Bunch, started a residency there. The Wild Bunch, who had been inspired by New York hip hop, had built their reputation playing illegal warehouse gigs and St. Paul's carnival, where they played through the night until dawn.

The club became the hangout for trendies from the Clifton area, locals from St. Paul's and working class youths from the outlying areas. With its low-ceilinged labyrinth of interconnecting rooms set out in the basement, and a lounge upstairs, it was more a scene place to hang out, smoke spliff and drink beer than a full-on dance venue.

While London at the time was mixing soul into hip hop, The Wild Bunch would drop reggae among their New York imports. Soon an exchange between London and Bristol developed, with

The Dug Out crew hosting sound clashes with London sound systems such as The Language Lab, while they were invited to London to join Nutriment, the Mastermind sound system and Notting Hill carnival.

Predictably The Dug Out was not popular with the police and after a campaign by the local street traders' association, the venue was closed in 1986. The scene briefly moved to The Moon club, a similarly dingy venue, but never recovered its legendary status.

Lest we forget:
Del Tha Funky Homosapien
Disposable Heroes of Hiphoprisy
Dr Dre

Best we forget:
Doves (dollops of speed passed off as MDMA)
Drink Prices
Door policies and dress codes

E In Aldous Huxley's *Brave New World*, the people were given Soma to overcome inhibition. In New Labour's New Britain there's ecstasy, MDMA or 3,4 methylene-dioxymethamphetamine to give it its proper name. First synthesised in Germany in 1912, it was later used for psychotherapy in the USA during the sixties.

Arriving in the UK in the late seventies, it originally appeared in gay clubs and among pop stars, fashion designers, journalists, in New Romantics clubs and later at nights such as Taboo. By the mid-eighties small groups of tourists started combining it with the sybaritic night life in Ibiza. Importing it into the UK, clubs such as Shoom, Spectrum, The Trip and Hot kicked acid house and rave culture into action – as documented in Matthew Collin's book, *Altered State*.

By the nineties pure MDMA had become rare in pills, with dealers peddling cheaper options, such as speed, caffeine and MDA. The rapid deterioration of the quality of the drug in the early nineties led to dealers selling quality MDMA by branding it with logos. Names such as Doves, Thunderdomes, MacDonalds, TNTs, Mercedes, Apples and Green Goddesses were adopted to describe the logo stamped on a pill.

For a limited period punters could choose better products, until the unscrupulous dealers copied the new pill's format but replaced MDMA with cheaper options. Like cigarettes, alcohol and red meat, ecstasy can be fatal. By the mid-nineties around 50 deaths had resulted from ecstasy use – usually through dehydration. Risks are greatly reduced by drinking water, even though it's also thought ecstasy inhibits the kidneys from working so water consumption should not be overdone. The long-term effects of ecstasy use are not known, although there's no shortage of guinea pigs.

Eastern Bloc Manchester and the north of England's most notorious record shop, Eastern Bloc was opened by Martin Price, who was later to find recording success himself with his 808 State band. Eastern Bloc became legendary as the purveyors of house and dance music, while also launching its own record label, Creed.

Among the artists and DJs that were launched by the label are K-Klass, Ariel and Justin Robertson, while many of the workers behind its counters, such as Robertson, Ariel and Greg Fenton, went on to careers as DJs or artists. In 1991 Creed was moved under the label banner of MOS (More O' Same) and Eastern Bloc launched its own brand label in 1993.

When the empire ran into financial difficulty, pop producer Pete Waterman purchased it and appointed Peter Taylor to take over the label. Eastern Bloc expanded their retail outlets to Leeds and then Toronto.

Eclectic As house and garage dance floor domination subsided in the mid-nineties, avant-garde DJs began to fill the vacuum. Eclectic mixing, which had dominated the early house and Balearic scene, began to replace the tired formula of repetitive beats, where DJs mixed records that were barely indecipherable from each other.

The style was a throw-back to the more catholic music of the mid- to late eighties, but eclectic took off in 1993 with Gilles Peterson and James Lavelle's That's How It Is nights at Bar Rumba and the Heavenly Social at the Albany. Playing contemporary, ground-breaking music alongside classics, they reworked house, hip hop and jungle to satisfy a new mood bored with four-four dance beats.

Leftfield DJs emerged from back rooms across the UK and stormed the main dance floors. DJs such as Ashley Beedle proved their versatility by recording house and techno as well as jazz and trip hop tunes. The focus is quality; play what you like as long as it's good and obscure enough never to reach the top 60.

Ever inventive, some eclectic DJs refined the art of clearing a throbbing dance floor at the flick of a crossfader.

Ecstasy Deaths According to Nicholas Saunders, author of *E for Ecstasy*, there are on average, five ecstasy-related deaths a year. The first recorded UK death was 22-year-old Ian Larcombe, who died of a heart attack after consuming 18 tablets in one go. The following October, Janet Mayes, also 22 years old, died after taking two ecstasy tablets at a disco in Hampton Court, Surrey. A media panic ensued as ecstasy was denounced as a killer drug.

Despite the outrage, and a series of horror story television documentaries on ecstasy, ecstasy use continued to proliferate. In September 1995, Daniel Ashton became the 51st person to die after taking ecstasy. Two months later Leah Betts went into a coma and died after taking a tablet at her home during her birthday party. While clubbers reacted by turning Apples, the brand that Betts had taken, into a status symbol, the mood perceptibly changed, even among those who still advocated the drug.

The E-vangelists, who previously preached its virtues, were replaced by people who, although not condemning the drug, encouraged greater knowledge about using it safely. Meanwhile magazines found a huge market in stories about the long-term effects of ecstasy use.

Even turning to other drugs, such as cocaine, began to take on a worrying health message. *Mixmag*'s biggest-ever selling cover was devoted to the potentially lethal effects of speed.

808 State Manchester-based 808 State was formed in the late eighties by Martin Price (owner of Eastern Bloc records shop), Graham Massey, Darren Partington and Andy Barker – the last two having been the DJ duo The Spin Masters. Originally the line-up also included Gerald Simpson (a.k.a. A Guy Called Gerald).

They released their first album, *Newbuild*, in 1988, but rose to fame recording their seminal *Pacific State* in 1989, which became an immediate club anthem and, later, a chart hit.

Pacific State was followed by a series of collaborations with vocal artists Bernard Sumner (of New Order) on 'Spanish Heart' and Björk on 'Oops' and 'Qmart' and two more albums, *Quadrastate* and *808:90*. A longer-lasting partnership was formed with rapper MC Tunes (Nicky Lockett), who later formed the rock/dance crossover band, The Dust Junkys.

MC Tunes worked with them for their fourth album, *North At Its Heights*. Price distanced himself from the band in 1991 to work on managing his new signing, the rap band Nu Conscious Kaliphz (later simply called Kaliphz), while the band went on to release a further album, *Gorgeous*, in 1993.

In 1998 they re-released *Pacific State* with updated mixes.

Electric Ballroom A vast warehouse of space and a favourite of Goths, students and lost Camden tourists, the Electric

Ballroom opened as a popular punk venue after the Music Machine, now the Camden Palace, closed. Following a brief incarnation as a roller disco, the Electric Ballroom opened as a night-club in the early eighties.

Cred is not a word that is associated with the Ballroom, but DJs such as acid jazz guru Gilles Peterson played there, alongside Glenn Gunner and Jay Strongman, who played anything from indie-dance, to classic disco, hip hop and house.

Nights such as the Warehouse, Rip it Up, The Slammer, Wavelength and The Crush fulfilled the role of weekend fall-backs when warehouse parties failed to materialise. Consequently a generation of clubbers cut their teeth within its walls.

Electric Chair Rising like a phoenix from the ashes of the Manchester rave scene, Electric Chair attempted to regroup and re-ignite the buzz of the Manchester scene that had been driven out of the city by the violence and corporate club culture of the early nineties.

Following the lead of the scene based around beat record shops such as Fat City, Justin Only Child (formerly of the New Fads) and Luke Unabomber (collectively called The Unabombers) formed Electric Chair.

Deliberately downbeat, they began looking for a suitably small venue that would challenge the dominant corporate club scene. In place of silk shirts they envisaged jeans and T-shirts, instead of champagne, beer, and rather than handbag and pop-house music they offered break beats, experimental music and eclectic mixing.

They booked themselves into the Road House, the only venue that would let them play their sounds, for their first night in the summer of 1995. The venue, a drab basement, was ideal. The first night attracted 100 people – nearly all of them friends and many of them part of the city's original house movement. By the fourth month the queues stretched around the block, despite the lack of any meaningful advertising.

Meanwhile other clubs with a similar ethos such as the seminal Feva, One Tree Island, Naked Under Leather and Headfunk enabled a new Manchester scene to flourish – splitting the city in two between the nu-groove and tired old corporate clubs.

Electro An experimental combination of hip hop and electronic music, Electro originated with Afrika Bambaataa's voyages into the outer limits of funk.

His and Arthur Baker's seminal 'Planet Rock' shifted rap music into a new genre and by the mid-eighties every shopping centre in the UK had its own break dance posse – equipped with baggy trousers, baseball caps, squashed cardboard boxes (for dance mats) and ghettoblasters pumping out electro. It spawned a string of compilation albums with titles such as *The Greatest Electro Album in the World, Ever – Volume Four.*

The re-emergence of break beat culture in the mid-nineties has seen electro sneak back on to the dance floor at nights such as Scratch in King's Cross, London. Like Hegel, whom Marx described as standing on his head, electro fans dance upside down.

Electronica Essentially big beat re-packaged for the USA market, Electronica was invented by confused music journalists and marketing people, who, on finding the predominantly rock-orientated North American market liked UK dance acts such as the Chemical Brothers and the Prodigy, had to find a way of categorising it.

The term, which bears little relation to the music, is used to describe anything from drum 'n' bass to downbeat techno, as long as it sounds British. This must have been very frustrating for America's little-appreciated domestic dance industry. Ironically, while UK dance acts were breaking in the states, the UK media was banging on about Brit-pop and bands such as Oasis taking the USA by storm – which of course they didn't.

Meanwhile UK clubs started describing their music policy as electronica – with their tongues so firmly planted in their cheeks they sprouted roots.

The End Boasting to be a club built by clubbers for clubbers, and owned by Mr C and Layo, The End swung open its doors in 1993. At first its blue boiler-suited staff and zealous door people were a little too pristine for clubbers who were turning to the beer-laced anarchy of the Hoxton scene.

Wear-and-tear and beneficial ageing, alongside a music policy that is as encouraging to rising underground movements as it is to big stars, has transformed The End into a thriving sound factory. Resident nights run by organisations such as Roni Size's Full Cycle Records, Skint Records, DTPM, Blackmarket and The End's own Tech-House night, Sub-Terrain, bring punters from the four corners of dance culture on to its spring-loaded dance floor. Alongside the club, The End runs its own record label, End Recordings, and represents its own roster of DJs.

In 1998 The End added to its attractions by opening a late night bar next door to the venue. But above all this, The End is notorious for its lush toilets, especially appreciated by female club toilet queue veterans, who are prone to swooning over The End's voluptuous row of 12 cubicles.

Epic House Epitomised in John Digweed and Sasha's *Northern Exposure* project and by DJs and producers such as BT and Perfecto, epic house is pitched somewhere between trance and house.

Opting for long drawn-out, pumping grooves, the records go on for ever and a night of them sees the DJ spinning endless records that sound exactly the same.

Lest we forget:
East West Records
8 Ball Records
Electribe 101 and Billy Ray Martin
Energy
Energy drinks

Best we forget:
Earning your living from nine-to-five jobs
Eating the contents of your fridge before going to bed
Not eating for three days

Fabio Frequently cited alongside Grooverider as the most influential DJ on the jungle scene, Fabio (Fitzroy Herbert) rose to prominence playing Fun City, at Shaftsbury's, in central London in 1989, and on the rave circuit, where he introduced harder beats to a young, energetic crowd.

But it was his collaboration with Grooverider, in the upstairs bar at the Rage nights, in Heaven, in 1990, that secured him lasting prominence. The duo were soon moved to the main dance floor, where a host of latter-day jungle DJs and producers, including Goldie and Kemistry and Storm, were introduced to their blend of hardcore and black dance music.

Fabio and Grooverider were experimenting with the decks, creating their own sounds by pitching records at plus eight, distorting the breaks and adapting ragga influences, such as Shut Up and Dance's '5, 6, 7, 8' to the rave scene.

As the acknowledged pioneers of the scene, when Kiss 100 decided to launch its first regular jungle show in 1995, Fabio and Grooverider were the obvious choice. This was in part out of respect to the duo but also because the jungle scene was by this point fraught with internal political division.

Meanwhile Fabio had been influential in taking the music to its next step. Teaming up with LTJ Bukem, the rising star of drum 'n' bass, and Kemistry and Storm in October 1994, he opened Speed at the Mars Bar. The club became pivotal in attracting a new audience to the jungle genre. His next role was to become the scene's ambassador to Europe and then the world, making tireless trips around the globe to introduce new audiences to the London vibe.

Fashion Just as music and fashion have always been inextricably linked, so club culture has at each stage informed the way people dress and their lifestyle choices – in books, film, home décor, holiday destinations, having kids and other trivia.

Dance music trends throughout the seventies, whether disco, soul or funk, pushed the boundaries of clothes credibility through oversized flares, lashings of glitter and stupendous Afro hair-dos – leading white men down to the hairdressers in droves for that Leo Sayer perm. The denouement came with George Clinton's extravagant sci-fi clothing for his Dr Funkenstein, Brides of Funkenstein and Mother Ship Connection shows.

In the UK the first wholly club-orientated fashion, in the contemporary sense of the term, came with the New Romantics movement at the Blitz club, Rum Runner and Club for Heroes. Here, disco, glam rock and punk themes, from acts such as the New York Dolls, were extended into a modern art form. Make-up and clothing became vehicles through which punters, like the Six Million Dollar Man, could rebuild themselves.

The next phase of club fashion came through the hard-times look. Rebelling against the luscious fabrics of New Romantics, the in-crowd at clubs such as La Beat Route, the Warehouse and The Wag wore ripped Levi 501s (at the time only available through import), Converse All Stars, beaten-up flying and baseball jackets and Mac Curtis flat top hairstyles. The look came to dominate the rest of the eighties, although the glam of New Romantics made a brief reappearance through Leigh Bowery's ecstasy and alcohol-fuelled Taboo club.

The rest of the scene became increasingly formulaic, with black 501s, Doctor Martin shoes and MA 1 jackets becoming ubiquitous until, in 1987, a bunch of nutters reliving their summer holiday in Ibiza, started showing up at clubs such as The Project, Delirium, Jungle, Shoom and Spectrum. Dressed in their holiday garb of brightly coloured baggy T-shirts, shorts and whatever else they wanted, the Balearic set broke the stranglehold on club wear.

Suddenly there were no rules – just pills. Naturally this free-form dress code soon became a rule book, with market stall-holders running off thousands of acid house smiley T-shirts and colour co-ordinated bandannas. Taking things to their logical conclusion, the Manchester rave scene introduced the baggy look in 1990, with flares big enough to parachute a tank under. Meanwhile the London scene had reverted to looking cool and ushered in an era of designer shirts and trousers. On the handbag scene, the babes had discovered wearing as little as possible: half-mast T-shirts, fluffy bras and slithers of material laughingly described as mini skirts.

On the rave scene people had started stripping to the waist or wearing boiler suits, white gloves, face masks and dummies. Layers were also to the fore, with endless tops (at least one of them hooded) being stripped off and slung round people's waists as they heated up on the dance floor, which would often be a disused aircraft hanger or a field.

As the scene diversified, so did the fashions that went with the music. By the mid-nineties you could spot a jazz head (by their goatee beard), B-boy (by their baggy trousers) and techno boffin (by their lack of hair and clothes sense) from a mile off.

Fat Cat Records Dave Crawley and Alex Knight's Fat Cat Record shop in London's Covent Garden was hugely influential in introducing many of London's DJs to quality techno. Originally opened in 1991 in Crawley, its reputation grew through supplying specialist music that covered the full range of electronica and experimental sounds.

In July 1997 the Covent Garden shop was forced to close after the landlords increased the rent from £17,000 a year to £40,000. After the closure Alex and Dave concentrated on developing the Fat Cat record label, which had released its first EP, 'E.V.A.' by Takuya Sugimoto, in October 1996.

Fat City, Feva and Grand Central Opened in 1992 in Manchester, Fat City records challenged the hegemony of house that dominated the city. Drawing on the city's overlooked tradition in seventies jazz and northern soul, they set up their stall in Aflex Palace, the city's labyrinthial indoor market. Fat City traded in old and new school funk, jazz and hip hop. The shop became the focus point for the city's black music scene with artists, producers and DJs using it as a meeting point.

Opening Feva in 1993, one of the first of a new wave of hip hop/jazz/break beat clubs, the Fat City collective showed the way forward, playing music that was rarely heard at the time outside London. The in-house band at Feva launched a series of artists such as the Freakniks and Laj who would, by the end of the decade, be making inroads into a range of musical genres.

In 1995 Mark Rae, one of the shop's founders, formed Grand Central Records. Taking advantage of his position behind the counter, he signed artists such as Aim and Funky Fresh Crew who had been regular customers at the shop, clearly buying old records for sampling.

But the label's first release was to come from Tony D, a New York-based artist who Rae had discovered on a fact-finding mission to the USA. After three single releases, Tony D's first album, *Pound for Pound*, was released to critical acclaim in 1997.

Meanwhile Rae had teamed up with Steve Christian and released their debut long player, *Northern Sulphuric Soul*. Continuing the label's collaborative tradition Rae and Christian invited artists such as Guru Tha Damaja, the Jungle Brothers, YZ from New Jersey and Texas to contribute to the album, blending hip hop beats with traditional song writing themes and nineties production techniques.

Festivals Once the preserve of hippies reminiscing about Jimi Hendrix at the Isle of Wight which, it soon became apparent, was their last clear memory, festivals in the nineties were invaded by the rave generation and transformed into mega dance-a-thons.

In 1989 the first sound systems took advantage of Michael Eavis' tolerant attitude towards travellers, whom he allowed into the festival free, and set up the first Glastonbury dance parties. By 1990 sound systems such as Club Dog and Hypnosis from London, DIY from Nottingham and Tonka from Cambridge were pitching up and transforming the festival into a series of raves. Whereas Glastonbury had at one time gone to bed after the bands played, the dance tents and sound systems only started after the official acts had finished. Glastonbury became a temporary 24-hour city of dance culture, with after-parties springing up all over the site.

The trend began to spread to other festivals, while the Universe organisation, whose illegal Tribal Gathering parties had moved to Germany to escape the UK's legal restrictions on raves, joined forces with the Mean Fiddler organisation in 1994.

Mean Fiddler, Vince Powers' huge entertainments empire which specialised in live music, gave Universe the clout and respectability to obtain a license to run the first legal rave in the UK. Meanwhile other festivals sprang up, such as Phoenix and T in the Park, all having a strong element of dance music.

After Mean Fiddler and Universe parted company, the former organisation joined up with Liverpool super-club Cream to put on Creamfields in 1998.

The Notting Hill carnival, which had a tradition of playing Afro-Caribbean dance music and a legacy that included the legendary Good Times and Mastermind Sound Systems, became a three-day celebration with music ranging from reggae to hip hop, rare groove, jungle, house, techno and garage.

Fetish Clubs Once considered a minority pursuit, fetish clubs had become a mass pastime by the mid-nineties, with clubs such as the Torture Garden and Skin Two packing the rubber-clad punters in. Whereas earlier fetish clubs had often concentrated on the gothic scene or had paid scant regard to music, the new breed appealed to seasoned fetishists, such as little old men dressed in school girl uniforms and what have you, as well as younger sussed clubbers who wanted to sparkle up their club/sex lives.

Beyond the confines of dress code (you had to come in fetish gear, whether that simply meant a leather waistcoat and a pair of shorts), the clubs were marked by an anything-goes attitude: master slave couples, whipping, bondage chambers, guys who like watching strangers shag their partners and whatever else the punters fancied – as long as all parties consented.

Naturally the clubs became popular with voyeurs and guys looking for an easy shag, who were tolerated as long as they kept their hands to themselves and dressed the part. Of all the fetish clubs, Rubber Ron's Submission became the most celebrated.

The Fez Held underneath the Great Western Hotel in Paddington in 1988, The Fez was part of Gilles Peterson's bid to rival the house revolution by injecting some of its energy into the acid jazz scene. Tracks such as 'Masterplan' kept the dance floor flaying and spinning madly, while the strict door policy kept punters guessing whether they'd gain access and ensured the unlucky ones would be equally mad – they probably flayed as well but in a different way.

Film Scores Film scores and sound effects have provided a plethora of out-takes and samples for clubbing's sound track, but whether dance music has taken from or added to cinema is a moot point. Herbie Hancock's seminal sound track to 1966's *Blow Up* (a take on swinging sixties London) and Issac Hayes' sublime funk film score for *Shaft*, certainly put the groove into celluloid.

In the nineties, sound tracks became a club land theme themselves, with DJs seeking out the scores of scores of films. Essential film tracks include Bob Crew and Charles Fox's *Barbarella*, a mutant, sci-fi-funk-driven work, Quincy Jones' Hammond grooves on *They Call Me Mister Tibbs*, Earth, Wind and Fire's contribution to Sweet Sweetback's *Baadaasssss Song*, Lalo Schifrin's avant-garde percussive breaks for *Dirty Harry* and *Enter the Dragon*, Curtis Mayfield's sweet funk on *Super Fly*, anything by Ennio Morricone and War's Low Rider contribution to *Up In Smoke*. Co-writer with Freddy Mercury on *Love Kills* and a contributor to the score for the movie *Flashdance* (which itself had an early influence on Sharam from Deep Dish), Gorgio Moroder's music for *Midnight Express* found itself sampled for a string of dance hits. Returning the compliment, films have taken themes from club culture to heart with releases such as *Wildstyle*, *Cruising*, *Good To Go Go*, *Loved Up*, *Young Soul Rebels* and *Clubbed To Death* basing themselves in club culture.

At the same time film footage has provided VJs with countless images to splice and project on club walls and hangings. All very multimedia, I'm sure.

Fist/FF FF stands for Fist Fuck. Designed for party people who in club terms are as hard as it gets, FF regulars started their partying on Friday night and cruised straight into work, or phoned in sick with a slight chill, on Monday morning. A predominantly gay night, FF attracted punters who developed weekend allergies to their beds. The party finally pooped at its regular Turnmills venue in 1996. Shame really.

Flares Derided as the epitome of bad taste sixties and seventies fashion, the more obsessive habits of flare-ware included stitching patchwork quilt 'darts' into seams to extend the ankle flap.

Ditched as the worst trait of hippie culture by punk, flares made an unexpected return in the eighties; first as a chic return to funk in the rare groove scene and then as a Madchester fashion necessity. The house nation flapped on to the dance floor with their trousers behaving like mobile sponges. The babes at the Hacienda might have felt less loved up if they'd known the damp, rising to their knees, came from the overflow of the men's urinal.

Flesh Run by Paul Cons, the promoter at the Haçienda, Manchester, Flesh, a monthly weekday club, led the charge of the club cognoscenti back into gay culture in 1992. By this time Manchester had been tagged Gunchester, after an article by journalist William Leith had described a night of violence, knife and gun-pulling in the Rainy City. The city was divided between drug gangs from Cheetham Hill, Moss Side and Salford, who were quick to establish themselves in any new club that dared open its doors.

Flesh's openly gay glamour and strictly camp door policy was enough to ensure no self-respecting arse of a gangster would go anywhere near it. The good times were back, but in place of the casual dress of the Summers of Love, Flesh operated theme nights, with everyone dressing up in cowboy gear or head to toe in white, depending on what extravagant theme Cons dreamed up.

Elton, whose pop career included guesting with the Grid and the Dub Federation, would turn up in elaborate mutant versions of the theme, while the drag duo of Coco and Chanel would spin and pout to Paulette's disco set in the basement. The sets would be as elaborate as the punters with swimming pools, snow storms and themed chill-out areas transforming the Hacienda's stark industrial interior.

Despite its door policy, Flesh led the way in transforming gay nights into mixed nights, with Cons letting in known faces from the straight scene, while forcing unknown boys to snog each other in the queue before letting them in – ensuring that, even if they weren't gay, their attitude was appropriate.

Fluffy Bras and Fluffy Stuff In the mid-nineties touchy-feelie clothing became the essential clubbing clobber, for a few brief months. As ever some people wouldn't let it lie and, rather than ditching the stuff, opted for ever-decreasing amounts of fluffy material, as if less is ever really more. Clubs became defined by whether they were frequented by girls in skimpy fluffy bras, skirts and knee-length white boots – an instant signal it was time to leave.

The upside of this was that it provided clubbers with a wealth of mirth as they played games such as 'spot the hypothermia case in a fluffy bra' at completely inappropriate venues, such as the somewhat chilly Creamfields festival. A case of fucking cold, rather than cool.

Flyers The traditional form of club advertising, the arrival of desktop publishing and the proliferation of club venues and nights during the eighties saw flyers develop into a boom industry. Initially consisting of scrappy pieces of paper or cardboard with printed text and maybe a rough-and-ready logo, as the competition grew the need for flyers to stand out and represent the quality of the night led to ever more elaborate design. Soon printers were gearing themselves up to specialise in flyer production and promoters were employing artists to design the artwork for their nights. Clubs such as Off Centre, Flesh and Pushca produced flyers that became veritable works of art.

Meanwhile the sheer volume of flyers being produced enabled organisations such as Steve Ball's Flying Blond to set themselves up as flying businesses, commanding a salary for handing out flyers on behalf of other promoters.

The label went on to release quality dance tunes from both UK and Italian artists, earning a formidable reputation.

4 Hero Frequently overlooked legends in the jungle scene, 4 Hero originally consisted of a north-west London quartet of Mark, Dego, Ian and Gus. Formed in the late eighties alongside their Reinforced record label, their second release, 'Mr Kirk's Nightmare' became an early nineties hardcore anthem, and a dark classic designed to awaken the worst paranoia of ecstasy users. The title referred to the media paranoia around ecstasy deaths, constantly repeating the line 'I'm sorry Mr Kirk . . . your son is dead . . . he died of an overdose.'

The original line-up split after Ian and Gus took over the reigns of Reinforced, while Mark and Dego concentrated on 4 Hero's output. In 1991 they released their first album, *In Rough Territory*. The first long player to come out of the jungle genre, it immediately attracted attention.

Revealingly, they were eventually noticed by Talkin' Loud Records, who at that point had yet to sign a drum 'n' bass act and so signed them in 1997. Their first album on their new label soaked up the freedom that a larger deal gave them as well as dabbling in the culture of their new home by using live instruments.

Meanwhile Reinforced went from strength to strength, releasing over 120 singles in nine years and nurturing the careers of artists such as Goldie, Nebulla II, Peshay, Nookie, Alpha Omega and Doc Scott.

France To quote French hip hop star DJ Cam, 'if you want to go to a town with a good club culture, don't go to Paris – honestly it's horrible.' Even so, the melting pot of cultures in Paris led to the birth of quality dance music emanating from the French capital in the nineties. Whether it was the hip hop of Cam, Da Funk Mob, Mighty Bop and MC Solar, the easy listening of Air and A Reminiscent Drive or the perverted house beats of Daft Punk, Bob Sinclar, St. Germain En Laye and DJ Dimitris, France had it. Alienated by the confines of the official French music industry, TV and radio, young acts developed a have-a-go mentality, developing their own record labels such as Yellow Production and F Communications and their own networks.

In fact the scene had been evolving for some time. DJs such as Dimitris had been playing on his own radio show, on NRG, for over a decade before he gained recognition over the Channel. Gradually France's radio stations recognised the country's domestic talent, although it remained heavily restricted. Stations such as Nova, FG (a satellite gay radio station where DJ Cam presents his own show on Fridays) began to open up to the scene.

Meanwhile the clubs remained moribund. Paris venues became notorious for wanting good DJs while not wanting to spend money on their fees. Surprisingly it hadn't always been that way. In the early eighties Paris had a thriving club scene, crowned by Les Bains Douche, the long-running It-Club and home for the poseurs and the élite. Architecturally splendid, the clubs were nearly always let down musically.

By the early nineties this had started to change, with clubs such as Erotica, in an old sex club on Pigalle, holding seminal hip hop and acid jazz nights. By the late nineties Parisian clubbers had taken refuge in gay clubs such as the 3,000-capacity Queen for nights such as Respect, where DJs slammed hip hop, break beats and intelligent house. Equally the Rex kept the faith playing techno and house for discerning punters. Meanwhile Paris has also caught on to the pre-club DJ bar phenomena providing an outlet for the new scene's music.

Outside of Paris, northern France has continued to be characterised by techno and gabber, while the south has remained a bastion of holiday-handbag/pop house and L'aeronef in L'Ille, a venue-cum-night-club, flew France's rave flag.

Freak Power and Fat Boy Slim Norman Cook, born Quentin, flew to fame as a member of the Housemartins in the mid-eighties. On their demise he formed Beats International, who shot to number one with 'Dub Be Good To Me' – much chastised for nicking the bass line from The Clash's 'Guns Of Brixton'.

His next venture, 'Freak Power', found similar chart success but also allowed Cook to explore more leftfield adventures, such as their limited edition *Trip Hop* CD and white label album.

Re-inventing himself as Fat Boy Slim, Cook headed for the beautiful south and signed on to Damien Harris' Brighton-based label Skint. His tunes helped popularise Big Beat. He now plays regularly at Skint's packed-out monthly nights Borrasic Beats, at The End, London, and Big Beat Boutique in Brighton.

Freedom To Party Growing out of Tony Colston-Hayter, David Roberts and Paul Staines' Sunrise organisation, Freedom to Party was launched at the Conservative Party conference of 1989 to oppose the introduction of the Bright Bill, which was aimed at penalising rave organisers. This loose group consisted of the main rave organisers such as Sunrise, World Dance, Biology and Energy.

Prior to discovering raving Staines had had a career in right-wing libertarian politics, organising support for the Contras in Nicaragua and working for right-wing fanatic David Hart (who later became involved in Freedom to Party) and the Adam Smith Institute. He applied his political knowledge and radical free-market philosophy to dance music, drawing up a manifesto for Freedom to Party which expressed their mission in terms of supplying a market need that young people were demanding.

Their first rally at Trafalgar Square in January 1990 attracted a few thousand people but disintegrated into a shambles. The second demonstration, in March, attracted only a dribble of demonstrators and the Bright Bill was passed by Parliament in July.

The Fridge Started by Susan Carrington and Andrew Czezowski, The Fridge opened in the first wave of new clubs in 1981 at 390 Brixton Road. The first club-cum-venue to have a video lounge and ambient chill-out room, with banks of TVs displaying the then new art of video scratching, it was decorated in clean frosty white.

Hovering somewhere between a post-punk and New Romantics venue, its early gigs included acts such as Eurythmics, Blancmange, The Pogues, Bronski Beat and last appearances of The Clash.

As its popularity grew, Carrington and Czezowski closed the venue and moved up the road to a disused cinema and opened the largest independently owned night-club in London in June 1985. Introducing many of the now-customary club effects such as split visual projections, The Fridge's custom rapidly expanded to fill its new home.

New club nights such as Mark Moore's 1988 house night Planet Love, Gilles Peterson's Talkin' Loud acid jazz night, Soul II Soul, The Daisy Chain, Roxy Motel, Indulgence, Cio Baby, Venus Rising, Glam and Slam, Escape From Samsara, Mother Brown and Love Muscle attracted a gay, mixed and straight crowd from across the spectrum of musical genres.

Funk 'I was lucky enough to be the one who created real funk. I used gospel music and I used jazz, brought it together and made a combination of non-stop music', says James Brown, who, as the godfather of funk, should know. Brown may have engineered the sound, but he relied heavily on his backing musicians such as Maceo Parker.

Hippie-influenced black artists such as Sly Stone and George Clinton took funk to a new level – their respective bass players, Larry Graham and Bootsy Collins, developing a new dance-driven attitude to bass. Their style still informs dance music – even in its most synthesised forms.

Much is made of the 'one' – politically a reference to unity but musically an arrangement emphasising the first beat of the bar.

Funk is the basic element of contemporary club sounds and Future Funk outfits, such as the Jedi Knights, have developed it into an updated and eccentric form. Old school funky nights such as Funkin' Pussy at the Africa Centre, Covent Garden still draw crowds of long-term disciples and recent converts to the groove thang.

Farley Jackmaster Funk Much-respected Chicago house DJ and producer, Farley Jackmaster Funk was a petrol station attendant and McDonald's assistant before getting booked to play at The Sheba and Copper Box 2 and launching his career as a DJ.

Between 1981 and 1987 he was the resident DJ at the Chicago Playground, a two-floor venue that held 3,500 people and was rammed every Friday and Saturday. Here he developed a Frankie Knuckles' trick and mixed Roland drum-machine patterns into Phily (Philadelphia International) disco tunes.

One of the earliest house producers, his first release came with 'Yellow House' on Dance Mania Records. His notoriety increased when he teamed up with Ralphi Rosario, Kenny 'Jammim' Jason, Mickey 'Mixin' Oliver and Scott 'Smokin' Seals to form the Hot Mix 5 on Chicago's WBMX radio station. The resulting mix shows spread the house faith over the city and inspired a second wave of Chicago DJs.

Funk scored an international hit with 'Love Can't Turn Around', reaching the UK top ten in September 1986. When WBMX went off air his career collapsed in the USA but he continued to play slots as a living legend in the UK.

Becoming interested in hip hop music in 1990 he also converted to born-again Christianity and consequently was notorious for answering all his questions in interviews with an acknowledgement to the creator. Moving back to his house roots he launched two new record labels in 1997, Q The Record and 2 Sided House.

Funkapolitan Although now-painful listening, Funkapolitan, a well-to-do west London early funk band, were instrumental in uniting the early London funk, soul and hip hop scene. Playing their first gigs on two consecutive Fridays, above the Wimpy in Notting Hill, the venue was packed with Holland

Park ragamuffins, south London soulboys and north London funkabillies.

By the second gig the venue was overrun and the third gig was pulled by the owners. They brought out one album, which should be avoided at all costs.

Funkin' Pussy and Jasper The Vinyl Junky A veteran funk DJ who had cut his teeth in the late seventies doing school discos, Jasper the Vinyl Junky played his first paid gig on a Wednesday night at the Horse and Groom pub in west London. Spinning deep funk grooves, the place was soon rammed and earned him and his Ace of Clubs sound system enough of a reputation to start organising gigs at larger venues, such as Acton Town Hall and warehouse parties, as well as playing the usual rent-money rota of weddings.

In the early eighties he secured his first radio slot on south London pirate station, Sky Line, before moving to the seminal pirate LWR, alongside DJs such as Tim Westwood, Derek Bolan, Maxi Jazz and Jazzy M. Leaving the station in the mid-eighties, he took his first legal radio slots at festival radio stations, before moving on to Kiss and then Choice FM in the early nineties.

Negotiating a deal with Choice that guaranteed he could play anything he selected, he finally left the station after five years, in 1997, when the programme controller tried to enforce a limited play list. In the meantime Jasper had teamed up with DJs Hooch and Tha Dump to start the Funkin' Pussy night-club in 1991. Originally held on a Saturday night at the Fish club on Oxford street, the music policy mixed P-Funk with contemporary funk-inspired tunes. At the time the rest of London's club scene was dominated by house music.

Funkin' Pussy immediately attracted a large and loyal following, which would cram into the tiny venue to sweat and dance in whatever corner they could find. The club became a favourite among London's musicians, with stars such as George Clinton making a point of stepping on to its dance floor whenever he was in London and the Hustlers of Culture liking the night so much they wrote a song about it.

New York hip hop legends Melle Mel and Africa Islam made a surprise appearance one night, with Mel taking the mike and Islam scratching and breaking on the decks. The venue erupted, with Mel directing the dance floor to take a step to the right – a command that the dance floor would have followed had there been an inch to manoeuvre into.

It was clear the club had outgrown the venue and, when the Fish closed to be revamped as Plastic People, Funkin' Pussy moved to Soul II Soul's old hangout at the Africa Centre. By the late nineties the club was still going strong and had moved on to embrace the re-emerging break beat culture. Its break dancers became legendary, with a photograph of one of them appearing on the cover of the Prodigy's 'Smack My Bitch Up' single.

Future Funk Marrying P-Funk themes to contemporary sounds from techno, drum 'n' bass and house, future funk emerged in the mid-nineties as the natural air to eighties electro. Pioneered by artists such as the Jedi Knights and labels such as Warp and Clear, the Future Funk moniker kept its underground attitude by failing to capture a clearly identifiable sound. Instead it united an odds-and-sods collection of artists, who also went under banners as divergent as drill 'n' bass and techno.

Lest we forget:
Farley and Heller
Finitribe

Mickey Finn
Freaky Dancing
Future Sound Of London

Best we forget:
Falling on the dance floor
Fellatio in the toilets
Feltching, anywhere
Flashbacks – thanks for the memory, but no thanks

g

Gabber As the rave scene ditched its loved-up roots, ecstasy became increasingly cut with speed and other alternatives. The music and mood took on a harder edge reflecting the dance rush of the drugs and the stark reality of urban life. Hugging strangers in clubs was more likely to induce a head butt than a reciprocal embrace.

By the early nineties hardcore had started to fill the UK's dance floors – an energetic brutal escape from economic depression that contrasted sharply with the happy-clappy house of the late eighties. But, however bad things were getting here, the Dutch must have been really narked. Gabber kicked into life in Holland in the mid-nineties with DJs and producers pushing the beats per minute to incredulous heights.

For binged-out dancers it's a delight. No matter the toxicity of the cocktail you've consumed, the music's so fast you'll never look out of time. Similarly mixing records loses its mystique: Gabber is the DJ's friend, which is perhaps where it gets its unlikely name. Gabber means mate in Dutch.

Gangsta Rap and G-Funk Used to describe West Coast P-Funk-driven hip hop, gangsta rap entered into use in the late eighties with the release of Ice T's *Rhyme Pays* album. The format followed Philadelphia rapper Schoolly D and grew through NWA's seminal *Straight Out Of Compton*. Rap lyrics had for a long time portrayed the intensity of urban life, but gangsta rap went straight for the jugular with an Uzi. Gangsta themes were laid heavy with references to hoes and bitches (women), gats (from Gatling guns), gang warfare and gangster attributes, such as smart cars and cash. They also kicked off Blunt culture (cigar skins packed with hash) and countless references to chilling on the streets with alcohol – think gin and juice.

Whereas mainstream hip hop had shifted into bland lover man and 'can you dance in this style?' lyrics, and the political trajectory of Public Enemy had run its course, gangsta caused a stir by reciting the daily struggle of the boys growing up in the hood. Not only did they live the lifestyle but they also died it – with artists such as Tupac Shakur being convicted for arms possession and ultimately being shot in a drive-by killing in 1996. Despite its uncompromising stance gangsta's often sublime use of break beat and production had notable success, with artists such as Ice Cube, the ubiquitous Dr Dre and Snoop Doggy Dog crossing over into the charts.

Gangsta's open acknowledgement of gang culture (how else would you explain Death Row Records?) naturally led to political interest with the US Congress starting hearings on the genre in 1994. In the UK it inspired a bunch of boys to wear hooded tops, hang out in gangs and talk about respect a lot. Luckily, 12-year-old Anglo versions mostly failed to transpose the lyrics of their mentors into reality.

Garage Used as a generic term for soulful house music that has a Disco Diva vocal over the top, and not to be confused with lo-fi guitar music, garage gets its name from Larry Levan's Paradise Garage club in New York. Levan played here every weekend between 1976 and 1987 and in the process transformed disco music and inspired house. He worked on electro and disco tracks – most notoriously Gwen Guthrie's 'Nothing Going On But The Rent' – but died of a heart attack in 1992.

At its worst garage is unadventurous commercial dance music but at its best it demonstrates the deep funky origins of contemporary music. Underground classics (alongside the odd chart breakthrough) continue to prove the music's vitality. Paul Trouble Anderson's long running Wednesday night at Camden's HQ has kept the torch burning, while recent media interest in Speed Garage has helped foster new disciples at London clubs such as Twice as Nice and Absolute.

Laurent Garnier Widely regarded as France's greatest exponent of techno, Laurent Garnier in fact started behind the decks in Manchester in 1987. His reputation was built through tireless schedules, playing up to four different European countries in a week. His fame can also be accredited to his considerable charm, which tends to win over all those who meet him.

Within techno circles he's often considered to represent the commercial end of the market, although he's also respected as an ambassador for the genre, having popularised it all over Europe. His influence was further increased by his record label, FNAC, which has now been superseded by the seminal F Communications imprint.

GBH/GHB Developed as an anaesthetic and used in the USA as a sedative, gammahydroxybutyrate (GHB), or GBH as it is commonly known, appeared on the gay club scene in 1993. Normally sold in small brown bottles, GBH is a slightly salty, colourless liquid that is usually drunk and rarely injected.

Also known as Liquid E, GBH in small doses breaks down inhibitions and gives a feeling of relaxed calm. Larger quantities can make the user retreat into their own world, cause sickness, muscle contractions, convulsions, collapse and possible coma. What a laugh.

By May 1994 200 people has been hospitalised in the UK after using GBH and there has been one reported death. Still in use, its popularity dipped in the late nineties, even though or perhaps because it was still legal.

Genres Despised, disliked and detested, genres of dance music have spread through and divided the dance scene like a plague. No sooner has a new form of dance music emerged, been tagged and appeared in the music press than a new sub-version branches off, gets a new name and spawns its own sub-genre, which begets another, and so it goes on. House begets techno and hardcore, techno begets tech house and intelligent techno, hardcore begets jungle, jungle begets drum 'n' bass, dark and jump up . . .

DJs, record-buying punters, who are faced by an ever-bewildering set of categories in their local record store, and those who remember the unity of the early house, hip hop or jungle scenes despise the fracturing of the movement. Meanwhile others point out that dance, in common with other forms of rhythm-based music, is differentiated by distinct beat and tempo changes. Each progression, although still broadly dance music, produces a marked change from what happened before, making a new title for the genre both desirable and inevitable.

Hate them as we may, genres are necessary – after all you would no more describe drum 'n' bass as hardcore than you would describe dub as ska.

Girl DJs Much was made of the growth of female DJs in the late nineties as attention focused on stars such as DJ Heaven, Lisa Pin up, Sister Bliss, Mrs Wood, DIY's Emma, Sexy Rubber Solo, Princess Julia, Smokin' Jo, Paulette and Bass Baby, to name but a few. In fact, although DJing has predominantly been a male activity, there has always been a number of female DJs on the scene and many of those who started getting recognition in the late nineties had been on the circuit for years.

In the rare groove period of the mid-eighties, Wendy May held sway over the largest overground club, the Locomotion, while DJ Elaine took to the airwaves at the seminal London pirate station LWR and on the jazz scene DJ Debra span with the best of them.

Glam After baggy had kicked the tight-arsed yuppie fashions of the eighties into touch, street style in the early nineties reverted to dressed-down casual and sportswear. Seventies Adidas trousers and tops swung on to the dance floor and dressing up was permitted only if it looked like you hadn't tried. Then glam pouted and strutted its way passed the door whores.

In common with so many club traditions, glam emerged from the gay club flamboyance of icons such as Leigh Bowery, with extravagantly dressed carnival transvestites leading the charge down the catwalk at clubs such as Kinky Gerlinky, in London, and Flesh in Manchester. Meanwhile early nineties underground clubs nurtured the growing scene, with seminal one-off nights being held in photo and film studios by organisations such as Cheeky Half, Respect, Sign of the Times, Solaris, Renaissance and Pushca.

The events were held in weird and wonderful environments, transforming the clubbing experience from being centred on music and dancing on a surreal journey through dreamscape settings.

As with many of the innovations of the club world during this period, glam's penchant for operating beyond the law fell foul of the Entertainments (Increased Penalties) Act and the Criminal Justice Act and many of the organisations were forced to wind up their operations. Those that survived within the law, such as Pushca and Renaissance, went on to become mega clubs filling venues such as Ministry Of Sound. Nice work if you can get it.

Global Communications The brainchild of Tom Middleton and Mark Pritchard, the Global Communications project was conceived in 1991 after the two met in a night-club in Taunton. Both shared a passion for Strictly Rhythm records, early Chicago house and Detroit techno. Middleton had previously been working with Aphex Twin, while Pritchard had produced hardcore tracks.

Their eclectic influences, which borrowed from deep house, techno and break beat, were soon honed into melodic, emotive techno tracks, released on Evolution under the Global Communication and Link monikers.

Releasing their first album, *A Collection of Short Stories*, in 1993, their reputation for single releases, remixes and long players grew through releases such as *Remotion* and 1995's *76:14*, the latter gaining massive critical success and being voted the eleventh best dance album ever made.

Following this with further albums, including a compilation for Warp Records, and a release for LTJ Bukem's Good Looking Records, they launched their Jedi Knights project. Prefiguring the re-emergence of electro, the Jedi Knights took themes from P-Funk and mixed them into contemporary aesthetics.

Go Go Arriving on the scene shortly after hip hop, go go was Washington DC's funk-influenced answer to New York's dance music. While hip hop developed DJ and rap skills, go go stuck with the more traditional band line-up, providing a non-stop music track and emulating the seamless sound track of DJ-led dance floors. It consisted of a leading MC/rapper/singer, usually supported by a team of backing singers or other MCs, a driving percussion section, an array of keyboards and, crucially, a funk-driven bass player.

Starting in the late seventies, go go was pioneered by Chuck Brown and The Soul Searchers, who released two seminal albums, *Bustin' Loose* and *Run Joe Run*.

Brown was followed by acts such as Rare Essence and Trouble Funk, who were to become the most successful chart band of the go go scene. Go go gigs resembled something of a cross between a live act, a club dance floor and pirate radio broadcast, with the lead MC holding a constant rapport with the audience, who often held up signs with messages on them for the MC to read out. By the late eighties go go had pretty much gone gone.

Goa Once students and young Bohemians would trek around India for a year to discover themselves. The deepest thinkers (or the slowest learners) settled in the hippie communes in Goa.

But that was 30 years ago. Today young executives can snap up the package-tour Goa experience in a week. The communes have given way to the sub-continents version of Benidorm and hippie culture has succumbed to dance, or more specifically trance, culture. Still catering in cheap drugs, the ultimate Goan pilgrimage is to a Full Moon party. Here you can trip to the deep throb of electronic music until the first rays of the Asian dawn lift dew from the palm leaves. Having found yourself, you catch your business class flight back to your comfortable office chair without so much as a rumble of dysentery. Who needs mother Earth when there's global clubbing?

Originally a Mecca for sixties hippies, Goa differs from the rest of India in that it's a Christian state. It became a fixed stop-off point on the international party trail from Ibiza to Amsterdam, New York and Mikanos but differed from these scenes largely through its base in psychedelic drugs, such as trips (LSD), which were cheap and readily available. By the early to mid-1980s Goa had become the scene of beach parties fuelled by early electronic music.

The scene was to develop alongside the house explosion of the UK in the late eighties, which it overlapped but remained independent from. The parties focus around the northern end of Goa, in the hippie market commune of Anjuna and the beach at Vagator.

More recently the Goan authorities have tried to clean up the area, encouraging package tours to fly into purpose-made hotels in the south. The embourgeoisement of Goa has led the hardcore trance devotees to abandon their idyll in the summer months and head to Manali in the Himalayas, where they can escape the monsoon and the package tourists.

Ironically Goa is at once home to a sprawling mass of Westerners, rabidly consuming too many drugs, and the favourite holiday destination of wealthy Indians who organise day trips to parties. It's not uncommon to see a group of well-dressed Indian families turn up mid-party to witness mad Westerners thrashing around on the beach. Being sandy affairs Goan DJs have learnt to improvise, using dust-friendly tapes rather than records.

While the partying may be fun and attracts hordes of visitors, government tolerance is intermittent, so, like wine, Goan parties have good years and bad ones.

Goldie Starting out as a graffiti artist in the Midlands, where his artwork led him to being employed by the local council and making several appearances on television, Goldie was originally a devotee of hip hop and B-boy culture. Alongside other UK hip hop graffiti artists, such as 3D, Goldie's talent gained him considerable attention, eventually taking him to New York and an appearance alongside Afrika Bambaataa in the 1986 graffiti film *Bombing*.

Moving to London in 1988, he became involved in the Soul II Soul sound system, providing artwork for Jazzie B. In 1991 he was converted to break beat jungle by DJs Fabio and Grooverider when he heard them play at Rage. Becoming a DJ pest, constantly asking them what track they'd just played, he immersed himself in the music and began doing the artwork for Reinforced Records.

His first record release for the label, 'Killermuffin', was a ragga-inspired cut that did moderately well. But his second single, released on Synthetic during the rise of dark in 1993, established him as a major mover in the scene.

Released under the pseudonym Metalheadz, 'Terminator' was a huge, unnerving dramatic storm, which captured the mood of the time perfectly. A series of releases on labels such as Reinforced, Moving Shadow and Synthetic further established Goldie's reputation. His Angel release of 1994 pushed drum 'n' bass into an new arena, blending samples from David Byrne and Brian Eno's 'My Life In The Bush Ghosts' with crunching metallic beats and the soulful jazz vocals of Diane Charlemagne.

By the time he released his first LP, *Timeless* on London Records, in October 1995, his reputation alone ensured it shot to number seven in the charts, despite the album receiving minimal air play. More than any other record, *Timeless* represented the crossover of drum 'n' bass into the mainstream.

His next step was an adventurous but ultimately mediocre attempt to recreate his music with a live band touring the UK and the USA. The shows sold out in the UK, despite being poorly received by Goldie's London audience. Abroad it was a different story and Goldie won a whole new set of converts.

By the late nineties his Metalheadz record label had expanded into an empire, hosting two weekly club nights in London and issuing its own merchandise, such as Metalheadz shoes.

Despite his success, Goldie has refused to compromise his music and his second album, *Saturnz Return*, released in 1998, featured a track called 'Mother' that's over an hour long.

Goth Growing out of the back of the punk movement, defining goth is an irritating process since most goths either refuse to admit they are or refuse to agree on what goth is. Either way, goths took their inspiration from the dark fashion of Siouxie Sioux and by the mid-eighties had spawned a thousand gloom-ridden followers.

Favouring black clothing, or dark colours such as deep purple, crushed velvet and leather, white make-up and black eye shadow and lipstick, elaborate silver jewellery, long dyed hair that's often semi-spiked, goth fashion drew in equal measure from Hammer horror movies and mutant sci-fi flicks.

How influential they were on the club scene is debatable. Certainly they had some influence in cities such as Edinburgh, although their cultish enclosed attitude has tended to keep them on the fringes of club culture.

In London, goths managed to survive in enclaves around Camden Town and at the Slimelight club. Held at the Electrowerkz, in Torrens Street, Angel, the unlicensed Slimelight ran through the night until 7 a.m. and was a long-running members-only club.

Over the years goth has proved to have immense staying power, although most clubbers would rather die than be a goth, which would probably be quite appropriate.

Grandmaster Flash Born in Barbados, Joseph Sadler (a.k.a. Grandmaster Flash) was raised in the Bronx, New York, where he discovered DJ parties being thrown by early heroes such as Grandmaster/DJ Flowers, Kool Herc, MaBoya and Peter 'DJ' Jones. Becoming Jones' protégé, Flash sought to combine Jones' timing on the decks with the break beat skills of Herc.

While Herc's mixes were rough and ready, Flash honed his style by finding a way to segue break beats together without jumping a beat. Locking himself in his 167th Street apartment for a year, he reappeared having mastered the art of playing the same record on two turntables and alternating between them to prolong the funkiest break beat in a track. The speed at which he alternated between each desk, spinning the record back to the start of the break and then mixing it in, earned him the name Flash. Having sorted his DJ skills out, he invited a vocalist to join him, working an original vocal line over the records – effectively creating a new tune and in the process starting a new form of music: hip hop or rap.

His first vocal partner was Lovebug Starski, who was followed by Wiggins (later to become Cowboy in the Furious Five). Becoming the star of the illegal block party scene, he was approached by Ray Chandler who suggested holding parties and charging people an entrance fee – until then hip hop nights having been free.

Doubting that anyone would pay to see him, Flash pulled together a team of New York's greatest talents, Melle Mel Glover and Kid Creole (a.k.a. Nathaniel Glover), to join Cowboy. Calling themselves Grandmaster Flash and the 3 MCs, their line-up was soon expanded to include Duke Bootee and Kurtis Blow, who were later replaced by Rahiem and Scorpio and became Grandmaster Flash and The Furious Five.

Hip hop culture took off, with rival sound systems such as Herc and Afrika Bambaataa playing sound clashes against each other –

the winner bagging their opponent's equipment. Meanwhile the Furious Five released their first record, 'Super Rappin', on Enjoy and made their debut proper on 2 September 1976.

After three further unsuccessful releases, Flash signed on to Joe and Sylvia Robinson's Sugarhill records. The first two records, 'Freedom' and 'Birthday Party', sold well but the third, 'Grandmaster on the Wheels of Steel', the first rap record to use samples, soared. Flash and his team were on a roll. Their next release, one of Joe Robinson and Bootee's earlier tunes, called 'The Message', went platinum and broke the band internationally.

Back at Sugarhill things were not going so well. Flash had fallen out with the label over money and eventually he parted company with them, moving to Elektra with Rahiem and Kid Creole.

The remaining members of the band stayed together as Melle Mel and The Furious Five, scoring an instant hit with 'White Lines', an anti-cocaine song. Ironically Flash was by now dependent on freebase cocaine.

Grid Formed by Dave Ball (previously half of early eighties synth-pop band Soft Cell and collaborator with Cabaret Voltaire) and Richard Norris (formerly writer for *Boy's Own*), the Grid met while playing with a band called Jack The Tab.

After recording one album, Ball and Norris split to form the Grid and notched up an impressive array of remixes for artists such as Happy Mondays, Pet Shop Boys and The Art of Noise. Their debut release, 'On The Grid' in June 1989, gained substantial praise, while 'Flotation' (1990) prefigured the growth of ambient house. But their recording career has been characterised by restlessness.

Having released four singles and *Electric Head*, an album released in 1990, they moved from East West Records to Rhythm King for one single before slinging their hook and moving to Virgin and then taking off to join DeConstruction at the end of 1993. Their release here, 'Swamp Thing', saw them safely into the charts with a Top Ten hit. Their 1994 album, *Evolver*, saw considerable sales despite lukewarm reviews.

In the meantime Norris set up his own label, Candy Records. In September 1995 they released *Music For Dancing* – a remix album and charted with the Diablo single. But the band had run its course and split up.

Grooverider Starting his DJ career in the mid-eighties, Grooverider teamed up with a group of mates and started the Global Rhythm sound system, playing hip hop, rare groove and funk music. By the late eighties he'd gained a slot on the south London pirate station Phaze One.

In 1988 he discovered the West End house clubs such as Spectrum and Land Of Oz. At the time Fabio was the only other DJ on Phaze One playing house music. The two naturally teamed up and started their own Thursday night-club at the tiny venue of Mendozas in Brixton.

As their reputation grew they became increasingly seen as a team, getting bookings up and down the country. Their most important booking came at Heaven, the home of Spectrum and Land of Oz, at a night called Rage, which Grooverider has described as the home of drum 'n' bass.

As the original masters of the scene, Grooverider and Fabio were asked to present Kiss 100's first permanent jungle show, while Grooverider's influence on Goldie, whom he promoted in his early years, also led him to become resident at the Metalheadz club nights.

Forming his record label, Prototype, he used it to release his own music before switching to promoting up-and-coming talent as well as supporting established artists. The label's output has included Ed Rush, Lemon D and Dillinja.

Guerilla Records Set up in 1990 by William Orbit and Dick O'Dell, ostensibly to provide an outlet for Orbit's Bass-O-Matic project, Guerilla Records immediately attracted attention from major labels after their first release, 'In The Realm Of The Senses'. Finally signing to Virgin, the label maintained its own identity and built a dedicated and influential following, releasing artists such as Spooky Moody Boyz, Outermind, D.O.P., React 2 Rhythm, and Trance Induction.

It was soon being seen as the chief exponent of early progressive house. Their compilation albums, such as their Dub House Disco and Dub House Disco 2000, were vastly influential on UK DJs such as Andrew Weatherall and Justin Robertson.

Guest Lists In the eighties getting into a club was a touch-and-go affair, as door staff vetted punters on their looks, clothing and attitude, dismissing clubbers on a whim. One way of securing entry was getting your name down on the guest list. Originally this was a rare event, even for the most connected of people. By the late eighties guest lists were common enough for rave anthems to be sung about them and for everyone to have access to at least one promoter's list. For some people clubbing became a hobby that centred around being on the guest list – their night being incomplete unless they could swank, nose in the air, to the front of the queue and gain priority entry.

By the nineties so many people had found a way of getting on the list that the queues for free entry were bigger than the ones for paying punters. Door staff would treat customers handing over the readies with respect, while contemptuously holding back the supposed guests, cramming them in a line against the wall. Being on the guest list had ceased to be fun, but worse was yet to come.

As promoters realised their clubs were three-quarters full with people who hadn't paid, the concept of the 'paying' guest lists was introduced. Usually costing half the price of a normal ticket, guests could now pay for the privilege of being made to wait outside for longer while the door staff abused them. Which somehow missed the point.

Gullivers Set on Down Street, behind the Hilton Hotel in Mayfair, at the end of the seventies Gullivers was notorious for attracting celebrities – especially from black culture – as well as for turning a blind eye to under-age clubbing. Among the stars sighted there were Mohammed Ali, Frankie Beverly from Maze and the glam disco outfit Imagination. DJs such as the latter-day house hero Graham Gold would spin soul, disco and jazz funk tunes.

In truth Gullivers was a dreadful dive and by the mid-eighties it had definitely passed its sell-by date.

Guru Josh Master of the three-word lyric, later copied by infinite pop house acts, Guru Josh (a.k.a. Paul Walden) was a vital component in the rise of DeConstruction Records.

Having run a night-club, Happy House, in Putney and sung with the rock band Joshua Cries Wolf, he signed to DeConstruction and released the sax-driven 'Infinity' and 'Whose Law Is It Anyway?'. His fame was cemented by his often-demented performances, where he would appear at raves and clubs, often uninvited, with a portable keyboard and saxophonist Mad Mick in tow.

Lest we forget:
Galaxy chocolate bars
Galliano

Gee Street
Genocide
Glasgow Underground

Best we forget:
Glosticks
Glue sniffing and other spotty habits
Gurning

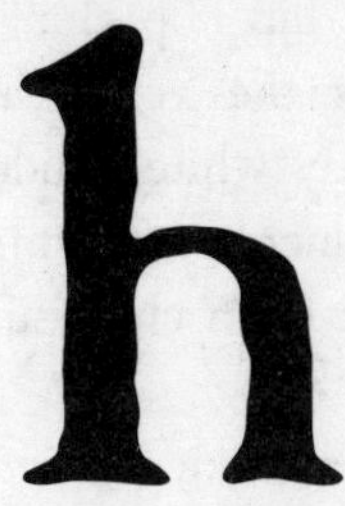

Haçienda Opened in 1982 and financially supported by electronic pop act New Order, who had crossed over on to the dance floor through their collaborations with Arthur Baker, the Haçienda was to become the most significant house venue in the north of England. A former yacht showroom designer Ben Kelly had made the most of its industrial features, creating a vast concrete terminus of a club, dotted with huge supporting iron columns, a sparce cathedral dedicated to dance.

Originally the Haçienda played host to an eclectic selection of indie dance, northern soul and rare groove nights. Wide, on Saturday nights, would have long-serving northern soul DJs Dean and Hedd playing hip hop, northern soul and indie to a packed crowd, which would normally fill the venue by 11 p.m. Hewan Clarke, another recruit from Manchester's soul scene, further locked the club into the city's underground dance scene.

One DJ in particular was to have a huge effect on the Haçienda's future. Mike Pickering, a former member of funk act Quando Quango, veteran of northern soul clubs and disciple of Larry Levan and the Puerto Rican New York club scene, was booked to play a new Friday night, Nude, in November 1984. Pickering and his sidekick, Martin Pendergast, began dropping new US dance grooves, such as electro, hip hop alongside funk and European electronic pop. Whereas the venue had previously been the domain of a predominantly white, student, indie-goth clientele, Nude began attracting an increasingly mixed audience as the city's jazz-funk crowd migrated from clubs such as Berlin, the Gallery and the Man Alive.

In 1986 Pickering started mixing an increasing number of house records into his set. The dance floor became frantic, as The Foot Patrol, a black jazz dance troop, led the punters through manic spins and turns.

Nude became a religion, with a hardcore of dedicated dancers turning up week after week. Among them were the figures who would lead Manchester through an incredible musical journey. Shaun Ryder and the Happy Mondays, the Stone Roses, Inspiral Carpets, the New Fast Automatic Daffodils, The Unabombers, 808 State, Justin Robertson, Louise Rhodes of Lamb and just about everybody joined the Nude crowd. In 1988 a young DJ called John Hibert (a.k.a. Jon Dasilva) returned to Manchester from London. He soon secured a booking from Paul Cons for a new night at the Haçienda. Hot, a night dedicated to sunshine and holiday partying, opened its doors on Wednesday 12 July and gave birth to the city's first Summer of Love.

The Nude crowd now had two nights a week and, with other clubs gradually taking up the theme, the party now lasted throughout the week. Meanwhile Pickering had been joined at Nude by Graeme Park, the house DJ from The Garage in Nottingham.

The Haçienda had captured the cream of the North's house DJs among its residents. Its fame, which was already considerable, went through the roof, with queues of coaches from cities across the UK lining up outside its doors. But fame has a price.

The ecstasy that fuelled the dance floor had become a boom industry, attracting dealers, whose only interest in the scene was the amount of easy money they could make and, of course, media attention.

Two days after Hot opened, Claire Leighton, a 16 year old from Cannock, Staffordshire collapsed and died after taking ecstasy. The Haçienda responded with a statement warning ecstasy dealers and users to keep out of the club, which did little to stop the police from focusing on it.

Despite a steady stream of arrests, the gangs from Cheetham Hill, Salford and Moss Side increased their hold on dealing in the club, pushing out the 'amateur' dealers through intimidation, muggings and beatings. The dance floor became increasingly divided between organised criminals with ever-increasing firepower to protect their turf. In 1990 the police finally moved against the club and attempted to remove its license. The Haçienda responded by employing George Carmen QC, the lawyer who famously represented Liverpool comedian Ken Dodd, to defend the club's case, as well as waging war on dealing inside the club. Intensive door searches were instigated, video cameras installed and suspected or known faces turned away.

Despite the searches and tough policy, the gangs became more determined to reach their market and after a series of threatening incidents, ending with the head of security being threatened with a gun, the club voluntarily closed its doors.

The Haçienda re-opened in May 1991. The club introduced metal detectors and yet more stringent searches at the door, but within six weeks a gang from Salford broke into the back entrance of the club and carried out a retribution knife attack on the security staff.

Further bad news was around the corner as Factory Records, part of the New Order/Tony Wilson empire that ran the Haçienda and Dry bar, went bust. The Haçienda continued, but the carefree party vibe of the early years had gone, only surviving at the monthly gay night, Flesh.

By the end of 1997 the Haçienda was racked with financial problems and an unshakeable reputation for violence. The club finally closed its doors.

Hair When clubs became hip in the post-punk New Romantic period, huge Flock of Seagulls creations and plastered-down, rigid wedges turned hair-spray manufacturing into an overnight boom industry. Then Rock-a-Billy quiffs arrived and dominated the eighties. Acid house had everyone washing the grease from their locks and letting their hair bounce around the dance floor. Pony tails became *de rigueur* and boys would practise pulling their manes through rubber bands three or four times a minute as they chatted up prospective shags.

Cue the mid-nineties and while the clubbers who were there from the start were still doing it, their hair has lost the plot. Suddenly it's no longer important. The shorter the better and no club is complete without its quota of well-polished slap-heads.

It might not be what Degrees Of Motion meant when they penned their club anthem 'Shine On', but it'll do.

Handbag and Hardbag As the rave scene died in the early nineties and clubbers sought to disassociate themselves from the increasingly macho and unfriendly hardcore scene, house music reverted to its camp disco roots.

Handbag, as the music came to be known, reflected a kitsch and glittery celebration of good times. The term was a deliberately ironic reference to naff early eighties fashion, when girls in white stilettos would dance in circles around their white handbags while boys eyed them up from the bar.

It was not meant to describe, let alone prescribe, a fashion where people actually danced around their handbags. Needless to say, it wasn't long before punters had removed the irony from the tag and dutifully placed their bags on the dance floor. Or perhaps they were stretching the irony to its logical conclusion.

Happy Mondays Formed in Manchester in 1980 by a group of scallies from Little Hulton, the Happy Mondays cut their teeth with the usual scally leisure activities, and copious consumption of drugs. Apart from the addition of backing singer Rowetta, the band retained its original line-up throughout with Shaun Ryder drawling caustic lyrics, his brother Paul on bass, Mark Day on guitar, Gary Whelan on drums, Paul Davis on keyboard and Mark Berry (a.k.a. Bez) on percussion and dancing like a lunatic.

Fame took its time coming and while waiting Ryder and Bez developed a lifestyle that was to earn them unrivalled reputations for indulgence and extreme hedonism. Playing their first gig in 1983 at the Haçienda, after being booked by Mike Pickering, they developed an association with the club that was to shape their music and in turn transform the venue and eventually the city. Already dressed in the scally fashion of huge denim flares, with shaggy haircuts, dubbed Baldricks by *i-D* magazine, they would huddle in a group on the dance floor caning whatever drugs were available (which would eventually be ecstasy), dancing madly and generally getting off their tits.

Releasing their first Pickering-produced single, 'Delightful', in September 1985 on Factory Records, it was another year before they followed it with 'Freaky Dancing' and, in April 1987, their debut album, *Squirrel and G-Man Twenty-Four Hour People Plastic Face Carnt Smile (White Out)*.

By the time they released their second album, *Bummed*, in November 1988, the Mondays were attracting national press coverage. Already notching up hits with releases such as 1989's 'Madchester Rave on EP', which took them into the UK charts for the first time, their first Top Ten came in 1990 with the release of 'Step On' – a reworked cover of John Kongo's 'He's Gonna Step On You Again'. Their next album, *Thrills, Pills and Bellyaches*, went straight to number one in the UK.

During this period they began a bizarre publicity partnership with sixties hippie singer Donovan, appearing in magazine photo shoots and even recording a tribute song to him. The pills must have been good.

While their drugs habits had helped get them publicity from the media, who were enamoured with Ryder and Bez's rock 'n' roll excesses, it was eventually to prove their downfall after Ryder admitted to going through rehab for heroin addiction. The press, who had previously fallen over themselves to cover Happy Mondays stories, suddenly turned cold, either ignoring the music or making spurious claims about Ryder's early lifestyle. On one occasion, after a story claimed Ryder had been a rent boy, he stormed into the Dry bar and smashed one of the huge mirrors behind the bar. Bad luck naturally followed.

Sent to Barbados to record their fourth studio album, *Yes Please*, the trip turned into a much-publicised, unproductive, strife-torn waste of money. Ryder, off heroin, had soon discovered an ample supply of crack. After six weeks Ryder had yet to record a single lyric and Bez had broken his arm and gone home.

The band's gradual break up followed, although the spirit of the Mondays lived on in Ryder and Bez's subsequent project, Black Grape. In 1998 Bez published his autobiography.

Hard Hands Formed in 1991 by Paul Daley and Neil Barnes, primarily to release their own material as Leftfield, the label made its mark after the band released their debut album,

Leftism, and their hit single, 'Open Up', with John Lydon. The label followed the downbeat techno trend of the early nineties, releasing artists such as Pressure Drop, Kerosene (the German techno team behind Pharama records), Solid Ground and Dark Globe.

Hardcore Rightly or wrongly, hardcore has attracted a bad press ever since its inception. Growing out of the rave scene of 1989, hardcore reflected the intensity of rave DJ sets, which were usually shorter due to the number of DJs that were booked to play and were consequently harder than more leisurely club sets.

Hardcore pitched the tempo of house music up and, rather than creating drum patterns on a drum unit, used sampled break beats that were left to kick and splutter at an ever-increasing b.p.m. A rough-and-ready music form, sampled lyrics were given the same treatment and, played back at 50 b.p.m. faster than they were originally recorded, gave rise to a wave of Pinky and Perky vocal lines. For the older dance set it was anathema, but for a younger generation moving into house culture it was testosterone-charged heaven.

By 1991 hardcore had become an identifiable genre with its own thriving scene of second-generation promoters. With legislation making illegal raves almost impossible, the new generation of rave promoters, such as Raindance, Rezerection and Amnesia, organised events in legal venues – albeit by twisting the law in their favour.

With them came a second wave of DJs such as Fabio and Grooverider, Slipmatt and the Prodigy, who would regularly play a live set at Raindance. The scene developed its own fashions, with gimmicks such as white gloves, paint masks, Vicks and light sticks – a playground of attachments designed to increase the buzz. As the tempo increased so dance style became more energetic. In place of easy-going arms in the air having it, hardcore had people running on the spot, arms contorting in a mass of air punches and prancing like deranged leopards.

Despite getting a general slagging in the style press, by 1991 hardcore had started notching up chart hits with the Prodigy's 'Charly', Altern-8's 'Active-8' and Smart E's 'Sesame's Treet'. Fuelled by an imposed self-sufficiency, hardcore had found its own network of record labels and promoters and developed its own market.

Hardkiss and West Coast Break Beat Formed by Scott Hardkiss, a San Francisco-born DJ who grew up under the influence of hip hop and the underground West Coast house scene, Hardkiss consists of Scott, Robbie Hardkiss and Gavin Hardkiss. Their music combines Scott's formative influences in a collaboration of techno and break beat hip hop and house.

The three met at college and made their name on the warehouse party scene, where a successful run of Sunny Side Up parties was eventually foiled by a rival promoter tipping off the police and losing the trio $10,000 worth of equipment.

Having earned a considerable reputation for their accomplished DJ sets, they established their Hardkiss record label, releasing the 'Magic Sounds Of San Francisco' EP. Becoming an underground classic, the track took samples from the Beatles and The Shaman and dropped them over hip hop beats. Known for their luxurious psychedelic packaging, further releases included '3 Nudes In A Purple Garden' and 'Raincry' and 'Phoenix' by God Within (a.k.a. Scott Hardkiss).

Meanwhile the trio continued to trot the globe as DJs, with Scott lining up records alongside live 303s and other fancy stuff.

Ron Hardy Widely regarded as the most inspirational of the Chicago DJs, Ron Hardy began perfecting his craft in the early seventies. Essentially a disco DJ, he was wild and adventurous in his choice of music and mixes, throwing in tunes that would completely change the direction on the dance floor. While other DJs such as Frankie Knuckles concentrated on smooth mixes, Hardy took a harder eclectic approach and happily played Led Zeppelin if it suited the mood on the dance floor.

Soon Hardy's nights at the Music Box had eclipsed everything else on the Chicago scene and dominated the house genre. Maybe house music had been named after warehouse parties, but now it didn't matter. According to Marshall Jefferson, if Hardy played it, it was house. 'Ron Hardy was the greatest DJ that ever lived,' says Jefferson. 'He mixed it all, took control of it and played everything. Every record had its own identity. He'd play a lot of the older stuff. I saw Larry Levan play in the Paradise Garage lots of times and he was a bit like Ron Hardy but a little less energetic – there were no rules.'

His mixes would roll along on percussive breaks for what seemed like hours before he would let the tune slam in – a trick that house producers have emulated ever since.

The crowd would be off their tits on PCP, acid or ecstasy, adding to the sense of complete submission to the music – one nation under a groove, indeed.

Soon regulars started producing music for Hardy to play, handing him tapes or poorly pressed 12in records to throw into his mix. As well as leading the dance floor, he was now inspiring a host of new musicians. One of them, a young DJ Pierre, handed him a tape one night that was overlain with squelchy noises created by a Roland 303 bass unit. The tunes, 'Acid Trax' by Phuture, started house's first sub-genre – acid house. Hardy died from AIDS-related diseases in 1994.

Harvey Starting as a drummer in the late seventies, Harvey played for a punk band, Ersats, when he was 13 years old. Through punk he discovered reggae and started playing records by Lee Perry, On U Sound and early electro in-between bands at pub gigs. By 1984 he was converted to funk and hip hop and was making regular trips from his native Cambridge to London to go to warehouse parties.

In 1985 Harvey went to the Bronx in search of hip hop records and clubs. By his return he'd learnt how to cut breaks. His DJ skills became an extension of his earlier experience as a drummer. His move into house was as accidental as his path into being a DJ. Choosing records he could mix into breaks, he found he was increasingly buying records from Chicago. At the start of the acid house, when clubs such as Hedonism, The Project and The Trip were taking over the scene, Harvey was working as a bus driver.

In summer 1988 he mixed ten pure house tapes, took them to Camden Market and set up a stall with his ghettoblaster. Within 20 minutes he'd sold all ten tapes for £5 each, leading him to slam the breaks on his bus-driving career.

Progressing from the market stall he began supplying boutiques and hair salons with mix tapes, while his DJ career began to take off in night-clubs. His eclectic style was accidental – at the time there weren't enough records available to play a whole night of pure house.

By this point he was involved in the legendary Tonka sound system and running regular raves on the sea front in Brighton. Securing a weekly residency at the Gardening club in London, he started his seminal club, Moist, with his wife Heidi, in 1992.

Harvey rebelled against the splintering of dance music while people split off into techno, garage, house and hardcore scenes, and so kept a deliberately open policy of playing across the board up-tempo music – or simply club music, as he described it.

It was here Harvey built his reputation for playing marathon sets, often playing solo all night. On the nights when he shared the DJ booth it would be with seminal DJs such as Larry Levan. In the late nineties he was booked as a resident DJ at Ministry Of Sound, first to play Friday night and then moving into playing both Friday and Saturday night. He went on to play regular slots at Cream, Back To Basics and the super-club circuit. In 1997 Harvey launched his own night, New Hard Left, at The Blue Note and returned to playing the whole night himself.

Richie Hawtin Richie Hawtin is frequently and mistakenly assumed to be American and part of the new generation of Detroit techno artists. It's a reasonable mistake. Hawtin was born either in Brandbury in the UK, or Windsor, Ontario in Canada, depending on whom you talk to. Having grown up under his father's influence and been introduced to Kraftwerk and electronic pop bands such as New Order, his progression into techno music was almost inevitable.

Hawtin began DJing at the age of 16 and was soon booked to play The Shelter, one of Detroit's two legendary techno clubs. Here he mastered his DJ skills before moving on to play Derrick May and Kevin Saunderson's Music Institute club alongside Juan Atkins, May and Carter.

After meeting John Acquaviva one night, the duo recorded 'Elements Of Tone' under the moniker State Of Mind. The EP was an immediate success and led to Hawtin and Acquaviva forming their record label Plus 8 in 1989.

Meanwhile Hawtin furthered his career, becoming the pioneer of nineties 303-driven acidic techno and undertaking an alarming number of remixes. Working under his two main aliases, FUSE (Future Underground Subsonic Experiments) and Plastikman, he released classics such as the unreservedly caustic and sparse 'Spastik' and 'FU' singles, and *Sheet One*, *Recycled Plastik*, *Dimension Intrusion Concept 1* and *Musik* albums.

Hawtin continued to build a dedicated underground fan base by usually releasing his material on extremely limited runs, while his legendary DJ sets and live performances marked him out for cutting-edge celebrity status among those in the know.

Heart and Soul Heart and Soul started in 1993 and remains one of the UK's few truly underground club nights. The DJs all play by their first names only and play cutting-edge techno and house that in most clubs would clear the dance floor – except that here they jump like lunatics. The club has thrived despite venue hassles.

There are no flyers, tickets are sold in advance by word of mouth and the promoters deny its existence to enquiring journalists.

Not a night that relies on passing trade.

Heaven One of London's largest and longest-running venues and the capital's favourite gay club, home to four dance floors (including the Soundshaft), a capacity of 1,500, the birth of seminal clubs such as Spectrum, Land of OZ and Rage, Heaven opened its doors in 1979.

As well as housing some of the most influential nights in the UK's club history, Heaven also hosted the UK gigs of performers such as Grace Jones and Madonna. Alongside its tackier disco and hi-NRG nights, in the early years of house music, Heaven gained a considerable reputation among the straight community for being one of the few places you could hear Chicago tracks.

In 1998 the club closed for a revamp, re-opening with extended dance floors, a coffee bar and more sedate areas for conversation.

Heavenly Growing out of Jeff Barrett's Head records, Heavenly Records was launched in 1990 with the release of Saint Etienne's 'Only Love Can Break Your Heart'. The subsequent release of the group's seminal *Fox Base Alpha* album secured the label's success.

Signing a deal with Sony music, the label progressed from strength to strength with acts such as Manic Street Preachers, Flowered Up and Espiritu joining the label. Further signings included Underworld, the Charlatans and the Chemical Brothers, who launched Heavenly into the club world with their Heavenly Social nights.

In August 1994 the legendary Sunday Social night opened its doors at the Albany pub, Great Portland Street, London. Originally intended to be a Sunday chill out, the venue erupted, ensuring the Chemical Brothers' (at the time called the Dust Brothers) rapid rise to stardom.

Progressing to a larger venue, Smithfield's in Farringdon, the night became legendary for its queues and eventually moved again to a Saturday night at Turnmills.

In August 1995 the label signed a new distribution deal with DeConstruction Records and added Beth Orton, The Hybirds, Dot Allison, Famous Times and PFM to their roster.

Hedonism One of the first acid house nights, Hedonism's infamous function in Hanger Lane was rammed with punters openly knocking back pills, snorting speed and smoking spliff.

Soul II Soul dropped Hawaii Five O in the middle of the night and suddenly everyone was on the floor paddling as if they were back in the school playground.

Herbal Highs and Herbal E By far the most common and well-known herbal, or legal, high, Herbal Ecstacy (note the misspelled name) is also the most expensive and is considered by many to be a poor form of herbal drug. As with most recipes that purport to provide a legal high, Herbal Ecstacy relies heavily on caffeine-type stimulants such as guarana, but its main ingredient is ephedrine, a plant-derived substance that is common in diet, allergy and asthma treatments.

Herbal Ecstacy consists of Tibetan *ma huang* (a source of ephedrine), Brazilian guarana, Chinese black ginseng, German gingko bilboa, cola nut, Russian gotu kola, Indonesian fo-ti-tient, green tea and nutmeg. People have differing views on the efficacy of the pills, although one reported effect was turning your tongue and ablutions blue, which is fun in its way.

Other herbal hits include Turbo Charge, which claims to last for six to eight hours and provides extra energy and an underlying feeling of euphoria. Its ingredients are remarkably similar to those listed above, with the addition of potassium chloride.

Hi-NRG and Nu-NRG Emerging in the gay scene in the early eighties, and reflecting the energy burst of poppers, hi-NRG specialised in speeding up bass lines and drum tracks on cheesy disco anthems. Unlike most gay trends, hi-NRG failed to find much of a following among the straight community in the UK outside of Scotland, where the punters couldn't get enough. It did however inform later perversions of disco music, such as house and some strands of techno.

Hi-NRG however found a greater support base in mainland Europe, particularly among the Italo disco community. It reached its height in 1984 with Stock, Aitken and Waterman's commercialisation of the sound on Dead Or Alive's 'You Spin Me Around (Like A Record)'. Picking up where hi-NRG left off, nu-NRG, as pioneered by DJs Blu Peter, Pete Wardman and the late Tony De Vit, is close to trance in tempo and sound but is favoured by the glamorous and pouting rather than crusty travellers. It glorifies in campness.

Handbag for those who excel on poppers: 16 tabs of E and 5,000 push-ups (stripping down to the waist is obligatory) and you're there.

Hip Hop Developing from the DIY disco period of late seventies New York, Hip Hop's essential instruments are two turntables and a microphone. While the DJ cut, scratched and looped fat-arsed funky tunes, a group of dudes in flared disco trousers would rap about their 'homies' (mates) and suck face with their 'hoes' (mates/girlfriends).

Fast-forward a couple of decades and the dudes are now in baggy trousers, workwear and wrap-around shades, but the principles are the same. Hip hop started in the Bronx, where early legends such as Kool Herc, Grandmaster Flash and Afrika Bambaataa made their mark. The last of these took the music into electro, until the second wave of B-Boys arrived with LL Cool J and Run DMC. A heavier politicised trajectory saw Public Enemy and NWA become spokespeople for a young black under-class and its anti-authoritarianism struck a chord with a large white and black following.

By the nineties hip hop had established itself as a commercial music force and influenced musical forms from jazz through to indie and house. In the UK hip hop helped launch club culture, with seminal clubs such as The Language Lab, in the early eighties, playing Sugar Hill b-sides while Londoners learnt to rap on an open mike.

French hip hop artists such as MC Solar, Cam and Da Funk Mob shocked the Anglo-Saxon world out of its France-ain't-hip xenophobia by producing continental music that is undeniably cool.

Nicky Holloway Starting out as a promoter by running events in fun pubs in the Old Kent Road, Nicky Holloway became the central figure in the Special Branch organisation, running soul weekenders in Rockley Sands and booking soul and jazz funk DJs into slots in pubs such as The Royal Oak and The Swan and Sugar Loaf in London.

Playing huge 4,000-strong weekenders such as the Livewire Prestatyn and the Barry Island events, his reputation spread beyond the south-east, pulling in punters from across the UK for seaside events and continental trips, to places such as Ibiza. In 1987 Holloway took other DJs such as Paul Oakenfold, Johnny Walker and Danny Rampling on a trip to Ibiza and met up with Trevor Fung and Ian St. Paul at their Project bar in Ibiza. The result was a mass conversion to Balearic beats.

Returning to London, Holloway opened The Trip at the Astoria, Charing Cross Road, in June 1988. The night was perfectly timed to pick up on the rapid growth of the acid house scene, the club being rammed wall to wall with punters discovering the buzz of ecstasy and dance music.

By 1990 Holloway had changed the name to Made On Earth, Sin, and then Alphabet City and had established it as the only legal alternative to raves such as Sunrise and Energy. Sin would explode on nights when raves failed to materialise.

Holloway's nights attracted mile-long queues, desperate to gain entry but frequently finding themselves turned away to seek out more dubious entertainment in one of Charing Cross Road's less salubrious drinking haunts. Holloway was of course making considerable amounts of money, which he ploughed back into the dance community by investing in a club, The Milk Bar and later Velvet Underground.

For the first time a club, rather than a night, was being run by someone who came from and was part of acid house culture. Others were to follow, such as Sean McClusky's The Brain and, later, Mr C's The End. Punters were treated to better sound systems, DJs and atmospheres designed for the music, although bar prices remained stubbornly high and only The End sorted out the toilets.

David Holmes Ireland's premier techno DJ and producer, David Holmes built his reputation as a DJ playing at the Sugarsweet night in Belfast. Originally recording with Ashley Beedle as the Disco Evangelists, he released 'De Niro' and 'A New Dawn' on Positiva in 1993.

His trademark cinematic qualities were already present in 'De Niro', for which he used samples from Morricone's score for 'Once Upon A Time In America'. Moving to Warp he began building his solo reputation and released 'Johnny Favourite'. He also simultaneously recorded under aliases such as Death Before Disco, the Well Charged Latinos and 4 Boy 1 Girl Action and with Andy Ellison and Pete Latham as the Scubadevils and remixed for artists such as Sandals, Saint Etienne, U2, The Aloof, Freaky Realistic and Sabres Of Paradise.

Setting up his own record label, Sugarsweet, with Ian McCready and Jim McDonald, he turned to releasing artists such as Wah Wah Warrior and his own Death By Disco project. Sugarsweet however failed to take off and was soon replaced by the Exploding Plastic Inevitable imprint.

In 1994 he signed to Andrew Weatherall's Sabres Of Paradise label, before moving to Go Beat. He released his first album, *This Film's Crap Let's Slash The Seats*, to critical acclaim in 1995. His 1998 album, *Let's Get Killed*, took its influence from the streets of New York, where, in the footsteps of Art Garfunkel, he recorded people's voices – a successful ruse, although many have commented that Holmes would have found a richer source of conversation in his native Belfast.

The first single from the album, *Don't Die Just Yet*, took its title from some graffiti Holmes spotted while walking around East Village.

The Horse Shoe Held in a pub next to the Dominion Theatre on Tottenham Court Road, Jazz Funk Double Disco at The Horse Shoe was run by seminal DJs Paul Murphy, George Power and Paul 'Trouble' Anderson in the early 1980s. Basic in its conception and practice (it consisted of a bar and a dance floor), it was populated by London's underground jazz scene.

Frowned on and misunderstood by the predominantly white music scene, The Horse Shoe played an important part in pioneering rare groove and jazz funk, which later took over the dance floor of clubs and warehouse parties across the UK. Despite its size, Murphy's dedication led him to invest thousands of pounds in inviting seminal American black musicians such as Tania Maria to the UK for the first time.

Murphy moved on to the legendary Sol Y Sombra, which became a magnet for jazz and Latin DJs and promoters from across the UK, while also taking over the upstairs bar of the Electric Ballroom, with Paul 'Trouble' Anderson, latter-day king of garage, playing electro and hip hop downstairs.

Revamping the Purple Pussycat club, in Finchley Road, in 1987, Murphy's jazz style was soon to be eclipsed by the rising stars of acid jazz and house music. Respect for his innovation remains strong within the DJ fraternity and he makes frequent appearances at clubs across the country.

House Derived from the disco music of Chicago of the early 1980s, house took its name from the city's warehouse parties and the Warehouse club, where luminaries such as Frankie Knuckles would cut up disco and electronic music on reel-to-reel tapes.

The music grew from roots in New York's gay club scene and in particular The Loft and Paradise Garage. Essentially house beefed up disco, with the DJ using drum machines to exaggerate the kick drum.

Chicago warehouse parties in 1983-4 took advantage of the city's plethora of disused industrial spaces. Held behind unmarked doors, recognisable only by the bouncer on the door and inaudible on the street, inside the party would explode: packed with gays, Puerto Ricans and black people, stripped to the waist, spinning madly and totally lost in the sound. Usually dark, the décor was minimal. Bars would be a geezer sitting on beer crates and where there was light the venue would be bathed in ultraviolet.

In particular one DJ, Ron Hardy, came to represent the house sound. The resident at the Music Box, he became the scene's messiah, although his musical style was in fact wildly eclectic.

While producers such as Marshall Jefferson would frequently record tunes for Hardy to play, it wasn't until Jessie Saunders started producing records that house artists began releasing their own tunes. According to Jefferson 'the guys who started making the first house music were Jessie Saunders and Jamie Principle. No one else thought they could do it as well as Jamie so nobody was making house music. When Saunders started he was making cheap bad house music, so everybody thought they could do better than Jessie. That's what got me into it, Farley Jackmaster Funk into it, Steve 'Silk' Hurley into it. Jamie Principle was playing it in the clubs, but then Jessie started putting records out and when I heard Jessie's records I thought "I could do this bad".'

House began seeping on to dance floors in the Europe in the mid-eighties, although it was initially confined to few clubs, mostly on the gay scene. Controversy rages over who introduced house music to the UK. It was certainly being played in clubs such as Jungle, The Pyramid, Black Market, Jive Turkey and Delirium long before the explosion of acid house popularised it. Generally Mike Pickering, Graeme Park and DJ Parot are cited as leading the way to house music in the north, while the Watson brothers, Mark Moore, Colin Faver, Kid Batchelor, Evil Eddie Richards and Derek Boland all spun house tunes in London clubs.

House Of God Starting in 1992 in Birmingham, House Of God's word-of-mouth reputation had soon made it one of the most hotly talked about techno nights in the country. This was techno with a capital T. Earth-shattering acid house and techno whipped the boys and girls into a sweltering gurning mass. Serious music for serious nutters, House Of God asked no questions and took no prisoners.

House Parties As club culture became increasingly corporate in the mid-nineties, former clubbers became less interested in what were often routine events held in predictable venues with average music. The seventies tradition of bring-a-bottle parties was re-introduced, although the lessons from warehouse and club culture meant a return to tapes and home sound systems was unthinkable. House parties were now expected to re-create a club environment, with decks and sound systems being hired and each circle of friends adopting their favoured DJs for their parties.

A new form of DJ emerged. The party DJ rarely played in a public space but was solidly booked playing the parties of people whom he or she only knew from behind the turntables.

Apart from being free, house parties also had another huge advantage. Unlike clubs, which eventually had some form of license restriction, parties could go on for several days if the owners wanted them to and there was no prohibition on drugs. The down side was that, unless a bar had been organised, in the cocaine hungry days the booze would always run out too early.

Tony Humphries Starting as a mobile DJ while working for the *New York Daily* newspaper, Tony Humphries was to become one of the most influential dance figures in New York. After he met Shep Pettibone in 1981 and was given a slot on New York's Kiss FM radio station he was booked by Larry Patterson to play the Zanzibar, which he transformed into New Jersey's most happening club.

Through his club slot and radio show he began to break underground dance artists such as Adeva, while also becoming a central figure in the emerging garage and house sounds. He went on to produce remixes for an endless roster of artists and was shipped over to the UK in 1992 by the Ministry Of Sound to take up a residency at the club.

Steve 'Silk' Hurley One of Chicago's earliest exponents of house music, Hurley built his reputation playing on WBMX radio in Chicago. His breakthrough came after he borrowed money from his father to release 'Music Is The Key' on Rocky Jones' DJ International record label. The record charted at number nine in the US dance charts.

Frustration followed after his song 'I Can't Turn Around' was covered by Farley 'Jackmaster' Funk as 'Love Can't Turn Around' in 1985 and went on to become the first house record to chart in the UK in August 1986. The record featured the vocals of Daryl Pandy, which rubbed the salt deeper into the wound, since Pandy was Hurley's former flatmate. But his following single, 'Jack Your Body', became the first house record to hit number one in January 1987. His reputation established, he collaborated with Keith Nunnally and released 'Let The Music Take You' as JM Silk.

Much remix and production work followed with artists such as Kym Sims ('Too Blind To See It'), Roberta Flack, Paula Abdul and Ce Ce Peniston ('We Got A Love Thang').

Lest we forget:
House Of Pain
The Hustle
Hustlers Convention
Hustlers Of Culture

Best we forget:
Hit Man And Her
Hooded tops
Hustling

Ibiza Once an impoverished rock that had economically relied on the salt trade since Roman times, this small Balearic island is now the Mecca of house music and club culture. Its transformation began under Franco's fascist regime in the sixties, when concrete hotels, theme pubs, fish-and-chip shops and package tourism usurped the sleepy feudal economy. The tiny fishing village of San Antonio de Portmany was transformed into a sprawling mass of holiday apartments, which by the mid-eighties catered for hoards of young lager-drinking Brits attracted by tacky discos, cheap booze and plenty of totty.

Other sides of Ibiza also thrived. The picturesque old Town of Ibiza remains relatively unspoilt by development and its winding alleys and numerous bars now host a flamboyant, international gay scene. Throughout the summer its streets are transformed into nightly parties until 2 a.m., when the bars close and groups of transvestites in unfeasibly high heels wobble their way down cobbled alleys towards the out-of-town clubs.

Despite its cheap and cheerful side, Ibiza became a playground for the rich. Vast, luxurious and celebrity-filled clubs such as KU (Privilege), Amnesia, Pascha, and Space competed with each other, producing ever more elaborate dance floors, sound systems and floor shows. It was here, in 1987, that a swathe of British DJs congregated and discovered the uplifting effect of ecstasy, music and all-night clubbing. On their return they recreated the effect in London and spawned the first Summer of Love.

Indie Taking its name from Independent record labels, Indie music is antipathetic to the corporate music industry and is essentially low-tech guitar music. It became prominent in the post-punk period of the late seventies and early eighties and is a catch-all term for music that is not commercial or influenced by dance music.

Often seen as the antithesis to club music, in fact the gulf is sometimes overstated. Bands that started the early club scene, such as Steve Strange's Visage, had musical roots in the psychedelic and experimental music that inspired post-punk bands.

In the early eighties the style setting London club scene became increasingly black dance music led, while much of the north stayed with indie – epitomised by bands such as the Smiths. Even here crossovers between indie and dance continued to thrive, with New Order opening the Hacienda club in Manchester. Here indie dance music shared nights with soul, rare groove, hip hop and house.

Meanwhile in London some acid house clubs mixed indie with the emerging house sound. Fusion, run by Simon Hobart (formerly of Bedrock and later to launch Popstars), opened as an indie/acid house club at the indie hang-out Marquee club in London. With DJs such as Carl Cox and Colin Dale gracing its decks, it attracted a dedicated weekly crowd. Initially Chicago house tunes were mixed in with indie dance, but gradually the music policy became increasingly dominated by house and techno.

As house increasingly ruled dance floors up and down the UK, transforming the north into a bastion of pure house dance clubs, guitar-based music lost its footing. It gradually re-emerged in the early nineties through clubs such as Smashing, Blow Up, Automatic and Hobart's gay mixed night Popstars.

Indie fans complain dance music is all the same. Dance music fans retort that Indie fans are better at drinking than dancing and enjoying themselves.

Intelligent Techno Invented by Dom Phillips, at the time writing for *Mixmag*, in 1992, the intelligent techno moniker was designed to differentiate between banging hardcore rave anthems, which also used the techno label, and the more subtle forms of techno music being created by artists such as the Future Sound Of London. The product of a specific period, Phillips now despises the term.

Internet Pirate Radio The possibility of broadcasting live events across the world made the Internet an attractive proposition to the music industry from the start. Technological constraints, cost and accessibility however restricted its use to large festivals and super-group concerts. Even then the number of people who had the facilities to tune in was limited.

Then Progressive Networks developed RealAudio Player Plus – a system that allowed the user to flick through Internet radio stations as easily as they turned a radio dial. The attraction for pirate radio stations was obvious. Instead of broadcasting to a limited audience within a two- or three-mile radius, they could now reach the world and, because the Internet isn't constrained by terrestrial broadcast laws, they could do it legally.

In early 1996 Steve Kennedy, an employee of Demon Internet, met a group of pirate radio DJs in a pub. Within a month

Gaia Live, the first pirate Internet radio station, began pumping underground London music across the world. It was soon joined by G-Force in London and Highlander Internet Radio – dubbing itself 'The Future Sound of Scotland' and InterFACE, Live. Other sites include Digital Flavour and Cyberville.

Italo House Kicked into the limelight in 1989 by Black Box's cheesy but effective Euro house anthem 'Ride On Time', Italo house dominated piano-led dance floors of the early nineties. An article in *Mixmag* coined the term Italo house.

Stars of the scene were Danielle Davoli, Mirko Limoni and Valerio Semplici, who released records as Black Box, Starlight and Wood Allen. Essentially marrying US and UK house and garage sounds to conventional European pop, Italo house opened the way for a flood of Euro-disco-inspired releases of varying, usually dubious quality. Among the classics of the genre were tracks such as Alexander Robotnic's 'Problemo d'Amour', Guacho's 'Dance Forever', Mixmaster's 'Take Me Away' and UF Force's 'Funk Express'.

Italo dance music had a long tradition. While disco's progression from early Philadelphia International tracks to tacky Bee Gees and Village People tracks had ensured its demise among clubbers in the UK in the late seventies, the Italians loved it. In the early eighties, the US DJs who were laying the foundations of house and garage music began to pick up on Italian imports such as Bari Centro's 'Tittle-Tattle' and 'Klien' and MBO's 'Dirty Talk'. Meanwhile the Italo disco sound also played a vital role in the emerging hi-NRG sound.

As the Balearic and house scene looked for alternatives to the mobbed clubs of Ibiza in the early nineties, eyes began to focus on the clubs of Rimini/Riccione and clubs such as Blow Up, Cocorico, Paradiso, Peter Pan and Slego.

From 1990 onward Italo house's boosted confidence led to a spate of high-production-value pop dance releases, creating the Media Records empire and introducing artists such as Capella, Korda, Double Dee and Flying Records (who were later to gain much credibility through their London arm).

Originally an Italian label and distribution company, the London arm of Flying was set up by Dean Thatcher and Charlie Chester in association with Cooltempo. Their first release was Thatcher's remix of Ian Dury and The Blockhead's 'Hit Me With Your Rhythm Stick', a track that had been previously remixed by Paul Hardcastle but not with as much support from the original band. The label went on to release quality dance tunes from both UK and Italian artists, earning a formidable reputation.

It's Obvious A Leeds-based, anti-club, club night, largely remembered for its ambitious and imaginative publicity gimmicks, It's Obvious announced its presence with baked beans cans with their labels removed and replaced by the club's flyers. Bearing no information apart from the club's name – the whole point being that it wasn't obvious – people were supposed to be confused but somehow they weren't and still managed to turn up at the venue on the right night. A case where less turned out to be more.

Lest we forget:
Ice Cube
Ice T
Inner City
Izit

Best we forget:
Vanilla Ice
The Incredible Giant Crab
'Intellectual' conversations at the end of the night

Michael Jackson Beginning his career with the Jackson Five when he was four years old, Michael Jackson is hardly from the underground. He modelled his stage presence on James Brown and the band soon found success, being signed on to Motown Records in 1968. Hits such as 'ABC' and 'I Want You Back' became early dance classics while Jackson probably still didn't know what pubic hair was, let alone have ambitions to grow some.

Jackson's solo career took off in 1972 with releases such as 'Ben' and Bobby Day's 'Rockin' Robin' – both chart hits in the UK and USA. The Jackson Five's record sales dipped in the mid-seventies and Michael Jackson's solo career was put on hold while the group re-launched as the Jacksons.

In 1979 he moved to Epic and collaborated with Quincy Jones on *Off The Wall*, a disco-fuelled album that introduced the now-mature Jackson to the world with considerable success. The album spawned two Number one singles, 'Don't Stop Till You Get Enough' and 'Rock With You'. His follow-up album with Quincy Jones, 1982's *Thriller*, was a milestone in dance music, selling over 42 million copies. A commercial take on the evolving dance music of the eighties, tracks such as 'Billie Jean' and 'Thriller' were driven by extremely influential bass lines and 'Beat It' was the first black artist video to receive rotational air play on MTV.

His success as a commercial artist was by now assured, but his influence on club culture from here on was negligible.

Norman Jay One of the UK's most influential DJs and fore-fathers of rare groove, acid jazz and house, Norman Jay's Good Times sound system organised the legendary Shake and Finger Pop warehouse jams in the mid-eighties. In a period when illegal parties ruled the day, punters relied on word-of-mouth networks for their party information and Norman became famous for telling punters on Kiss during its pirate days 'If you were there you knew, if you weren't, shame. Next time you'll know.' He still didn't tell the punters where it was.

Born in west London to Caribbean parents, Jay was immersed in the black music culture in the late sixties from an early age, playing his first gig when he was 10 years old. By the late seventies he was already an avid collector of Motown, Stax, Atlantic, jazz and the Sound Of Philadelphia disco records. He had experienced US disco first-hand while visiting a DJ relation in Brooklyn, where he met Larry Levan at his legendary Paradise Garage. He also formed friendships with the then-unknown David Morales, Tony Humphries and Louis Vega.

Returning to London he formed the Good Times sound system and played the Notting Hill carnival. Soon he was attracting up to 1,000 people to his gigs, leading to an invitation to do a slot on the pirate radio station Kiss, in 1985. His involvement led to the recruitment of fellow club and warehouse DJs Jazzie B, Dr Bob Jones, Danny Rampling, Gilles Peterson and Judge Jules to the station, despite their lack of any broadcast experience. Calling his slot The Original Rare Groove Show, his Shake and Finger

Pop outfit, alongside Judge Jules' Family Funktion, led the rare groove movement.

Despite the rare groove tag, Jay's parties would play anything from old school to the earliest house imports. By the beginning of the nineties Jay had set up his club night, High On Hope, with Patrick Lilley and started importing the original US gurus such as Marshall Jefferson, Humphries, Blaze, Ten City and Adeva.

Meanwhile he maintained his eclectic music taste, joining Gilles Peterson on his Talkin' Loud record label and playing regular rare groove nights at the Bass Clef until it was taken over by The Blue Note. Jay continues to play old school jazz and funk and cutting-edge dance music.

Marshall Jefferson A disciple of the late Chicago DJ Ron Hardy, Marshall Jefferson began his house music career in the early 1980s at legendary Chicago clubs, the Warehouse and the Music Box, where DJs such as Hardy, Jamie Principle and Frankie Knuckles played. An early innovator of house music, Jefferson is fondly remembered as the creator, alongside DJ Pierre, of the acid house sound.

He started making tunes when he had to stop going to the Music Box after landing a job at the post office doing the graveyard shift – from midnight to eight every morning. The Music Box was open from midnight to seven, so Jefferson made tapes of his music for people to take to the Music Box for Ron Hardy to play. Soon his reputation as a house producer took off.

Whereas early house had concentrated on stripped-downbeats, Jefferson tried to inject a musical element into the mix – not always to a rapturous reception. When he released 'Move Your Body', which included a now-familiar keyboard refrain over the drum pattern, he recalls baffled house fans complaining, 'Hey!

Where'd all the fucking piano come from? There ain't no fucking piano in house music.'

In 1985 he recorded songs using a Roland 303. Two years later DJ Pierre asked him to produce some records he'd been producing on a 303. The resulting releases, 'Acid Trax' by Phuture, kicked acid house into being.

Jive Turkey Run by promoters Mathew Swift and John Mattan and DJs Parrot (who found record success with his All Seeing Eye project in 1998), Winston Hazel and Allister Whitehead, Jive Turkey, in Sheffield became legendary among the funk and jazz fraternity in the mid- to late eighties. Punters would travel from all over the UK to soak up the atmosphere. Frequented by Richard H. Kirk of Cabaret Voltaire and the Warp Records crew, by the late eighties Winston, Whitehead and Parrot started introducing house into their sets, taking their devoted following with them.

Held in the ballroom of Sheffield's City Hall, a venue that was used more for tea dances than raving, it was described as a shit hole by its regulars. In fact the ballroom consisted of three rooms stuck in the basement among a network of corridors. What it lacked in décor was amply made up for in atmosphere and its surprisingly good sound system. Despite the few thousand capacity of the venue, the door was restricted to 850, allowing plenty of room for the punters to groove and spin.

After closing in the late eighties. Jive Turkey returned in 1991 to re-introduce eclectic mixing and take on the dictatorship of rave. Alongside The Blue Note in Derby and Graeme Park's Garage in Nottingham, Jive Turkey kicked the north of England into house sounds.

Juice Bars Juice bars have a surprisingly long association with club culture, with Ron Hardy's seminal Music Box night being held in one, but their real proliferation came in the mid-nineties as a last-ditch restorative for the near terminally drug fucked.

Having binged on all manner of chemicals for 48 hours, clubbers would desperately try and delude their vitamin-drained bodies that they did really care about them, and quaff litres of fruit juice or smoothies in a vague attempt to emulate a healthy lifestyle. Soon there was enough of a market for juice bars to spring up in stylish urban areas, offering fruit cocktail tonics and claiming all manner of curative effects.

Fashionably decorated and populated by the hip and trendy, clubbers were fooled into paying way over the odds for a glass of mashed fruit.

Jump In 1992 the American-Irish hip hop band House of Pain notched up a top ten hit with 'Jump Around' and momentarily changed the way B-boys looked at dancing. The hip hop fraternity, urged on by the style press, began to bounce around dance floors commanding each other to 'Jump' at the top of their lungs. Clubs that had previously boasted about representing the re-birth of cool were transformed into tidal waves of inverted pogo-ing baseball caps.

Soon people realised that losing your keys and wallet on the dance floor was not the most enjoyable way to spend Friday and Saturday night and, like Zeberdee, Jump was put to bed.

Jumping Jack Frost Infamous for turning up at Shock nights in Cold Harbour Lane, Brixton in the late eighties, Jumping Jack Frost would slam sped-up hip hop breaks on the turntable, playing 33 r.p.m. records at 45 r.p.m. and mixing from break to break. Many credit him, alongside Fabio and Grooverider, with spawning the jungle sound.

Starting out as a rare groove DJ with his long-time collaborator Bryan Gee on Brixton's Passion pirate radio station, by the late eighties and the arrival of rave Frost was lining up behind the decks with the likes of Dave Angel, Kenny Ken and Carl Cox.

While hardcore kicked in, Frost worked on developing the hard break beat science that was to become jungle. By 1993 he and Gee had set up V Records and, revealing their knack for predicting the future, released Roni Size's 'Made To Fit' as their first single.

Taking advantage of the talent around Size, V quickly became one of the scene's most respected imprints. After releasing 'The Burial' under the Leviticus moniker, Frost and Gee set up a sister label, Philly Blunt, to release more mainstream material. Winning a show on Kiss FM in London, Frost helped take jungle overground.

Jungle Jungle grew out of the London hardcore scene of the early nineties. The music and its name immediately inspired controversy. In common with hardcore, the tempo of the rhythms and the urban intensity of Junglist sounds jarred on the ears of happy house enthusiasts.

Musically Jungle is a hybrid, combining break beats from hip hop and the tempo of hardcore with samples and ragga's half tempo, subsonic bass lines. The roots of the music can be traced back to bands such as Shut Up And Dance and tracks such as '5,6,7,8' (which was unexpectedly adopted as a rave anthem), A Guy Called Gerald's 'Voodoo Ray', Metalheadz's 'Terminator' and 4 Hero's 'Mr Kirk's Nightmare'.

The term jungle came into use some time in the early nineties, although it is unclear where it came from. One theory is that the term was taken from a sample of Jamaican sound system MCs, who would identify people from the Tivoli Gardens area of Kingston, Jamaica as junglists. The first record to use the term jungle, 'Jungle Techno', was released on the Ibiza Rave record label. Controversy over the name arose from its possible racist connotations and an unease among its originators towards giving the music a definitive name.

The music was pioneered in clubs and raves by DJs such as Randall, Micky Finn, Ron, Jumping Jack Frost, Kenny Ken and, most importantly, Grooverider and Fabio and by producers such as Rob Playford and his label Moving Shadow. Legendary nights such as Rage, at Heaven and AWOL, at the Paradise, attracted a dedicated following of enthusiastic junglists.

On radio Jumping Jack Frost and Fabio and Grooverider's Kiss FM shows brought jungle out from the underground, while pirate stations such as Kool FM, Transmission One and Don FM nurtured the burgeoning scene. Early indications of it crossing over into the mainstream came with Genocide II's 'Narra Mine' and Rebel MC's 'Comin' On Strong', but the first proper jungle hit came in 1993 with SL2's 'On A Ragga Tip'.

The music found greater popularity as the more experimental wing of the jazz and leftfield movements adopted it as their own. Inspired by labels such as Good Looking, Mo Wax, Metalheadz, V recordings and Moving Shadow and artists such as Goldie, LTJ Bukem, Wax Doctor and BLIM, jazz and beat heads began to find a home in drum 'n' bass.

As more subtle and melodic variation than the earlier dark and ragga periods of jungle emerged, drum 'n' bass soon found its way into the mainstream of clubbing. In its wake the more aggressive and dance-friendly jump up began to replace drum 'n' bass rhythms as labels such as Congo Natty and Ganja Crew and DJs such as Zinc and Hype reintroduced club kids to the harder elements of jungle. Nights such as Metalheadz, at the acid jazz-owned night-club The Blue Note, Speed and Movement became flagships of clubbing. Jungle finally knew it had arrived when Roni Size's Bristol-based collective, Reprazent, claimed the Mercury prize in 1997.

As jungle developed it became divided into an increasing number of camps.

Ambient drum 'n' bass, which is also known as artcore, is distinguished by its lush dreamy string arrangements, which flow over and break up the break beats.

Darkcore, or simply dark, was the earliest form of jungle, identified by a brooding menace and use of horror film samples.

Drum 'n' bass, the form that popularised jungle, came into use in 1994 to describe the more intelligent use of jungle rhythms with complex musical structures. It became massive among the post-acid jazz set.

Hard step is stripped down, crisply produced minimal form of jungle, which usually emphasises the second and fourth beats of the bar. It was eclipsed by drum 'n' bass in the mid-nineties.

Jazz step combines hard step with drum 'n' bass' jazzier excursions.

Jump up is a rougher variant closer to original jungle but with greater emphasis on the music's hip hop rather than ragga influences. It became the most prominent form of the music in the late nineties.

Ragga jungle, as the name suggests, does the opposite to hard step and borrows ideas from ragga sound systems, such as samples from ragga tunes or live toasting in a hybrid of Jamaican patois and inner city slang.

Justified Ancients of Mu Mu Formed by Bill Drummond (a co-founder of Zoo Records) and Jimmy Cauty, the Justified Ancients of Mu Mu are not so much a band as an anarchic project. They began releasing records in 1987 under the moniker The Jamms, but gained notoriety when they changed their name to KLF and released 'What The Fuck is Going On?' Taking advantage of the growth of sampling (KLF stands for

Kopyright Liberation Front), they laid other people's music over hip hop beats.

In 1988 they had an early house hit, reaching number one as The Timelords. The song, 'Doctorin' The Tardis', pinched the *Dr Who* theme tune. In 1989 they played the Helter Skelter rave in Oxfordshire. Demanding their £1,000 fee up-front in pound notes, they scribbled 'We love you' on each one and dropped them from a crane into the crowd.

Their heyday came between 1991 and 1992, when the KLF scored a series of hits with 'What Time is Love?', '3AM Eternal', 'Last Train to Transcentral' and 'Justified And Ancient', featuring Tammy Wynette on vocals. After winning the Brit Awards for Best British Group, they announced their retirement from the music industry and turned their anarchist tendencies on the art world.

In 1993 they lampooned the Turner prize by running their own £40,000 competition for the worst piece of art. Rachel Whitbread won both prizes. The following year they caused outrage by burning a million pounds in a field in Scotland.

They returned, briefly, to the music world in 1997 as 2K and released 'Fuck The Millennium'.

Lest we forget:
Chad Jackson
Jon Pleased Wimmin
Grace Jones
Juan Trip
Judge Jules

Best we forget:
Jellies
Jive Bunny
Jungle Brothers re-releases being re-released

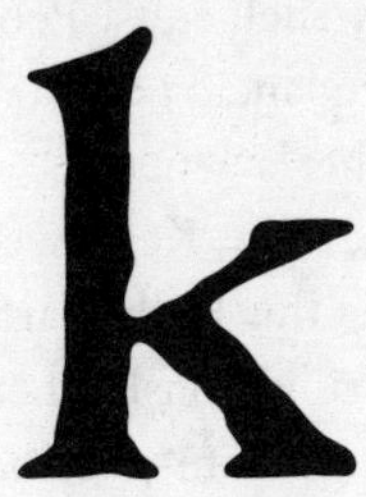

Kahuna Brothers One of London's early big beat clubs, Dan (from Leeds) and Jon (from Dewsbury) Kahuna opened their Big Kahuna Burger club night in Finsbury Park in May 1995. Before DJing, Dan had been a communications student and worked in marketing for Beat Wax Concrete and Heavenly. Jon had been an industrial plastics salesman.

Moving to Smithfield's, Farringdon during 1995, the night and the Kahunas gained a reputation for alcohol-fuelled evenings in which they'd frequently get as messy as their punters. They were soon known for their chaotic mixing, which launched a new school of beered-up, deliberately crap DJing.

They still attracted most of the rising stars of the UK's freestyle break beat community to spin behind their decks. Moving the club to a monthly residency at the Mars in central London in 1998, the duo took time off to begin organising their record label, Kahuna Cuts.

John Kelly One of the north-west's first-name DJs, John Kelly started playing house at the Underground, in Liverpool. A members-only club, you had to know or be known to get in, yet the Underground was rammed full of hard-as-fucking nails scallies, clad in obligatory shell suits. People who would normally punch your lights out for glancing at their pint would be wrapped in the ecstasy of each other's arms.

Continuing in the same vein, Kelly went on to play the raves at Quadrant Park. Following this Kelly started G Love in Liverpool's Mardi Gras venue, with ridiculously cheap door prices. The club downstairs resembled a pub-cum-pool hall, while upstairs people immersed themselves in beats and dry ice.

Kemistry and Storm Disciples of Fabio and Grooverider's sets at Rage, Kemistry and Storm are jungle's foremost female DJ duo. Their entry into jungle is deeply entwined with Goldie, who appeared with them as their MC at their first gig at Mindblown, Wolverhampton in 1992.

Before DJing Kemistry had been a make-up artist from Birmingham, and Storm, from Kettering, had been a radiographer. The two moved to London together and shared a flat in 1989, where they began raving and soon discovered Rage and heard Fabio and Grooverider. Inspired, they bought a pair of decks and began mastering their DJ skills.

In 1995 they fulfilled one of their dreams, when Goldie booked them to play alongside their two heroes at his party in Heaven. Their big break came when they teamed up with Fabio, LTJ Bukem and Doc Scott to play the weekly Speed night. As well as DJing, both work for the Metalheadz record label.

Ketamin Mistakenly thought to be a horse tranquilliser, ketamin (K or special K) was first introduced by the University of Michigan in 1965 during the search for a safe general anaesthetic for surgery. Noted for having a rapid recovery and wide safety margin, it was used extensively in the Vietnam war and produces a 'disassociative' state, where the mind is separated from bodily experiences. Ketamin is still in use as an anaesthetic for humans, although in the UK it is used by veterinary surgeons on animals.

The drug can be administered by IV injection, sniffed or taken orally. Users have likened the effects of injection to being smacked around the head by a crow bar. Despite this, in the post-ecstasy dance community, ketamin has become a drug of choice for a significant minority. The disassociative effects means users are usually easy to identify.

Convinced their mind and body no longer exist in the same space, they chase themselves in manic circles around the dance floor trying to re-unite their cognitive and physical sides. More risky effects occur when users imagine they've died and decide to climb into someone else – which doesn't always go down well.

Kinky Gerlinky The club that relaunched the over-sized glam of the mid-eighties, Kinky Gerlinky was the brainchild of Michael and Gerlinda Kostiff. The Kostiffs were veterans of the London club scene and had been regulars at Leigh Bowery's legendary Taboo nights and Bowery was in turn one of Kinky Gerlinky's most loyal punters.

Glittering with drag queens and costumed club trendies, like other glam nights of 1992 such as Flesh and Pushca, Kinky Gerlinky held regular theme nights where the crowd would turn up in purpose-made costumes. The club had been conceived as an excuse for the Kostiff's glamorous friends to dress up – and they weren't let down. Boys who normally dressed in downbeat trendy clothes became overnight drag queens, spending weeks before the next party preparing their costume.

Kinky Gerlinky maintained its sense of uniqueness by being held irregularly at Legends night-club in London. Its popularity soon outgrew the venue and it moved to the larger space of the

Empire on Leicester Square. A tacky tourist club that in normal circumstances wouldn't have been touched with a barge pole by any self-respecting London clubber, it suddenly became the most desirable night in London.

The party came to an abrupt halt after the sudden death of Gerlinda Kostiff, who died of a brain haemorrhage in 1994.

Kiss The first legal dedicated dance music radio station in London, Kiss began broadcasting as a pirate station in 1985. Picking up on the rare groove-, funk- and disco-inspired music scene developing in the capital and concentrating on playing tunes rather than talking, it immediately found a home in the hearts of London club land. After the UK government announced plans to liberalise the airwaves, Gordon McNamee, Kiss FM's managing director, took the station off air and applied for a licence.

In 1990 the station began broadcasting as a commercial radio station, bringing the whole range of dance music to London 24 hours a day. Inevitably commercial pressures chipped the edges of the station's radical beginnings, but the station maintained connections with dance floors across the nation by rostering club DJs for regular shows.

In April 1992 Kiss took a further step away from its underground origins and joined the Emap media empire. Kiss expanded to Manchester and then Leeds, but the two stations were sold to Chrysalis in 1997 and re-branded as Galaxy.

While club heads are prone to dismissing Kiss for 'selling out', it pioneered a radical change in the content of music radio. Kiss DJs are now on the fast track for a career in Radio One.

Kit Kat Club More than any other night, the Kit Kat club gave birth to the Leeds house super-club scene. This was to develop into the city's heyday with clubs such as Vague (which was the Kit Kat by another name), Back To Basics, Up Yer Ronson, Hard Times and the Cooker drawing in punters from across the country.

The Kitchen A seminal illegal blues party during the Summers of Love in 1988-90, The Kitchen was based in two flats that had been knocked into one, in Charles Barry Crescent on the Hulme council estate in Manchester. Opening after the Hacienda and PSV closed, it operated erratically, relying on word of mouth to let it be known when it was happening.

On the nights it did function crowds would flock to get in. This was not surprising when the only other post-2 a.m. entertainment in the UK's rave capital was going back home to watch the tacky club programme *The Hit Man and Her* on television.

K Klass Formed in late 1988 by Andy Williams and Carl Thomas, who later invited Paul Roberts and Russ Morgan to join them, K Klass originate from Wrexham in Wales but became associated with the Manchester scene through their contacts with 808 State. They soon added a vocalist, Bobbi Depasois, to their line-up.

Their debut EP, 'Wildlife', was funded by the government-run Enterprise Allowance and by Roberts' British Telecom redundancy money and was an immediate dance hit.

After touring the UK extensively with 808 State they released 'Rhythm Is A Mystery' on Eastern Bloc records – the label run by 808 State's Martin Price. The single sold well and after six months and a move to a new label, it hit the top ten at the end of 1991. Further hits followed with 'Don't Stop' in 1992 and 'Let Me Show' in 1993.

Frankie Knuckles One of the original Chicago house DJs, Frankie Knuckles was raised in New York where he grew up listening to his sister's jazz records and learnt to play double bass. He went to Dwyer School of Art in the Bronx and studied textiles at FIT in Manhattan.

Starting his DJ career at the Better Days venue, he would regularly go to watch his former work colleague Larry Levan, who eventually booked him to play the Continental Baths club, one of New York's most famous gay Bath Houses.

In 1977 he was invited to Chicago to play the opening of the Warehouse club. Securing a residency, he initially played sets of mainly Philadelphia International and Salsoul, derived from the New York gay scene. Importing the NYC sound into Chicago he soon made a name for himself.

As disco ebbed away he began to play with the records, editing and looping chunks on reel-to-reel tapes – a trick Levan was already practising in New York but which was radically new in Chicago.

Moving to the Powerplant in 1984, Knuckles brought a Roland TR909 drum machine and began programming drum clatters to play between tracks or boost the kick drum of a song.

By now Chicago music was being called house and Knuckles, along with DJs such as Ron Hardy and Farley Jackmaster Funk, was being credited with starting a new genre.

By 1988 the Powerplant, which Knuckles had helped set up, had been targeted by the city's criminal fraternity and was witnessing sporadic outbreaks of violence. The venue closed and Knuckles moved into production and recording with Rocky Jones' DJ International, releasing 'Tears', with Robert Owen on vocals, and producing 'Baby Wants To Ride' for Jamie Principle on Trax. Furious with Knuckles for recording with Trax, Rocky Jones obtained a copy of 'Baby Wants To Ride' and released a rival single of the track on his label.

Having started editing and remixing records for his own DJ sets, he was soon in demand as a top remixer, being asked to work on projects for everyone from The Pet Shop Boys to Chaka Kahn.

Hooking up with Dave Morales, the two formed the Def-mix production team and attracted yet more prestigious remix work. Meanwhile his reputation secured him DJ slots all over the world.

Konspiracy Based underneath the Corn Exchange near Manchester's Victoria Station, Marino Morgan, Chris Nelson and the Jamm MCs' Konspiracy followed in the footsteps of the Hacienda in 1990 and took the city's acid house explosion to a new audience.

Based on the northern side of the city centre, it attracted a rougher-edged, locally based crowd from Salford and Cheetham Hill. In place of the touchy-feelie atmosphere of the Hacienda, Konspiracy was packed with hard-faced wised-up kids. Also attracting the Hacienda originals, Justin Robertson and Greg Fenton span a Balearic set to a crowd who had followed them through the early Spice days, while the main room throbbed with north Manchester's harder-edged rave heads.

The venue itself, despite the chilling corridor leading to the dance floor, provided a brilliant arena for punters to immerse themselves in the harder beats that were breaking into the rave scene, despite the violence.

The club was clearly doomed from the start, as gangs moved in at breakneck speed, charging punters a fiver to slip in through the back and ripping off the takings at the front cashier desk. DJs would frequently return home empty-handed after gangs held up the promoters and stole their takings.

Kruder and Dorfmeister Hailing from the unlikely city of Vienna, Peter Kruder and Richard Dorfmeister immediately attracted attention among jazz, techno and downbeat enthusiasts with their first EP, released on their own G-Stone record label, in 1994 – not least because of the pastiche of a Simon and Garfunkel's *Bookends* photograph they used as a cover.

Specialising in warm, laid-back, stoned grooves that has the listener itching to build a joint by the third bar, they soon found themselves being enlisted for remixes by artists such as William Orbit, Japan's leftfield jazz heads, United Future Organisation and Bomb The Bass, among others.

The two met in the early nineties while Kruder was in the Austrian hip hop band, The Moreaus and Dorfmeister was in Sin. Their music is wildly eclectic, borrowing from Brian Eno, Bill Laswell, Brazilian jazz artists Airto and Edu Lobo and lolloping hip hop beats.

Lest we forget:
K7
Roland H. Kirk
Knights Of The Occasional Table
Kold Sweat
KRS-1

Best we forget:
Kriss Kross

Language Lab London's first dedicated hip hop night, the Language Lab became the focus for a London-wide scene that was to become crucial to the early warehouse parties. Kids from north, south and west London would congregate in the confines of the upstairs of the old Gossips night-club, also home to nights such as the long-running Gaz's Rockin' Blues, Soul Furnace and The Lift – a mixed gay disco and hi-NRG energy night.

Bunking in was a preoccupation at this period, mainly because the clubbers were too young to afford the door price, and Gossips was particularly useful for this. A stream of punters would gain access to the club via a side alley, from where they could clamber on the roof and jump through the gents toilets. Like a Benny Hill sketch, for every person that went into the toilet, four would come out.

This was before the days of big-name DJs and before Londoners had learned to rap. While DJs spun Sugar Hill b-sides, young dudes such as Nutriment would practise rap licks and toast over the hip hop beats.

Latin House Latin music has a long history in UK club music, stretching through jazz and clubs such as Sol Y Sombra and Club Sandino in the mid-eighties through to Salsa and Brazilian clubs kept alive by the Latin American and Caribbean populations of the UK.

Latin house however kicked in through New York as DJ/producers such as Masters At Work who worked Latino grooves into the four-four formula. Legend has it that UK DJs actually introduced New York DJs to Latin licks, who at the time were nonplussed by the idea of people dancing to such traditional sounds.

Timothy Leary The legendary intellect of the sixties drug culture, Timothy Leary led the rational behind the 'tune in, turn on, drop out' culture of the hippie years, pointing to a utopian higher state of consciousness that could be reached through drugs such as LSD. Putting his radical message into practice, he was fired from his professorship by Harvard University in 1968 for administering the drug to his students.

In his later years Leary took his passion for drugs to new technology and teased the world with the promise of cybersex. On learning that he was dying from prostate cancer in 1995 he planned his death in full cyberview of the world by plugging into the internet. He died on 31 May 1996 having eased his passage with an endless lust for cigarettes, coffee and drugs.

Leeds While clubbers from Leeds were among the ravers who took part in the house music explosion of the late eighties, they had to travel across the Pennines to Manchester and Blackburn to join in the party. Somehow the house vibe eclipsed the city's clubs. Early house clubs, such as the Downbeat, which closed in September 1989 and specialised in Chicago tracks, did exist but remained on the underground – much loved by those who went but completely unknown to everyone else.

Joy, a monthly club run by students, took over Downbeat's mantel but played a London eclectic mix of hip hop and house rather than capturing the northern energy of the Hacienda. Next to open was Awechasmic, a pure house and techno mid-weeker that by its second week was rammed with 1,000 ravers. Meanwhile DJs Mark and Farrar introduced Italo house at Kaos at Ricky's.

Then in 1992 Paul Fryer and Suzy Mason started a night that was to transform the city's club culture. Originally called the Kit Kat club, held at the Arcadia (now Bar Basics), the club added acts such as magicians and sword swallowers to appear over the eclectic mix of music.

After its popularity began to attract pissed-up punters who were abusive to the club's female and gay clientele, the club reacted by announcing a ladies night and invited Leeds drag act Lips 'n' Lashes to perform.

Meanwhile they billed Danny Rampant and Jeremy Feely as the DJs and the legendary TWA (Trannies With Attitude) were born. Moving venues and renaming the night Vague, Leeds' most legendary night-club started on 10 April 1993 at the High Flyers club.

In its wake a series of legendary clubs such as Back to Basics, Hard Times, It's Obvious and Up Your Ronson transformed the city into a northern clubbing capital. After Vague closed and Fryer and Mason parted company, Mason went on to open I-Spy at the Nato venue.

Leftfield A term that has its roots in jazz-influenced music, describing almost anything that was experimental and underground but particularly related to cut up break beats and techno. It lost popularity after Neil Barnes formed Leftfield the band, at once killing the efficacy of the term and causing some confusion among beat heads trying to describe their musical preferences to the uninitiated. In fact Barnes chose his title well, since his band was involved in the very boundary-breaking musical style that the term tried to describe.

Nonetheless it infuriated the leftfield scene, since part of its charm was exclusivity. People were not supposed to know what leftfield music was, let alone buy it and make it chartable, which is exactly what Leftfield did when they teamed up with John Lydon to produce Open Up in 1992.

Larry Levan Possibly the most influential DJ of all time, Larry Levan was born Lawrence Philpot in Brooklyn in 1954. He rose to fame as the resident weekend DJ at the Paradise Garage in New York, where he built an international reputation for driving dance floors crazy.

Scores of DJs came to worship at his altar, and his adventurous mixes influenced the birth of house, techno and, most obviously, garage. In fact Levan had eclectic tastes, reworking disco, soul, gospel, electro pop and anything else that enabled him to lift the dance floor.

He thrived until the Paradise Garage closed on 26 September 1987, when his love of narcotics, especially heroin and cocaine, took over. A sufferer from a lifelong heart condition, Levan died of a coronary on 8 November 1992, aged 38.

Locomotion Run by one of the first club heroines, Wendy May's Locomotion was held at the vast Town and Country club (now The Forum) in Kentish Town, London. Trading on the popularity of rare groove that had been slowing burning since the early eighties, May's club was the commercial face of the scene. Despite high ceilings and the overall impersonality of the event, the large dance floor would be heaving with Levi 501-clad north London trendies nimbly working their DMs to late sixties and early seventies soul and funk grooves.

More intimate, heaving and sweaty, the Locomotion's second venue at the T&C 2 (now The Garage) in Islington was a low-tech, larger-fuelled dance excursion. Ultimately the Locomotion was the mid-eighties equivalent of a nineties corporate club and it was soon populated by the tragically unhip.

Lost Emerging from the underground in 1992, Steve Bicknell and Sheree's irregular dark and deep techno outings would have fans from all over the country making regular trips to London to hear an unrivalled line-up of DJs such as Jeff Mills, Ritchie Hawtin and Bicknell himself. Relying on word of mouth rather than heavy publicity, Lost took a rammed season at Bagley's warehouse in 1995, before deciding to live up to their names and disappear underground again. You may not know it, but Lost are somewhere out there.

Lil' Louis One of the easiest DJs to confuse with his namesakes, Lil' Louis was born Louis Jordan but shouldn't be mistaken for the jump jazz giant of the same name, and also should not be mixed up with Little Louis Vegas of Masters At Work.

A Chicago house DJ and producer, his releases include 'War Games', 'Video Clash' and 'Seven Days'. Lil' Louis scored a UK club and chart hit with the release of 'French Kiss' in 1989, despite the single being banned by the BBC for its heavy breathing female vocal. The censorship was not confined to this side of the Atlantic. New York DJ Frank Bones was handed his P45 for playing the tune at his club.

Further piano-led releases included 'I Called U But You Weren't There', an account of a relationship with an ex-girlfriend which got so out of hand he had take out a restraining order on her. The subject was unusually serious for the hands in the air dance genre – being a more likely subject for his father Bobby Sims, a leading blues guitarist, to write about.

Releasing his debut album, *From The Mind Of Little Louis* in 1989, his second album, *Journey With The Lonely* (1992) is considered a house classic. Later releases such as 'Freedom' revealed a more jazz-orientated side to his style and in the early nineties he relocated to New York, which by that stage had a thriving jazz house scene. Subsequent releases such as 'Clap Your Hands' continued to ensure his lasting presence.

Loungecore Emerging in the early nineties, loungecore was a deliberate side swipe at the 180 b.p.m. manic hardcore scene. In place of the mayhem of rave, loungecore clubs such as Indigo at Madame Jo Jo's in Soho, London introduced epic film score, easy-listening carpet-shoe shuffles.

A small but dedicated scene emerged around clubs such as Multipulciano and Double Six, while DJ James Karminsky and Plastic People scored underground hits. Often featuring performances such as poetry reading, the loungecore scene swung somewhere between Berlin Cabaret clubs of the thirties, sixties bohemian London and the nineties.

Love Parade Europe's largest techno festival, the annual Love Parade attracts over a million scantily attired ravers and over 40 trucks loaded with 15,000 watts of sound system apiece, to parade from Berlin's Tiergarten to the Siegessaule every July.

A mammoth event, it's naturally financially lucrative and the city's bars, hotels and venues take in the region of 110 million Deutschmarks a year from the revellers. The amount of money that Planetcom, the festival's official organisers, make from the parade is a well-kept secret.

Starting in 1989, the festival has managed to gain official approval despite its overtly hedonistic atmosphere by masquerading as a political festival. The brainchild of the charismatic and eccentric Dr Motte, a German techno enthusiast, the parade was inaugurated after Motte found a legal loophole that enshrines the right to demonstrate in the German constitution and so held a street party under the slogan 'Peace, Love and Pancakes'.

The first festival attracted 150 people, mostly friends of the good doctor, but over the years it has swelled to over 6,000 times the original turn out. Along the way Motte has put his surreal imagination to good use, penning a series of seemingly meaningless 'political' slogans such as 'We Are One Family' and 'Let The Sunshine In Your Heart', all of which have been enough to satisfy the authorities of the parade's legitimacy.

Naturally the throng has its detractors as well as supporters. On the left a group of anarchists, who in 1997 called themselves the 12th Of July Movement, had organised direct action against the march using tactics such as firing water pistols at the sound systems in an attempt to short-circuit them.

The Green Party has objected to damage done to the Tiergarten park, which turns into an enormous cesspool as ravers take advantage of the bushes to relieve their full bladders. The officials at Berlin's Bund for the Environment estimate that a litre of urine is deposited in the park for every raver present. The Greens also claim the sound systems cause birds to drop from the trees with heart attacks.

Right-wing opposition has come from German professionals who naturally object to that many people having a good time and playing loud music in their back yards.

Despite the opposition, the Love Parade shows no signs of stopping – unless it's momentarily to take a piss.

LSD and Trips The hallucinogenic of the sixties hippie era, LSD's popularity proved to have greater staying power than flares and long hair, although it tended to have greater use among small groups of friends at home rather than in clubs, for most of the eighties.

Discovered in 1943 by Dr Albert Hoffman, who self-administered a dose of lysergic acid diethylamide tartrate on 19 April of that year.

The first deliberately inflicted acid trip was spent riding around Basel, Switzerland on his bicycle, which can't have been a bad way to spend the war.

Twenty years later his discovery was fuelling a cultural movement, as hippies discovered the psychological power of the drug and sought to change the world through the drug's mind-bending effects.

Naturally it had been outlawed in the mid-sixties, before mass consumption kicked in. Usually ingested orally, the dosage in the sixties tended to be high enough to leave the user completely monged. In the nineties its use on the dance floor is usually administered in smaller doses.

Wrongly identified by journalists as the drug behind the early lunacy of acid house parties in 1987, strangely the real culprit had been identified two years earlier in the *Daily Mail*, in an article about the Taboo night-club.

LSD did however, begin to appear more frequently on the dance floor in subsequent years, especially among the psychedelic trance movement.

Lest we forget:
Last Poets
Limbo Records
Lisbon
LL Cool J
Loaded Records

Best we forget:
Lager theft
Laser pens (ha, ha)
Ligging
Loss of memory

MA 1 Jackets The ubiquitous clubwear of the mid-eighties, MA 1 jackets were everywhere at trendy nights at The Wag, the Mud club and the Warehouse. If ever club fashion had gone stagnant, it was now.

Below the MA 1s, black Levis with turn-ups and Doc Martin shoes ruled, as did T-shirts with slogans on them. Dull but safe clothing, this was the period where mates would mock each other's clothes if anyone tried to stray too far from the consensus. Then acid house came along and blew it all away.

Well, not quite. Bouncers never quite got the message, as if their style catalogue had become permanently stuck in a terrifying ground hog day of MA 1 jackets.

Mad Professor Born in Guyana, the Mad Professor (a.k.a. Neil Fraser) moved to London when he was 13 years old. Getting into early dub music in the mid-seventies, he bought himself an Akai 4000-DS tape machine and began experimenting. By 1979 he had set up a recording studio and started recording bands and his own material.

Constantly seeking to push technology and experiment with sound, he blended dub with electronic bleeps and squelches. His output was prolific, recording 25 albums between 1980 and 1985. By the nineties Mad Professor was producing ten albums a year, while also being called on to work on remixes for a startling amount of artists.

Madchester Renown as the home of seventies and eighties guitar bands and underground dance clubs such as Berlin, in the late eighties Manchester became the most intense club capital outside Ibiza.

In 1982 New Order opened the Hacienda, a vast industrial warehouse of a club. Although it was set up on firmly indie territory, DJs such Mike Pickering and bands such as the Happy Mondays started to play there. Pickering played an eclectic mix that embraced disco, electronic music, hip hop and funk. In 1986 he played his first house record in the Hacienda and within two years ecstasy had infiltrated the dance floor.

At this point Manchester was still dominated by the jazz funk scene, with nights such as Berlin attracting students, often from the south, and enthusiasts from across the country.

The local black/mixed dance scene however had already lit the flame of house music. Influenced by jazz funk, dancers such as The Foot Patrol applied jazz steps and turns to the new music, spinning wildly in front of the stage at the Hacienda's Nude night on Friday's, where Pickering had been joined by Graeme Park.

House was still firmly underground and Nude would attract a mixture of black people, locals and the odd musically clued-up student. Other clubs such as The Fizz at the Man Alive were already following suite and mixing in house sounds among eclectic funk and rare groove sets.

But it wasn't until a new night, Hot, began on Wednesday nights that Manchester exploded. DJ John Dasilva moved back to his home town and Hot opened on 13 July 1988. The first Summer of Love kicked in. Ecstasy culture took hold and the Hacienda developed a tribal congregation which would return faithfully week in and out. For two years the city was awash with happy faces, baggy T-shirts and flares.

But by 1990 the gangs, inspired by the easy profits from drugs, had moved in. Media hype about Gunchester did little but fuel the problem, as dealers from Moss Side, Cheetham Hill and Salford built up firepower. Clubs such as Konspiracy were taken over by the gangs, who acting as bouncers closed the front and charged people at the back door – depriving promoters of door money. Any money the promoters did manage to obtain was frequently taken by gangs anyway.

In the early nineties the original scene moved into the safety of gay clubs such as the small and fiercely hot Number One and then, later, the Paradise Factory, only returning to the Hacienda for the monthly euphoria of the gay Flesh nights.

Meanwhile the straight club scene became increasingly corporate, taking advantage of the city's reputation and attracting coach-loads of tourists and increasingly violent scallies.

In 1992 John Dasilva and Greg Fenton's Space Funk attempted to rescue the scene by moving against grand-scale clubbing and holding their night in an extension of an Italian restaurant. The setting was reminiscent of early hip hop clubs, when promoters were forced to take any space available and transform it with drapes and projections. The night was successful, until it finally succumbed to a new crowd. Within a few months the venue had been burnt out.

Simultaneously a new jazz, funk and hip hop community began to flourish. First to arrive in 1992 was Mike Chadwick and Dave Norton's The Planet, a popular but doomed affair.

Clubs such as Cubop, at Home, and Feva, at the State, took up the break beat flame. By 1995 nights such as Electric Chair and record shops such as Fat City were leading a new musical expression. Meanwhile an IRA bomb ripped the city centre apart in 1996. Destroying the area around the Corn Exchange, the bomb forced many of the smaller record shops and artistic community to relocate to Manchester's Northern Quarter.

The effect was to concentrate record companies, record stalls, recording artists, clubs, promoters and studios into a defined area. The once-derelict Northern Quarter is now a thriving community.

Once again Manchester is turning heads, although it doesn't have so much to answer for today.

Madonna Starting her musical career as a drummer/singer with the Breakfast Club, Madonna entered the world of dance music when she joined up with Detroit drummer Steve Bray and released 'Everybody' for Sire Records in 1980. The track was a US club hit. Branching into pop via her collaboration with John 'Jellybean' Benitez for the single 'Holiday', she secured an international hit in 1984. Her follow-up, 'Like A Virgin', was the first of ten US number one hits.

With her career and star status firmly established, Madonna's club links may have been expected to be severed. But tracks such as Vogue, which introduced the world to the new LA club dance of the same name, and her return to Bray for their collaboration on 'Into The Groove' showed her roots in dance had not been forgotten.

Meanwhile her raunchy and powerful use of her own sexuality pre-figured the rehabilitation of strong feminine images. Showing a breathless ability to reinvent herself, Madonna could hardly be described as coming from the underground.

Magazines and Fanzines As club culture kicked off in the late seventies and early eighties a series of magazines emerged catering for the new fashion and lifestyle of the UK's bright young things. Fanzines such as *Sniffing Glue and Other Rock 'n' Roll Habits* had played a prominent roll in the punk movement, but with the dawn of club culture a new crop of more professionally and artistically produced magazines sprang up.

In 1980 the first editions of two influential titles were published. *The Face* and *i-D* in different ways reflected a new culture. Containing little of the glossy quality they would all eventually adopt, the titles documented the events, clothes and clubs of the emerging dance culture from different perspectives, between them capturing the activities of the hip and happening people who by the end of the decade had changed the culture of a generation.

They also introduced a generation to a new form of literature, discovering a market that was to spawn tens of rival magazines. In February 1983 *Mixmag* was launched by DMC to accompany its 'DJ Only' Megamix tapes.

Edited by Tony Prince of Radio Luxembourg, the magazine acted as a trade journal for radio and club DJs, featuring reports on people such as Bruno Brooks as well as introducing its readers to new sounds such as hip hop and later house. By 1984 the magazine had 1,000 subscribers and DMC held its first international DJ convention. Two thousand DJs attended and a young Greek called Sanny X won the competition, introducing the other delegates to live sampling for the first time.

By 1986 *Mixmag*/DMC was organising the first DJ trip to Ibiza and world tour of DJs including Chad Jackson and Sanny X in the line-up. In 1989 a young DJ called Dave Seaman took over as editor and *Mixmag* finally appeared on magazine stands and broadened its horizons, gradually increasing its coverage of the club scene and including articles on related subjects such as drugs. The magazine had moved from being a DJ talking shop to club-land bible.

Major Force Set up to release 'Tycoon To$h' and Terminator Troops' 'Live Wire Voodoo' and 'Guess What?', Major Force Records was established to release leftfield excursions by five Tokyo producers: Gota, Tosh, Kudo, Kan and Hiroshi.

Meanwhile the label's administration was handled by Yosh Temple Island Terashima in the UK. Its superb sample and break beat compositions were soon attracting increasing attention from DJs across the world – something Major Force themselves failed to notice until they started receiving offers from major record companies.

A determinedly underground organisation, Major Force only ever released 1,000 records at a time, meaning their much sought-after 12in records changed hands for silly money. Turning down large sums of money themselves, and only accepting license deals, Major Force maintained their commitment to producing high-production-quality records.

Being in a position to secure a deal they were happy with, they eventually agreed to release their Love TKO project via Columbia Records, while Walt Disney's Hollywood Records snapped up the Major Force back catalogue in 1991, which by this time was frequently being re-released on poor-quality bootlegs. Later projects also included collaborations with James Lavelle's abstract break beat label Mo Wax.

Manumission In 1994 Andy Manumission was having the summer of his life. A regular at Selinus beach, Ibiza, carrying a Manumission flag and doshing out flyers for his new night-club, his Summer holiday job was earning him enough money to live for the rest of the year.

Manumission opened at KU as an instant hit – reviving the flagging fortunes of the Ibiza scene. Theatrical performance was an integral part of the Manumission experience – famous for its processions of dwarves, drag shows, trapeze artists and the customary plunge in the pool under the dance floor. Innocent pleasures indeed.

But in 1995 brothers Andy and Mike hit on the formula that would ensure lasting media interest, when Mike's girlfriend, Claire, began performing a live sex show. Initially this involved Claire getting it on with another women wearing a strap-on, but in 1996 Mike joined in at an Aids benefit in Paris.

To comply with French decency laws they performed under a sheet, but such inhibitions have long since been disregarded in Ibiza. But this is no cheap thrill. The door and drinks prices are legendary.

Howard Marks Born Dennis Howard Marks in Kenfig Hill, south Wales, Marks grew up a scientific nerd, or 'weak swot' in his own words. Appropriately enough he found his vocation at Balliol, Oxford, where he discovered cannabis and started selling it to his chums. After leaving university he began dealing in larger quantities, shipping dope into Europe and America, stowing it away in the furniture of Pakistani diplomats and in the speaker stack of a fictional rock band called Laughing Grass – the clue's in the name.

He was caught in Amsterdam in 1973, but skipped bail and went on the run, picking up the moniker Mr Mystery and attracting gossip about him being abducted by the IRA or MI5. In 1980 he was arrested again for smuggling 15 tons of cannabis into Scotland. His defence that he was smuggling on behalf of the Mexican Secret Service to buy grass from the IRA under MI6 orders was described as 'the most ridiculous defence I ever heard in my life', by his lawyer. Marks was acquitted.

By the mid-eighties his smuggling activity was a multi-million pound industry, earning him the name Narco Polo. He had 43 aliases, 89 phone lines and ran 25 businesses, all of them fronts for dope dealing.

In 1988 Marks was arrested by the US Drug Enforcement Agency and sentenced to 25 years in Terre Haute Penitentiary. He completed seven years of his sentence and was released in 1995, a year later securing a publishing deal for his best-selling autobiography *Mr Nice*.

Becoming a celebrity he teamed up with fellow Welshmen the Super Furry Animals, who had already released 'Hanging With Howard Marks', and recorded 'The Man Don't Give A Fuck'. He stood for election in 1997 for the Legalise Cannabis Party and applied for the position of Drugs Tsar for the Labour government. He launched himself as a club promoter in 1998.

Massive Attack A seminal Bristol collective based around the key figures of former graffiti artist 3D (a.k.a. Rob Del Naja, a.k.a. D, a.k.a. Delge), Daddy G (a.k.a. Grant Marshall) and Mushroom (Andrew Vowles), Massive Attack were the direct descendants of The Wild Bunch hip hop sound system, of which they were members.

Inheriting the collaborative ethos of The Wild Bunch, the band formed in 1988, releasing their first single 'Any Love'. They then spent a couple of years working with other artists such as Neneh Cherry, for whom Del Naja penned some of the lyrics of 'Manchild' and Mushroom helped on mixing her *Raw Like Sushi* album.

Through Cherry, Massive met with Cameron McVey, who produced their first album, *Blue Lines*. Released in 1991, *Blue Lines* was a masterpiece that combined hip hop with the Bristol influences of dub reggae and soul and spawned three hit singles, 'Daydreaming', 'Unfinished Sympathy' and 'Safe From Harm'. The album took eight months to complete, which turned out to be extremely quick compared with Massive's subsequent working pace. Creating downbeat dance music made for home listening rather than club dance floors, the album proved to have incredible longevity, improving on every listening.

Their next album wasn't to appear for three years and in the interim many of the artists they'd collaborated with on *Blue Lines*, such as singer Shara Nelson and rapper Tricky, left to start solo careers, while Massive Attack-influenced acts such as Portishead took the limelight.

The second Massive album, *Protection*, arrived in 1994, with former Wild Bunch and Soul II Soul collaborator Nellee Hooper taking over as producer. Other contributors to the album included Tricky, Nicolette, Tracey Thorn and Horace Andy.

As with *Blue Lines*, the album proved to be another slow-burning long player, with many critics dismissing it only to have it grow on them over time. Not to be stung by repeating the same mistake, their third album, *Mezzanine*, was released to critical acclaim in 1998.

Masters At Work Formed from the partnership of Kenny Dope Gonzalez and Little Louie Vega, their first collaboration resulted in the release of 1991's 'Ride On The Rhythm'. Individually they already had established reputations. Vega began DJing at college parties when he was 18 years old, before securing a slot at the Devils Nest and then Studio 54, where Todd Terry would hand him his latest tracks to test on the crowd. Soon the duo were turning out an alarming array of remixes for acts such as St Etienne, Chic, Debbie Gibson, Lisa Stansfield, Deee-Lite and Tito Puente.

Leading the way in developing New York's bass-line-driven, soulful house, jazz house, Latin house and garage signatures, they also recorded a string of club hits under their joint name, while continuing to release material individually or collaborating with other artists. Gonzalez's Bucketheads anthem, 'The Bomb', was played to the point of tedium in clubs throughout 1995.

Their ability to reinvent themselves, just when critics are writing them off as a spent force, is breathtaking. At the end of the nineties Masters At Work increased their popularity by releasing their Latin- and jazz-influenced NuYorican soul project. Revered as a masterpiece, some UK DJs point out that it was UK DJs who reinvented house, injecting Latin and jazz, and shipping it back to its American roots. One story has it that Kenny and Louie's jaws dropped in disbelief when they heard that UK punters danced to tunes such as 'Prince of Peace'. Luckily their disbelief was short-lived.

Derrick May Alongside Juan Atkins, Carl Craig and Kevin Saunderson, Derrick May was one of the creators of Detroit techno music. A former school mate of Saunderson, and partner in running the Music Institute club, his work of the late eighties such as 'The Dance', 'It Is What It Is' and his seminal 'Stings Of Life' are regarded as classics of the genre. His early influences included European artists such as Kraftwerk and Yello, to whom he introduced Atkins while May was still studying at Bellville High school.

He played his first DJ gig after being booked by Darryl Tiggs to play downstairs at a pub. He says he bombed. Synthesising European electronic music with electro, he recorded under the names Mayday or Rhythim Is Rhythim, released his debut single 'Nude Photo', followed by 'Strings Of Life', and established his own label, Transmat, to release his tracks.

Despite his popularity, he was in no rush to release records, hanging up his gloves for a couple of years after 'Strings Of Life', and proved to be an elusive DJ.

In 1990 he released 'The Beginning', followed by 'Innovator: Sound Track For The Tenth Planet', a retrospective EP, for Network records.

In the early nineties May moved to Amsterdam and in 1998 he released his *Innovator* album on Belgium's R&S techno label. May took to greater self publicity in the late 90s claiming his right as one of the originators of techno. He even appeared in a US advertisement campaign for backpacks.

MCs Growing out of the Jamaican sound system tradition of DJs or toasters bantering to the crowd while the records were spinning, the first DJ to recruit MCs (Masters of Ceremony) to support his sets was Grandmaster Flash, whose team of rappers became known as the Furious Five.

While hip hop continued to employ MCs to support DJs, eventually leading to the rappers being more famous than the DJ, MCs went through periods of decline and popularity in other musical areas.

In the UK, with its strong urban Jamaican population, the tradition of MCs already had roots and hip hop rapping quickly caught on, while many MCs adapted the toasting of existing sound systems to new musical styles such as house, garage and jungle.

Meanwhile a new language was being formed, which combined inner city slang with Jamaican patois.

Mega Dog Formed from the ashes of the long-running Club Dog in 1992, Mega Dog continued Club Dog's tradition of unpretentious clubbing, which had originally been a reaction to the stuck-up door attitudes of mid-eighties London clubs.

Dog had blended World music with dub and psychedelia, but had progressively moved into dance and, in particular, trance and techno. Mega Dog kept this eclectic outlook, but aimed to bring showmanship back into dance music by featuring live performances. Also inviting circus performances and stalls, the club created a festival atmosphere – a theme that enabled them to transform the usually drab but cavernous Rocket Venue, on Holloway Road, into a carnival atmosphere. The roster of artists that have appeared at the club is impressive and eclectic, with acts such as Jah Wobble, Cabaret Voltaire, Ozric Tentacles and Senser.

In 1992 Mega Dog booked Orbital to play. It was a gig that was to change the club's destiny, as it almost immediately organised a live techno tour of the UK, showcasing artists such as Aphex Twin, the Drum Club, Spooky, System 7 and Eat Static.

Orbital may have transformed Mega Dog, but in turn Mega Dog had transformed techno by pulling the UK's major producers out of the studio and pushing them on stage for the first time. Other artists were to follow, such as the Chemical Brothers, Underworld, Lionrock, CJ Bolland, Dave Angel, Ken Ishi, Transglobal Underground, Banco De Gaia and many more.

In keeping with their eclectic spirit, they went on to book jungle, house, trance and techno artists, featuring them in the same room rather than dividing them into separate rooms as other clubs were doing at the time.

In 1995 Mega Dog decided to move into festivals proper and organised the dance tent at Glastonbury festival. The result was 30,000 people flooded to get into a tent with a capacity of 3,000. The same pattern was repeated at Phoenix later that year, where the tent capacity had been expanded to 5,000. After further Mega Dog tents at the following Glastonbury, Womad, Phoenix and Essential festivals, they organised a tour of the USA in 1997 before organising their first Mega Dog festival at the Lizard Peninsula in Cornwall.

Megatripolis The brainchild of Frazer Clark, Megatripolis started as the collaboration of a like-minded collective. Clark, one of the club scenes more obscure characters, had been preaching the psychedelic message since the sixties and had started publishing *Encyclopedia Psychedelia* in an attempt to anchor the acid house scene to a deeper philosophy. He found a more natural home among the Goan-influenced trance posse.

Hooking up with Slack 1993, a Brighton-based rave organisation already renown for their beach parties, they started organising new-age-influenced nights at the Marquee, with festival-inspired trippy décor, proper chill-out spaces, Internet connections and educational lectures on spiritualist philosophy and environmentalism.

An unrivalled experience in club land, the nights soon outgrew the venue and moved to Heaven. The peace and harmony of the events soon shattered as the original crew fell-out.

Many of them jumped ship, and some of them regrouped to form Escape From Samsara. The nature of the nights changed and eventually Megatripolis relaunched as Altered States.

Middle Youth Having discovered the joy of all-week clubbing, been through ecstasy and found a new music form that seemed to be capable of endless transformation into new genres, the generation that grew up through the eighties dance music hit middle-age in the nineties. By now many of the nuttiest ravers, most dedicated groovers and tireless night owls were holding down steady jobs with huge responsibilities. It was time to settle down. Was it bollocks! Middle-age was no obstacle to this generation.

Clubs now teamed with an age range that stretched from 18 to 40. Many of the DJs were in their late thirties, but they were still being booked to play clubs across the world and dictating the music that fashionable young things would flock to buy.

In mainland Europe clubs had always been more cosmopolitan in their age range. In the UK the advent of older clubbers was little short of a cultural revolution and naturally attracted much media interest. Arguments raged over the causes and consequences of these middle-aged people who in their minds had stopped growing up after the age of 18. Naturally they needed a name, and were duly christened middle youth.

What they'll be called in their old age will have to wait for a subsequent edition, but maybe twilight youth will do.

Jeff Mills Born in Detroit in 1963, Jeff Mills started DJing in 1987 and began to produce his own music two years later. In 1990 he joined up with Mad Mike Banks to form his record label Underground Resistance.

Releasing under records such as 'Punisher' and 'Seawolf' under a series of monikers, including X-101, he attracted a dedicated following in the UK, where techno had begun to take off as interest began to transfer from house to the Detroit sound. Consequently Mills found himself being booked for an increasing number of UK and European gigs.

Leaving Underground Resistance, Mills moved to New York and Chicago and established his own label, Axis, before, having obviously got the label bug, setting up yet another company, Purpose Maker, in 1996.

Mills is renown for whizzing through records in his sets, often spinning through 50 discs as he selects what he sees as the cream of each tune before slamming in the cream of the next one. His sets bond a variety of styles, playing house, techno and even gabber.

Strangely, considering his awesome style and the considerable respect that is shown to him, he doesn't consider himself to be a DJ. Well, who is then?

Ministry Of Sound The realisation of DJ Justin Berkman's long-held dream to recreate New York's Paradise Garage in London, and financed by James Palumbo, the Ministry Of Sound opened its doors in September 1991. The first licensed 24-hour dance club in the UK, it was dismissed by a director of Rank Leisure as a fad. Within four years the club had grown into the world's largest club, fashion and merchandise company, employing over 80 full-time staff.

It runs its own record label, with sales of two million pounds a year, a clothes company and shop in Covent Garden. Ministry Of Sound also pioneered the concept of club tours, has a TV show, runs a radio broadcast and a website that records 500,000 hits a month. Its magazine, adventurously titled *Ministry*, hit newsagents in 1998 amid general praise from the media.

Ministry Of Sound turned clubbing into a corporate enterprise and has reaped the profits. Naturally it has also reaped scorn and die-hard clubbers renamed it the Misery Of Sound, while omitting to recall the weekends they've lost there or that at some time or another their favourite DJ has spun on its decks.

Mixed Clubbing Gay clubs have a historical position as the innovators of dance music. Meanwhile straight clubs, which have gone through their ups and downs of excellence and loved-up atmosphere, have always had their violent and stagnant down side. Consequently gay clubs have periodically appealed to straight clubbers, wanting to escape the bone-head attitude of heterosexual night life. This was recognised by clued-up promoters in the mid-eighties, who catered for knowledgeable dance kids unable to find their groove in other legal venues.

Clubs such as the Mud club, at Buzby's, and on Wednesday's, The Pyramid, at Heaven, opened their doors to attitude-free straight people, who flocked there even though entry was far from guaranteed. This was the era of high energy and early house, as DJs such as Jay Strongman entertained a popper-fuelled dance floor.

The pattern was to be repeated in the early nineties, when refugees from the Haçienda, Home and Konspiracy, in Manchester, found salvation from gangland hassle in the Gay Village and clubs such as Paradise and Haçienda's Flesh nights.

Mo Wax Set up by James Lavelle, Mo Wax Records rocketed into record shops in 1992 with carefully crafted releases by artists such as Raw Stylus, the Repurcussions, RPM, DJ Krush, DJ Shadow and Lavelle's own Men From Uncle project.

The label's initial material reflected the burgeoning funk and urban soul market, but soon releases such as Shadow's 'In Flux' revealed an abstract, hip hop eclecticism.

Having released a more conventional and long-awaited single by the Bristol-based Federation, Lavelle suddenly flipped into a more adventurous project and commissioned an EP of dub remixes of the track. The result was to have a huge influence on the trip hop scene. This was in keeping with Lavelle's earlier tastes: he'd compiled electro tapes when he was 10 years old and had a long-standing passion for hip hop, although he had also been exposed to acid house, techno and, particularly, acid jazz. Lavelle however railed at the trip hop moniker.

Joining up with long-time acid jazz guru Gilles Peterson, Lavelle united the old and new waves of the leftfield jazz scene and launched the seminal That's How It Is, at Bar Rhumba in 1993. Within weeks there were queues stretching down Shaftesbury

Avenue, while the dance floor spun, twisted and jumped to ever more adventurous break beats and deep sub-bass kick drums.

Lavelle was quick to spot drum 'n' bass moving into the jazz field territory and so signed up Alex Reece, securing the label's reputation for living so far out on the cutting-edge it hurt.

Mobile Phones The ubiquitous tool of yuppies, pimps and drug dealers, the mobile phone became the essential piece of clubbing equipment during the rave years of the late eighties.

As police surveillance of illegal 'pay parties' increased, promoters took to announcing venues at the last minute on the night by giving out a 0898 Voice Bank phone number for punters to call.

Mobiles became the vital link, with the promoters using them to change their message once they had secured the site of the party, while punters used them to call from pre-arranged meeting places such as motorway service stations.

New forms of communication had to be invented when ICSTIS, the telephone watchdog body, ordered the withdrawal of Voice Bank numbers in late 1989.

Moby Christian, vegan, philosophy graduate and New York DJ, Richard Hall (a.k.a. Moby) took his nickname from the story of *Moby Dick*, which was written by one of his ancestors, Herman Melville. Originally a 15-year-old member of a speed metal hardcore punk band, the Vatican Commandos, he also sang with Flipper. A skilled self-publicist and committed environmentalist, he refuses to go anywhere by car because of the damage cars cause to the environment.

Musically his biggest hit came in 1991 when he released 'Go', a remix of the theme from the *Twin Peaks* television series. He was soon being hailed as techno's first star. Follow-up tracks included 1993's 'I Feel It' and 'Thousand', which was classified as the fastest-ever single, peaking at 1,015 b.p.m.

Typical of his irreverent anarchistic attitudes, he trashed his keyboard at the end of his set at the 1992 DMC/*Mixmag* awards ceremony. Signing to Mute in 1993, he released 'Ambient', a collection of unissued tracks from 1988-91, and 'The Story So Far', before releasing his 'Hymn' single – a 35-minute religious techno odyssey. His work as a remixer includes tracks for The Pet Shop Boys, Erasure, Orbital and Depeche Mode.

His seminal 1995 release 'Everything Is Wrong' blurred the boundaries between electronic and classical music. Typically he shocked everyone by following this with a punk-driven album, *Animal Rights*. In 1998 he released his 'Honey' single.

David Morales Born to Puerto Rican parents in Brooklyn, New York, David Morales grew up to be one of America's leading remixers. As a youth he frequented The Loft and the Paradise Garage, where he was booked to play by Judy Weinstein's For The Record organisation. Developing a deep understanding of garage and disco he used his knowledge to execute sublime remixes and was soon turning out an alarming number of them. Demand grew and he released classics, such as Robert Owen's 'I'll Be Your Friend', while also working prolifically with his long-standing collaborator Frankie Knuckles as Def Mix.

Amongst his output tracks such as Will Downing's 'A Love Supreme', Aretha Franklin's 'A Deeper Love', Incognito's 'Always There', the Brand New Heavies' 'Dream On Dreamer' and his work with Jody Watley on 'I'm The One You Need' have made him one of the best-known house producers.

Inspector Morse As rave culture took hold it was only a matter of time before clubbing would make an entry into mainstream television dramas and soap operas. Its most legendary appearance came in an early nineties episode of the detective series *Inspector Morse*. It became notorious for its comical story line, which reflected the media's paranoia about ecstasy at the time. The basic plot revolved around a batch of pills that were so good that teenagers started topping themselves rather than face a drab boring life.

Some classic scenes included a teenage girl's parents ripping down her bedroom posters to reveal a collection of flyers she'd stuck behind them. The club nation was crapping itself – but with laughter rather than suspense. The best was yet to come as the chubby old inspector eventually turns up at a rave. The rest is probably best left to your imagination. Cult viewing.

Moving Shadow Founded by seminal hardcore/jungle producer Rob Playford in 1990, Moving Shadow Records has been a prime mover on the jungle scene ever since.

Playford had spent the previous four years playing hip hop, house and acidic techno as well as running raves, such as Voodoo Magic, before he released his first track, 'Orbital Madness'. Since forming the label he has been responsible for pioneering many of the sounds and production techniques of jungle/drum 'n' bass scene.

Starting out by selling records out of the back of his car, Moving Shadow soon began attracting attention as well as a wealth of imitators, and by 1992, through releases such as 'Waremouse' and 'Bombscare' by 2 Bad Mice and 'Music Takes You' by Blame, it had established itself at the forefront of the growing scene.

Spotting the shift to more ambient drum 'n' bass early on in 1993, Playford released Omni Trio's 'Mystic Stepper' and 'Renegade Snares' and 'Four Plays Open Your Mind'. Further seminal tracks followed, taking the distinctive drum patterns of drum 'n' bass into ever more experimental territory such as jazz step. By the late nineties Playford had signed 20 acts to his label.

The M25 (London Orbital) Central to London and the south-east's rave culture, the London orbital became the scene's umbilical cord linking party punters to heady nights of unremitting hedonism as well as to legendary games of hide-and-seek with the police. Petrol stations, and in particular South Mimms on the M1, were favoured meeting places, where conveys of cars, stuffed with pill-popping youths would swarm on unsuspecting and bemused service station staff and wait for further instructions. This was the era of the mobile phone. Promoters would outfox the police's Pay Party Unit by announcing the location of the party at the last minute, often through a series of treasure-hunt locations where ravers gathered to receive the next piece of information.

On nights when the first venue fell through, the convoy would head back to South Mimms and wait until a new location had been found. Regulars soon noticed the first vehicle to get the call would always be the drinks van and, like the pied piper, it would lead a procession of cars around the M25 in the early hours of the morning. Laden with equipment and drinks, they could rarely travel faster than 50 m.p.h., thereby providing a bizarre spectacle of hundreds of cars snaking round the slow lane of an otherwise empty motorway. Needless to say nobody ever overtook the van.

Mud Club and Mark Moore Opened in 1983 at Subway, Leicester Square and then Buzby's (now the LA2) on Charing Cross Road, London, Philip Salon's Friday night Mud club became the most seminal regular London club of the mid-eighties. Attracting a mixed, gay crowd and north London funk-a-billies, who defined the hard-times look, the queues to get in would be policed by Salon, who was famous for tersely turning people away and getting boys to perform tricks for him, such as standing in a sarcophagus he had by the door.

The door policy was strict, but mostly dependent on whether Salon thought you looked right for the club – for example, suits were definitely not allowed. Amazingly the club ran until 1990 and had a renaissance at Bagley's Studios, King's Cross, in 1992.

Inside, the dance floor heaved to the disco beats of resident DJs Jay Strongman, Tasty Tim and Mark Moore, who span old seventies and new disco records. Moore, one of London's pioneers of house music and later lead member of S-Express, had started to DJ at the Mud when Tasty Tim couldn't play one night and asked Salon if Moore could stand in for him. At this stage Moore hadn't been DJing but he'd been handing Tim records to play for some time. Tim persuaded Salon to take a risk and it paid off.

Moore was to become one of the most influential DJs of the eighties, at first spinning an eclectic selection of deliberately cheesy tunes, including tracks by Dollar, Bee Gees, Abba and Julie Andrews. He switched when everyone started copying his sets and started playing old school disco and funk. When this also caught on he moved into ever-harder hip hop and hi-NRG. By 1986 he was liberally sprinkling his sets with house music. Moore went on to play clubs such as the Opera House, Sacrosanct, The Asylum and The Pyramid, at Heaven, one of the first house nights in 1997.

Murk Record label-cum-dance producers, the Miami-based Murk crew of Ralph Falcon and Oscar Gaetan have released some of house music's most seminal classics, such as the Funky Green Dogs From Outer Space's 'Reach For Me', Liberty City's 'Some Lovin', Interceptor's 'Together' and Coral Way Chief's 'Release

Myself', as well as providing Warp Records with their 'Miami' EP. Having been notoriously hard to find, the label agreed to the UK's Network Records licensing the first three tracks above and released a DJ sampler in 1992. Further releases as The Funky Green Dogs From Outer Space included 'High Up' in 1994 and 'Fired Up' in 1997, while 'Reach For Me' was again re-released in 1998.

Paul Murphy Probably the most seminal jazz DJ in London during the late seventies and eighties, Paul Murphy's nights at The Horse Shoe, Electric Ballroom and Sol Y Sombra became legendary. In 1987 he moved to the Purple Pussycat club in Finchley Road, revamped it and opened it as The Cat club. By then the acid house revolution was about to launch music into a new direction and Gilles Peterson was to lead jazz in a new direction.

Lest we forget:
Mastercuts compilations
MC 900ft Jesus
MC Solaar
Mix Master Morris
Georgio Moroder

Best we forget:
Master Mix and other DJ-only CDs for mobile jocks
Mixing when you're too gone to see the turntable
Mobile discos

Nation Records Inspired by early fusions of world music with Western pop such as Mory Kante's late eighties classic 'Yeke Yeke' and Bappi Lahiri's 'Habiba', Katherine Canoville and Aki Nawaz (of FunDaMental) joined up in London to promote work on a cultural-cross fusion project that would combine traditional multi-ethnic rhythms and music with hip hop, dub and house. Having approached several major record companies and been given the cold shoulder, they decided to branch out on their own and establish Nation Records.

Their first release, a compilation, introduced artists such as Talvin Singh and Pulse 8 (featuring David Harrow/James Hardaway, Jah Wobble and Justin Adams). Other acts soon followed, such as Trans Global Underground (who became 1994's darlings of the festival circuit), FundDaMental, Joi and Loop Guru. Their 1993 *Global Sweatbox* compilation album took their crossover ideas further into club territory with remixes of Nation's back catalogue being carried out by the Sabres Of Paradise, the Drum club, Fabio Paras and Youth.

Anti-racism ran to the core of Nation's philosophy and after a British National Party member was elected to Tower Hamlets council in 1993, FunDaMental released their anti-racist classic, 'Dog Tribe'.

In 1994 Nation came across a trio called Asian Dub Foundation, who mixed politics, hip hop and rap with Asian themes and dub and jungle. By 1998 Asian Dub Foundation were attracting considerable attention and were invited to tour with Primal Scream. Meanwhile Talvin Singh had recorded an album for Island Records, while Joi had been snapped up by Peter Gabrielle's Real World label and Natacha Atlas had moved to Beggars Banquet.

Determinedly underground and sincere, Nation had succeeded in launching a new breed of crossover music during a period when the major labels had given up on world music.

Joey Negro The UK's champion of disco house, Joey Negro (a.k.a. Dave Lee from Essex) first appeared on the Republic record label, where he learned the art of remixing. Teaming up with Mark Ryder, he released several records for the label under aliases such as Masters Of The Universe and Quest For Excellence.

Releasing 'Together' as Kid Valdez of Mystique, Negro scored a dance chart hit in the US and attracted the attention of journalists, who tried to track down the real Kid, who of course didn't exist outside Lee's fertile imagination.

From then on he started working as Joey Negro and built a formidable reputation as a disco remixer. Not afraid to take risks, his debut album, 1993's *Universe Of Love*, included a reworking of 'Ooh What a Life' by the Gibson Brothers, with Gwen Guthrie on vocals.

In 1998 Negro was seen by many as the forefather of the emerging nu-disco house school in the UK and he celebrated by releasing a compilation album, *Disco Connection*.

Nervous Records New York's purveyors of quality house and street sounds, Nervous Records established themselves in the public imagination as much through their clothing and distinctive logo as through their garage and house music.

Launched in the summer of 1990 by Michael Weiss and Gladys Pizarro (who soon returned to Strictly Rhythm Records), their first releases, 'Feel It' by Niceguy Soulman (a.k.a. Roger Sanchez), 'Good Feeling' by Swing Kids (a.k.a. Kenny Dope Gonzalez) and 'I Want To Know' by Latin Kings (a.k.a. Todd Terry), quickly built their reputation. Further releases such as Masters At Work's 'NuYorican' track kept interest bubbling, while the label's quick turn-round policy kept their music fresh and close to the street despite international success. Notwithstanding this, they are still best known for their T-shirts and record bag logos.

Network Records Starting as an off-shoot from Neil Rushton and Dave Barker's Kool Kat Records in Birmingham, Rushton had been a successful northern soul DJ in the seventies before starting Kool Kat in 1988. Through his US connections, he was introduced to Detroit techno and Kevin Saunderson, whom he later managed. After releasing a techno compilation for Virgin, he and Barker, who had been a jazz funk DJ, set about releasing techno and Chicago house tracks in the UK, while nurturing up-front UK artists such as Altern 8. Despite its success on the dance circuit, Kool Kat began to face financial difficulties and in a bid to save the company, the duo launched Network Records.

The new label had a much broader musical policy than its sister label. Its first top ten chart hit came with Altern 8's 'Active 8' and, with their financial crisis abating, Network followed 'Activ 8' with KWS's 'Please Don't Go', a catchy slice of pop dance which stayed at number one in the UK charts for five weeks.

By now money really wasn't a problem. Altern 8's debut album, *Full on . . . Mask Hysteria*, was released in 1992 and found further success, although the label had a slight hiccup with Rhythm Quest's 'The Dreams' EP, which put the boot into the police for closing down raves. The police were concerned it could incite ravers to violence and the record was reissued with the offending material removed.

In August 1993, after almost a year of negotiations, the company sold 49 per cent of its shares to Sony. Network from now on was part of the Best Beat Dance Ltd. company.

Disappointed with the commercial leanings of Network, the company launched SiX6 (a.k.a. Six by Six) and released Glam's 'Hell's Party'. Meanwhile other sister labels had been launched, such as New York's First Choice, Stoke On Trent's Baseroom Productions and has close relations with a host of other US and UK labels.

New Romantics In the post-punk period of the late seventies and early eighties, clubs such as The Blitz in London and the Rum Runner in Birmingham began to attract glammed up boys and girls who melted punk fashion sensibilities, such as wild dyed and lacquered hair and make-up, with camp disco clothing. Deriving from the futurism of bands such as Kraftwerk and Can and the post-punk and Acron punk of artists such as Devo and Tubeway Army, the music mixed disco beats with guitar and electronic music.

On the more exploratory side Steve Strange's Visage managed to find chart success with 'Fade To Grey', while ultimately the less challenging format of Duran Duran shot from one chart success to another.

Forming the link between punk and disco, the movement opened a wave of new interest in clubbing, leading to the establishment of venues such as the Camden Palace, of which Steve Strange went on to become an integral part.

Nice 'n' Ripe London's pioneering independent garage label was formed by George Power (one of the original founding members of Kiss FM) in 1993, when it released Integration's 'Loosen Up', featuring the influential Grant Nelson. The label went on to produce a series of quality UK garage releases and established itself at the forefront of the growing London garage scene, with tracks such as the Ambassadors Of Swing's 'Coming Up' and the Dangerous Brothers anthem, 'Can't Stop The Feeling'. Its roster of artists includes Grant Nelson, Jeremy Sylvester and Victor Suarez.

Ninja Tune Coldcut's eclectic and influential label, its music policy, although fluid, is identified with leading the dance world back to downbeat break beat, while its off-the-wall attitude ensured it fitted neatly in the punk ethics of the late nineties.

Ninja was born out of Coldcut's frustration with major labels and the label has been used to nurture the UK's more exploratory artists. Respected in the UK, Ninja Tune is worshipped in Japan. Signing up artists such as Herbaliser and Mr Scruff, while also using the label to release Coldcut and Hextatic's collaborations, Ninja expanded to form a sister label, Ntone, to release experimental electronic music.

North Versus South With the advent of the funk of artists such as Sly Stone, James Brown and George Clinton in the seventies, the unity of the UK's dance scene fractured. Northern soul clubs had already started to prefer the harder more obscure cuts of US soul artists; then, as London became progressively funkier, the two scenes began to find a greater musical divide between them.

Further changes in musical styles, such as disco, punk, reggae, dub and modern soul, in some cases (as with punk) united the country while in others (dub) it further divided it. By the early eighties London and the South were, in their funk traditions, embracing hip hop and then, in the mid-eighties, rare groove. Meanwhile, through DJs such as Graeme Park, Mike Pickering, Parot and Winston Hazel, the North was progressively moving towards house. While London DJs such as Mark Moore and the Black Market boys were playing house, their sets remained eclectic, mixing in rare groove and hip hop.

The division became sharp enough for magazines such as *i-D* and *Mixmag* to note with alarm that, because of the flood of London students to cities such as Manchester, rare groove nights were proliferating in the North and threatening to wipe out the indigenous house scene.

The differences were not only musical. The eclectic attitude of London suited its more laid-back style. Northerners, perhaps because of traditions such as northern soul, were used to having it large and going mental to a continuous pumping beat.

So much for mythology.

While divisions between North and South no doubt exist, and inform the subject matter of many fine beered-up pub and club conversations, there are numerous examples of clubs and communities that support and detract from the theory. Quite how Trade, Rage and Freedom in London or Spice, Berlin and Electric Chair in Manchester fit in is probably worth a late-night heated debate. But then again . . .

Northern Soul Coming hard on the heels of the R&B explosion in the UK in the sixties, young mods were introduced to the contemporary US dance acts on the Motown and Atlantic record labels. It was the beginning of a mod soul tradition that was to inform dance culture in the UK through to the early nineties. The scene found particular resonance in north-west England, where clubs such as The Twisted Wheel in Manchester, The Golden Torch in Stoke-on-Trent, the Mecca in Blackpool and the legendary Wigan Casino introduced young Britons to the latest cutting-edge US black dance music.

A drug-fuelled scene, the parties would last all night, with the punters driven through a dance frenzy driven by amphetamines such as speed and prescription drugs such as black bombers and French blues.

Some 20 years before acid house, northern soul fans were having it large in marathon dance sessions that left them weak and sweaty in the waking hours of the following day. Not satisfied with 12 hours of dancing, northern soul introduced the concept of weekenders, with soul organisations taking over holiday camps and ramming them with thousands of punters who had one thing in common – taking drugs to keep them up and dancing non-stop to four-four beats. At its height the Wigan Casino, an alcohol-free, drug-powered club that opened between midnight and 8 a.m., boasted 100,000 members.

Unlike most musical genres, northern soul is based in the culture and not the music, which tended to come from the US cities of New York, Chicago, Detroit, Los Angeles and Philadelphia. Yet the culture was strong. While the London scene, with a few exceptions, progressed into funk in the early seventies, the North stayed firmly in the soul vibe.

Punters dressed variously in polo shirts, pinned-down collars, vests and the ubiquitous flares would sprinkle talcum powder on the floor to ease the friction between feet and dance floor, making the characteristic hip swinging side shuffle and manic spins easier. Meanwhile they snorted a different powder that similarly made dancing easier.

The drugs naturally attracted media and police attention and the authorities moved in, mounting police raids and gradually closing the major clubs. By the late seventies and early eighties modern soul and funk had captured the scene, although a hardcore of DJs such as Richard Searling kept the faith.

Meanwhile a scene emerged in Europe in the late eighties and nineties, with clubs such as Spellbound in Hamburg and Mod Soul Nuit at Glaz'art in Paris attracting a small dedicated crowd. Back in the UK the scene was still swinging in the late nineties, with new converts spending months tracking down the by now-rare original 45s and albums.

Northern soul nights, usually monthly, re-emerged at nights such as Happiness Stan's in Smithfield's, London, Lowton Civic Hall, near Wigan, Lancashire, Soultastic in Alferton, Derbyshire, Manchester Ritz all-nighters and the Oakenfold club in Sale, Cheshire. Meanwhile Richard Searling had secured his own Sunday show on the Jazz FM radio station.

Nu Med Describing the emerging late nineties Balearic disco sound of record labels such as Glasgow Underground, Nuphonic and Tummy Touch and artists such as FAZE Action, Ashley Beedle, Joey Negro, DJ Q, Idjut Boys and Mateos and Matos, the term Nu Med came about as a joke. The name was invented by Richard Moon Boots (from Eastern Bloc) and Phil Mison while they were eating in a restaurant in Manchester.

The restaurant's menu pitched itself as Nu Med and, just for a laugh, Richard used the term in reviews he was writing for *Mixmag* at the time. The name stuck and a veritable movement was born. Chaos or conspiracy? Take your pick.

Nuphonic Established as an independent record company in November 1994 by Ballistic Brother Dave Hill and Sev Remzi, who had met while Seb was in-house promoter at Rathbone's night-club, Nuphonic rapidly found its mark as an underground disco/Balearic-house label. It aimed to establish a core group of artists who would work consistently with the label and develop its sound, as well as releasing one-off licensing deals with exotic and sometimes bizarre collaborations. Initially concentrating on DJ-friendly 12in vinyl releases, label highs included FAZE Action's 'Full Motion' and 'Turn The Point' EPs, Larceny's 'Who Are They?', Ashley Beedle's 'Black Jazz Chronicles', Yellow Sox's 'Flim Flam' and Idjut Boys' 'Roll Over And Snore'. The artists' influences and label sound range from disco, techno and early electro through to the African funk of Fela Kuti and break beat and drum 'n' bass. Balearic references infuse the label's output and in the late nineties it led the Nu Med movement.

NWA One of the most influential and controversial hip hop groups, Niggaz With Attitude's line-up included rap luminaries such as Dr Dre, DJ Yella, MC Ren and Eazy E. Most notable was Ice Cube, who formed the band and then departed for a solo career after falling out with the band's manager.

Cube went on to initiate the trend of rap stars crossing over into movies, but not before inciting an investigation by the FBI in 1989 over the band's tune 'Fuck Tha Police'.

NWA's first single, 'Boyz 'N' The Hood' set out gangsta rap's themes of heavy funk beats and explicit lyrics about guns and violence and women (read bitches and hoes etc.). In the UK the government seized copies of the band's first album, 1991's *Efil4zaggin*' (Niggaz4life inverted), under the obscene publications act – having been unimpressed by their staple diet of expletives, oral sex and violence, let alone references to gang rape and paedophilia.

Naturally the legal attention encouraged sales among spotty teenage suburban males – with attitude.

Lest we forget:
(spot the odd one out)
Shara Nelson
Neneh Cherry
New Order
Nicolette

Best we forget:
Network 7
New Age Nonsense

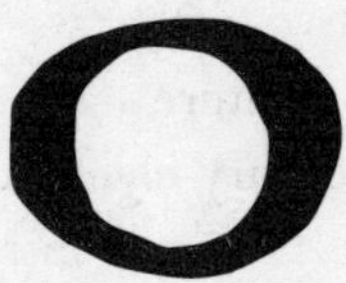

Paul Oakenfold One of the original Balearic DJs and an early exponent of hip hop in the UK, Oakenfold, a trained chef, started to DJ in 1981 when he was introduced to the decks by Trevor Fung in a bar in Covent Garden, London.

Ditching his cooking career he ventured into the music business and, failing to find work in London, headed to the dance Mecca of New York, where he became a regular at the Paradise Garage.

After working for Arista Records, he moved back to the UK and secured a job with Champion Records, importing US hip hop into the UK and snapping up acts such as Jazzy Jeff and Fresh Prince and Salt 'n' Pepa.

In this period he also made an appearance on *Blue Peter* to explain what hip hop and break dance was to somewhat-perplexed presenters. Success in the hip hop world began to be superceded in 1985 when Oakenfold discovered Chicago house and took his first trip to Ibiza.

During this period he also began a residency at The Project club in Streatham, south London. In 1987 he spent the summer in Ibiza, playing at clubs such as Amnesia and hanging out with formative figures such as Nicky Holloway and Danny Rampling. It was the year ecstasy arrived.

Returning to London he held an invite-only Ibiza reunion party at The Project and introduced the UK to its first Balearic house rave. He went on to start two further legendary nights in London's West End (Spectrum and Phuture – named after the original acid house act) and play at legendary nights such as Sch-oom and Land Of Oz in London and the Haçienda in Manchester.

He became a national figure through his association with the Ministry Of Sound, for whom he prepared compilations, and established himself as a prominent remixer, working with acts such as the Happy Mondays, M People, The Shaman, Massive Attack and New Order, usually under the Perfecto moniker with co-producer Steve Osborne. Perfecto also operates as a record label, alongside his other label, Fluoro. By the late nineties he was the main resident at Cream in Liverpool.

Old School Originally used in the late eighties to describe the original hip hop sound such as Sugar Hill releases, old school (or old skool) gradually crept forward in meaning as time went on. Eventually it was being applied to more or less any night in the early nineties that wasn't playing one or other variant of house music. To allow even greater flexibility an additional word was added to give 'old skool flavour', allowing the DJ to play recent records that had the old skool vibe.

Quite unnecessarily, promoters also began describing their nights as old and new school flavours. Meanwhile, presumably to add to any confusion that might reasonably have developed, house DJs began to refer to their not-very-old-really records as old school.

Now you could go to an old school night with absolutely no idea what music you would be treated to. Which was really quite progressive.

Orb Ambient house DJ Alex Paterson's project, the Orb, was formed in 1988 with Jimmy Cauty. Taking their name from a line in Woody Allen's film, *The Sleeper*, the band's first release, 'Tripping On Sunshine' came through the *Eternity Project One* compilation album.

Following this with 'The Kiss' EP in 1989, their next release, the cumbersomely titled 'A Huge Ever-growing Pulsating Brain Which Rules From The Centre Of The Ultraworld', led to the group signing with Big Life Records in 1990. After an acrimonious split with Cauty, Paterson joined up with Youth to record 'Little Fluffy Clouds', before finding a more permanent partner in Thrash in 1991.

Their first fruits came in the form of the Orb's debut album, *The Orb's Adventures Beyond The Ultraworld*, which rose to the top of the UK album charts. Meanwhile the band had recorded a set for John Peel, which was shortly released as an album.

A further acrimonious split in 1993, this time between the Orb and their record label Big Life, led the Orb to join Island Records, while also leading them into the High Court to resolve their dispute with Big Life.

Meanwhile the Orb joined the growing trend for dance acts to play live. Their first release for Island Live '93 was followed by the *Pomme Fritz* album in 1994, which was greeted harshly by the press. After releasing 'Orblivion' in 1997, Paterson establish Le Petit Orb in 1998 to play live in smaller club venues.

The Orbit Among the first of the new crop of techno clubs that appeared at the back end of the rave period in 1991, The Orbit was considered by many to be the best of the UK's techno nights – it was also the longest running.

Set in the Afterdark in Morley, near Leeds in West Yorkshire, it attracted the cream of the world's techno DJs to its decks.

Sven Vath, CJ Bolland, Claude Young, Westbam, Dave Angel and Luke Slater all joined residents DJs John Berry, Nigel Walker and Mark Turner, despite the fact they'd probably never heard of Morley before.

Orbital Formed by brothers Paul and Phillip Hartnoll, Orbital took their name from the M25, which at the time formed a link between the massive raves being held in the south of England – although it's also said to allude to their use of loops.

Prior to becoming the UK's hottest ambient techno outfit, they lived in Sevenoaks, Kent and Paul played with Noddy And The Satellites and worked as a labourer, while Phil was a bricklayer and a barman. They made their mark playing and improvising electronic music live in a period when much dance music was studio based.

Having been snapped up by FFRR Records they hit the top 20 with 'Chime' in March 1990. In 1991 they released their first album *Untitled 1*, which was followed by *Untitled 2* in 1993, and moved to Internal Records where they released their political concept album *Snivilisation* in 1994 and *In Sides* in 1996. Their live reputation continued to extend their fan base with performances in clubs and their seminal appearances at Glastonbury in 1994 and 1995.

Meanwhile the cinematic quality of their music was affirmed in 1996 with the release of 'The Box', which was accompanied by a film and an awesome video and entered the UK charts at number 11. They followed this in 1987 with a live rendition of 'Satan' and their version of the theme from the cult ty programme *The Saint*. Both singles entered the charts at number three.

Despite success, the brothers have maintained their down-to-earth anarchist attitude: they're frequently spotted quaffing a pint in Hoxton and they recorded tracks on *In Sides* using solar power. Their fifth album was released at the end of 1998.

Outcaste One of the longest-running nights in London's burgeoning Asian underground scene, Outcaste is more of a multimedia circus than a club. Its mission is to explore and showcase new British Asian art as well as to provide an eclectic mash of beats that share an Asian influence.

The Outcaste experience acts as a conduit for Bombay B movies, mad theatre, comedy, poetry and acoustic music – all played out against a backdrop of drum 'n' bass, hip-hop, tabla groove and cyber sitars. Alongside their successful monthly nights at London's Notting Hill Arts club, Outcaste set up its own record label, releasing home-nurtured talents such as Badmarsh and Shri's 1998 sublime 'Dancing Drums' LP.

Having already run one-off events in Belgium and Holland, they spread their message further into Europe through club nights in Paris and Amsterdam, while also starting monthly clubs in Manchester, Brighton and Bristol.

Lest we forget:
The O'Jays
Outside and Matt Cooper
Robert Owens
Oops up side your head

Best we forget:
Ottoway

Jose Padilla The most famous of the original Balearic DJs, Jose Padilla moved to Ibiza in 1973 and followed Alfredo in creating a DJ style that would change dance floors across the globe. His rolling ambient sun-down evening sets at Café Del Mar became legendary, leading to him being signed to release a series of compilations on React Records.

Paradise Situated on the current site of The Blue Note in Angel, London, the Paradise began life as a single room (now the bar area) that operated as a steamy late-night pick-up disco and drinking joint. The addition of a second room upstairs brought new music, mostly notably hip hop, into the club.

A long association with black dance music evolved, with nights such as the legendary Awol, where Randal and Bukem played the warm-up slot, attracting a packed mixed crowd.

In the mid-nineties a new night called Popstarz started on Sunday evenings. The first club to rehabilitate indie dance in London, it burst at the seams until the Paradise was taken over by the Mean Fiddler organisation. They promptly closed and revamped it as the Complex – a lush venue with none of the spit-and-sawdust charm of the original. In July 1988 the venue was renamed The Blue Note.

Paradise Garage The club that gave its name to garage music, the Paradise Garage was a vast alcohol-free venue that ran between 1977 and 1987. Based on David Mancuso's seminal Loft club, DJ Larry Levan and his sound man Richard Long installed an awesome sound system. They soon attracted the most energetic dancers from New York's Puerto Rican and black gay community, although the club was supposedly straight on Fridays and gay on Saturdays. Levan's DJ sets became legendary, as he cut his own edits of dance hits on reel-to-reel tape, mixed in adventurous tracks from unlikely sources, such as Led Zeppelin, Ian Dury and the Steve Miller Band, among the pumping disco. Levan would change mood on a whim and usually take the audience with him. But his fondness for drugs sometimes led to the odd dance floor error – such as being so smashed he'd forget to play the next record.

Graeme Park One of the first DJs to pick up on house music in the UK, Graeme Park converted a plethora of DJs to the Chicago sound, playing records such as Adonis' 'No Way Back' in the mid-eighties.

A classically trained clarinettist and saxophonist, Park was switched on to DJing after taking a job behind the counter of Select-A-Disc in Nottingham. His first slot on the decks came after his boss, Brian Selby, took over a reggae club called Ad-Lib. In the absence of another DJ, Selby booked Park to play.

Discovering emerging hip hop and electro imports, Park's sets became increasingly adventurous and his legendary nights at the Garage in Nottingham were responsible for introducing scores of people to house music. Securing a residency at the

Leadmill in Sheffield, he went on to secure slots at Kool Kat in Nottingham and teamed up with Mike Pickering at the Haçienda, Manchester.

There's naturally a lot of controversy over who introduced house music to the UK and, although it was certainly being played in clubs long before the end of the 1980s, most cite Park or Pickering as the originals. Going on to become a remix king – including 1990's New Order's 'World In Motion' football anthem – he was voted DJ of the Year by *Mixmag* in 1992.

Gilles Peterson As a young teenager Gilles Peterson spanned the early eighties London dance scenes revolving around the suburban soul Mafia, the inner city black dance music of sound systems such as Mastermind and post-New Romantics club culture.

Gaining his first DJ bookings when he was 17 years old, he played alongside seminal DJs such as Bob Jones, Froggy, Pete Tong and Chris Hill, while also securing a show on Invicta radio alongside Steve Devonne, Mastermind and Soul II Soul.

His most important break came when legendary jazz DJ Paul Murphy put Peterson forward to take over his upstairs room at the Electric Ballroom. While most punters at the Ballroom contented themselves with Paul 'Trouble' Anderson's electro beats downstairs, Murphy's room was rammed with a predominantly black élite, such as the I Dance Jazz (IDJ) posse, who had honed their dancing skills, combining jazz and funk movements and creating new steps and spins. The crowd there were the hub of London's new dance culture, a phenomenon that was being repeated in the north, where clubs such as Berlin in Manchester had DJ Colin Curtis spinning way-out mixes to an equally inventive dance floor. Murphy was by this time becoming a star and was head-hunted from the Ballroom to play The Wag. A more exclusive central London venue, many of Murphy's original crowd found themselves turned away at the door and, in what was to be a fortuitous turn of events for Peterson, instead became devotees of his sets at the Electric Ballroom.

By now being booked to play Nicky Holloway's nights at pubs such as The Royal Oak, he started teaming up with Chris Bangs – a partnership that would have an important influence on Peterson's musical development. Bangs had a reputation for being the Eric Morecambe of the jazz and black music scene, banging tracks such as 'Tequila' into his sets, wearing off-the-wall costumes and generally having a laugh.

While DJs and promoters were behaving according to the straight-laced attitudes of the eighties, Peterson and Bangs were having fun and increasingly came to be seen as the rebels of the dance circuit.

Undeterred, Bangs and Peterson delved deeper into beat habits, reading Jack Kerouac and turning up at one of Holloway's Rockley Sands events dressed in hippie gear and encouraging punters to do creative writing.

The introduction of the Balearic vibe and ecstasy culture was to have a profound effect on Peterson and London's dance culture as a whole. While those that had been to Ibiza embraced chemical culture, Peterson and those around him stayed on an organic, rather than chemical tip.

Taking up residency at The Belvedere, Peterson found himself playing to a divided scene that was strangely united by his sessions. While Rampling, Jimmy Jewel, Chris Butler and the Shoom posse chilled out to his sets, the jazz enthusiasts were going crazy to leftfield dance beats.

By now acid house had taken hold and one night Peterson and Bangs were booked to play one of Holloway's events in Brentford Community Centre. Paul Oakenfold was playing before them, dropping relentless up-tempo acid tracks. Armed only with their usual fare of jazz- and funk-inspired tunes, Bangs and Peterson were stumped as to how to follow Oakenfold. Working in a frantic guitar intro, they announced 'fuck acid house, this is acid jazz'. The dance floor went mental and acid jazz was born.

Having always played alongside the house scene, it suddenly became obvious that London's dance music traditions could be mixed to capture the energy of an acid dance floor.

Peterson's next club, Cock Happy, was to become Shoom set to different grooves. Attracting key figures from the Shoom posse, such as Jewell and Butler, the venue was divided into two rooms, one playing acid jazz while the other laid out on a trippy vibe, where poet Rob Galliano would perform poetry. At the beginning, the club still emphasised the difference between organic and chemical-driven music, but acid house nutters were soon alternating between Cock Happy and the Balearic clubs.

The new mood continued with Babylon at Heaven, a club that captured London's dance grooves with Colin Faver playing techno in one room, Peterson and Marco spinning acid jazz and Paul Oakenfold dropping Balearic beats in future.

By this point the seminal Talkin' Loud And Saying Something club at Dingwalls, which started in 1986, was well and truly established. Starting at midday on Sundays, the music would work through black jazz dance, when the dance troupes would spin and circle madly, move on to a live band and end with a full-on session picking eclectically through dance styles.

Meanwhile Peterson had started the Acid Jazz label with Eddie Pillar, but was becoming increasingly frustrated with the label's output, with acts such as James Taylor Quartet veering towards mod culture rather than the experimental eclectic dance music that Peterson envisaged.

Breaking away in summer 1988, he established his own label, named Talkin' Loud after his Dingwalls sessions. By this time dance music was beginning to become monolithic, often missing its black sound system roots. Talkin' Loud was set up to incorporate the range of black music styles and promote UK artists who were otherwise ignored by acid house culture.

With the closure of the Dingwalls venue, Peterson moved his Talkin' Loud nights to the cavernous Fridge, where James Lavelle, a young devotee of the Dingwalls sessions, began working with him.

Alongside his London commitments, Peterson now moved to spread the word internationally, taking up residencies in Soul Seduction, Vienna, Beat Box, Wuppertal, Germany and Sherezade in Paris. His excursions helped establish Talkin' Loud and leftfield dance music, while bringing attention to developing dance cultures in places as far flung as Japan.

In 1993 he teamed up with Lavelle, who was now running the Mo Wax record label, and started their seminal That's How It Is night at Bar Rumba, re-introducing eclectic DJing and in the process kick-starting trip hop and popularising drum 'n' bass among a new audience.

P-Funk, Parliament and Funkadelic The brainchild of the enigmatic, eccentric George Clinton and his Parliament/Funkadelic band-cum-collective, P-Funk came into general use to describe their sound after Parliament released 'P-Funk (Wants To Get Funked Up)' in 1974.

The music emphasises funk's obsession with the first beat of the bar, which James Brown described as The One. In Clinton's fertile imagination, The One was transformed into an intergalactic philosophy of racial emancipation, awareness and unity, as expressed in songs such as 'One Nation Under A Groove' and 'Chocolate City'. The latter contained the lyric 'they still call it the White House, but that's just a temporary condition.'

Alongside the philosophy, Clinton invented a new language, alias names and personae for his band (such as Star Child, the Brides of Funkenstein and Dr Funkenstein) and extravagant camp clothing, including space-age uniforms and nappies.

By adding disaffected members of James Brown's backing band to his collective in the early seventies, Clinton surrounded himself with the giants of funk such as Bootsy Collins, Maceo Parker and Bernie Worrel. The result was ground-breaking, dance-driven, space-age funk music that has continued to influence dance acts ever since.

Phat Whether it's a result of communal dyslexia, drug-induced slackness or just for the fun of it, misspelling has been a long-time clubbing pastime. Some misspellings such as Phat (pronounced fat) are gloriously onomatopoeic. Describing the low-down funky bass end of chunky hip hop in the early nineties, the word was synonymous with spliffs, blunts and the downbeat trends of the era.

By 1993 the word had spread across all genres of dance music, although it remained most common in the hip hop fraternity and had become shorthand for good or cool – just as 'bad' had once meant good. As with most words that express a common link between their users, phat soon lost its efficacy after it caught on. Irritating related words include phunky, phucked and phull on. Not big, clever or phuny.

Mike Pickering Legendary DJ behind the Hacienda's Nude nights and the explosion of house in Manchester, Mike Pickering's upbringing was soaked in music. He cut his teeth dancing to northern soul at clubs such as the Blackpool Mecca, had seen the

Pistols play their seminal first gig in Manchester and had played saxophone for the dance band Quando Quango.

Having worked in a fish factory and an engineering warehouse, his DJ career took off after his old flatmate and New Order manager Rob Gretton booked him to play a residency at the Hacienda on Friday nights. Quando Quango had scored dance hits on the New York black gay scene and Pickering immediately set about recreating the vibe of clubs such as The Paradise Garage and The Loft.

His Friday night-club, Nude, started in November 1984 and lasted until 1990. Originally partnering with Martin Prendergast, the pair would spin electro, electronic pop, hip hop, funk and US dance imports. Whereas the Hacienda had previously been the domain of goths and indie kids, Nude attracted a mixed crowd of students, scallies and the predominantly black dance scene.

In 1986, according the now-legendary story, Pickering permanently changed the Hacienda's sound, dance floor and culture, by playing his first Chicago house imports in his set. The hard-edged grooves slotted perfectly into his eclectic music and picked the dance floor up into a thumping whirlwind. From then on house came to appear regularly in his set and eventually dominated it.

When Pendergast departed, Graeme Park, the resident DJ at Nottingham's Garage club and early house DJ, was the natural choice to compliment Pickering's style. Both of them had already worked together on the Northern House tour in 1988, and they now became a legendary partnership at the epicentre of Manchester's first Summer of Love.

As well as earning the accolade of being described as the country's most respected DJ by *The Face* magazine, Pickering was also working in the music industry as a successful A&R man for Factory Records, booking The Smiths to play their first gig and signing James and the Happy Monday's and working with the T-Coy house band.

From here he progressed to becoming a junior director of DeConstruction Records and set up his band M People with vocalist Heather Small and Paul Heard (former member of Orange Juice and Working Week). Styling themselves as a pop dance act, the band released their first record, 'Colour My Life' in May 1991, which was followed with the anthemic 'How Can I Love You More'. By 1993 the band's success was ensured, as they released hits such as 'Movin' On Up', their third album *Elegant Slumming* and received the Brit Awards for Best UK Dance Act.

DJ Pierre The most often-credited creator of acid house, DJ Pierre began DJing under another name in 1983, but was forced to change his moniker after playing a disastrous party.

Going on to play several Lil' Louis parties, he hooked up with his partner Spanky in 1986 and one night set about reprogramming a recently purchased Roland 303 bass unit. As he attempted to clear the machine's memory bank it started making weird squelching noises. Laying the noises over a drum track Spanky had been working on, they passed the tape on to producer Marshall Jefferson, who had already been making tracks using 303 bleeps. The resulting sounds were given to Ron Hardy to play at his Music Box club, the tunes becoming known as Hardy's Acid Trax. From here, the act Phuture was formed in 1987, issuing the seminal Acid Trax.

Having established himself, Pierre moved to New York and helped set up the Strictly Rhythm record label empire. Pierre's output has been varied and prolific, releasing records such as 'Annihilating Rhythm', 'Darkman', 'Masterblaster', 'Rise From Your Grave', 'Musik', 'Generator Power', 'More Than Just

A Chance', and 'I Might Be Leaving You'. He perfected the slow-building sound of Wyld Pitch.

Pirate Radio Following a long tradition in illegal radio stations broadcasting cutting-edge music, pirate radio proliferated rapidly in the UK in the early eighties with stations such WBLS, JFM and Studio FM broadcasting in London. Unlike countries such as New Zealand, which had opened up its airwaves, the UK was grid-locked with restrictive legislation prohibiting new stations from broadcasting.

In 1985 the government promised a series of licences would be granted in the near future. The pirates dropped their broadcasts and prepared for the transition to legal status, but it soon became apparent the promise would at best be a long time coming if it ever materialised.

Gradually some stations crept back on to the airwaves. One station in particular, called Kiss, was to capture the mood of the forthcoming decade. While commercial and state-owned stations such as Radio One and Capital played minimal amounts of dance music, pirates became dedicated to specialist genres.

Kiss made its name by recognising the growing interest in underground soul and funk and by booking DJs who were building the scene in clubs and warehouse parties. Beginning 24-hour week-long dance broadcasts in October 1985, Kiss soon had a dedicated London following. One DJ, Norman Jay, christened his show rare groove and defined a new musical movement. By the late eighties Margaret Thatcher's *laissez faire* Conservative government had moved to liberalise the airwaves.

Kiss applied for, and won a license to broadcast legally in London. Becoming a commercial station its radical music policy was gradually watered down as it wrestled to maintain a market share and thereby revenue from advertisers.

Meanwhile the promised liberalisation failed to appear as the few independent stations that were granted licenses were swallowed up by large media groups such as Chrysalis, Virgin, Capital and Emap.

In its wake new pirates sprung up to promote music forms such as ragga, street soul, jungle, hardcore and underground house. Broadcasting non-commercial music to a niche selection of targeted listeners, pirates faced the risk of fines and the confiscation of their equipment, but were consistently able to outrun licensed radio in picking up new musical trends, even when the quality of broadcast was patchy.

Pirates also introduced a new vernacular to broadcasting and club vocabularies – not least the oft repeated mantra of 'big shout going out to . . .' whoever was the last person to call.

Platforms The periodic perennial hangover from early seventies fashion, platform shoes just wouldn't let themselves be put away. Whether it was the nimble creations adorning the feat of drag queens on the gay club scene, the ludicrous high-soled creations of Leigh Bowery in the mid-eighties or the Buffalo shoes creations of the late nineties that the Spice girls popularised, platforms were always high on the club footwear agenda.

Giving the wearer that extra few inches of height, they also carried with them the disadvantage of the potential to bring you crashing down to ground level. A drink to many, an awkward indent in the floor or an over-enthusiastic dance step, and down would come wearer, image and all.

Poppers Properly described as amyl nitrate, poppers have driven the dance floor in the gay community for 20 years, although they're also used for sex and hence are often distributed through sex shops. Unlike most other drugs, which are illegal, poppers are legal unless they're being used as 'room odorisers'. The impact of poppers – a bursting, heady, energy flash – is immediate.

Generally sold in small brown bottles, poppers are taken by sniffing their vapours. The resulting rush is caused by the arteries and veins being dilated, causing the blood to flow faster through your body to your brain and heart. Taken during dancing, the effect is a momentary and complete subservience to the music and many clubs have been rumoured to add it to their air-conditioning. During sex it feels like your body has become one giant sex organ. The down side to poppers is the renowned headache it can leave you with.

Popstarz Simon Hobart's gay-indie night started on Sunday nights at the Paradise, in Islington, London in 1995. Challenging the dance music's domination of both the gay and straight club scenes, Popstarz picked up on the popularity of Brit pop and bands such as Blur and Oasis. The main dance floor would sway and jump to classic and contemporary indie dance tunes, while downstairs a gloriously camp disco set would have everyone reeling and pouting.

After the Paradise was taken over by the Mean Fiddler organisation and revamped as the Complex, Popstarz moved to the cavernous Bagley's Studios in King's Cross, where they adopted a curious 'pay-as-much-as-you-want-to' policy on the door. With the added space, Popstarz could now have a bit of fun and started including fairground rides on the dance floor.

Moving to the Hanover Grand, the second room was replaced by an eighties room, which had to implement a one-out, one-in policy, causing the bizarre spectacle of a club with an interior queue. By the late nineties the club had moved venue again to the Leisure Lounge in Holborn.

Pork Recordings Pork Recordings, a leftfield eclectic record label which is fiercely independent, was formed in Hull in late 1990. The product of a collaboration between Porky and Steve Cobby, its first release came in 1991, but it really appeared on the scene with the release of Opik's 'Feel Yourself'. Opik were soon snapped on to a licensing deal with DeConstruction. Meanwhile Fila Brazilia was turning heads with releases such as 'Mermaids', 'Rankine' and the seminal 'Pots And Pans'. The band proved themselves to be extremely versatile, prefiguring big beat and downbeat trip hop sounds.

The equally jazz-tinged Solid Doctor's 'Losing Patients' series provided the label with experimental, film score, crossover house epics. Other members of Pork's roster, such as Heights Of Abraham, Bullitnuts, Baby Mammoth and Akotcha, proved to be equally able in attracting a global following for the label, despite Pork shunning collusion with major labels and the obvious distribution and publicity advantages that it would bring. Proof that small is beautiful and definitely underground.

Portishead One of the central bands to push trip hop music and the Bristol sound up from the underground, Portishead was formed by Geoff Barrow after he secured an Enterprise Allowance grant – a government scheme designed to help unemployed people set themselves up in business. He enlisted guitarist Adrian Utley, drum programmer Dave and singer Beth Gibbons, whom he discovered while she was making a living singing Janice Joplin covers in a pub.

The band took its name from the sleepy West Country town in which Barrow grew up. After they had produced a film, *To Kill A Dead Man*, the band's first white label, 'Sour Times', seeped into specialist record shops. Featuring a bewildering number of immaculately produced remixes, including a crashing guitar version, the band immediately attracted attention.

Despite being notoriously reclusive in their early years, the band displayed a gift at self promotion. For example they publicised their first album, *Dummy*, by bathing the Royal Festival Hall in blue light and placing mannequins around central London. Throughout, the band were noticeable in their absence. Their second album, *Portishead*, was released in 1998.

Jamie Principle The father of house records rather than DJing, Jamie Principle entered the world of music by accident, first studying the clarinet and then moving on to drums and keyboard. Recording tracks at a friend's (Jose Gomez) studio for his own pleasure, Gomez took one of Principle's tunes called 'Your Love' to Frankie Knuckles.

Knuckles liked the tune and played it at his club. 'Your Love' was later to become available in the UK via a much sought-after bootleg. The tune was released on Trax Records, but it was the b-side, 'Baby Wants To Ride', that would launch Principle to fame in Chicago and later the UK, where Steve 'Silk' Hurley remixes were issued on the FFRR label.

Principle and Hurley were to form a lasting on-off collaboration on tracks such as 'Rebels'. Meanwhile one of Principle's earliest house works, 'Waiting On My Angel', resurfaced on a bootleg. Other singles such as 'Date With The Rain' further built Principle's reputation, and he re-united with Hurley in 1991 to release the US smash hit, 'You're All I've Waited 4'.

Prodigy Formed after Liam Howlett, a hip hop devotee who had been converted to the rave scene, recorded ten tunes in his Essex bedroom in 1990. Taking his influences from Joey Beltram and Meat Beat Manifesto, he presented his roughly hewn tracks to XL Records, who immediately snapped four of them up and pressed the first Prodigy EP, 'What Evil Lurks', in February 1991. The record sold a respectable 7,000 copies, but the next single, 'Charly', flew out of the shops and launched a series of toytown techno tunes.

Creating a band with dancer Leroy Thornhill, dancer-cum-vocalist Keith Flett and MC Maxim, the Prodigy began touring tirelessly at raves such as Raindance, where they ditched the usual keyboard-dominated performances of other dance outfits and put on frantic, often lunatic shows.

Follow-up releases such as 'Everybody In The Place', 'Fire' and 'Out Of Space' shot into the charts and their debut album, *Experience*, went gold, staying in the Top 40 for 25 weeks.

By 1993 the rave scene that had spawned them had been all but driven out of existence by legal restrictions. Howlett began laying the foundations for a shift in musical direction and, drawing influences from guitar acts such as Nirvana and the Smashing Pumpkins, the band released 'One Love' on a white label. Despite no one knowing who had released the track, the record was well received in the press and on its official release in summer 1993 it charted.

After being recluse for a year, Prodigy released their second album, *Music For A Jilted Generation*, in July 1994. The album went straight to number one and went gold within a week.

Prefiguring the direction the band was taking, the first single from the album *Voodoo People* was backed by a remix from the Chemical Brothers.

By the release of 'Firestarter' in March 1996, the band had adopted an intense punk big-beat sound. The single literally exploded into the charts at number one. By the release of their third album, *Fat Of The Land*, in June 1997, Prodigy had started to lead a British dance invasion of the US, with 'Firestarter' creeping into the US Billboard charts.

Progressive House Coined as a genre in 1991 by journalist Dom Phillips, progressive house distinguished between the dominant rave scene and the new school of UK house. At the time the scene was split between rave and the more soulful and funky US garage and house of people such as Steve 'Silk' Hurley.

Progressive house artists such as Laurence Nelson combined the rougher edge of European music with the funk of US grooves. Growing out of the Balearic scene, Progressive house was fostered by DJs such as Charlie Chester and the *Boy's Own* crew.

UK artists such as The Aloof and Leftfield, whose 'Not Forgotten' was an early classic, twisted US house into new formats, adding dub bass lines and a leftfield edge. The sound was pioneered at clubs such as Love Ranch, at Maximus, Shave Your Tongue, Open All Hours at Ministry Of Sound and by DJs such as Darren Emerson, Billy Nasty, David Holmes, Andy Weatherall and Justin Robertson.

Progressive house record labels such as Cowboy and Gorilla promoted the form, but its popularity brought complications. Identifying what the tag meant became increasingly confusing. What it means now is anyone's guess, but it's not what Phillips, Chester, Weatherall and co. meant.

Promoters Until Steve Strange started his Blitz club night in Covent Garden in 1979, night-clubs would have their own internal promoter, booking in-house DJs and running nights that would simply be named after the host venue such as Whiskey A Go Go, Gullivers or Crackers, every night of the week.

Strange changed all that by becoming the first promoter to hire his venue from the owners. The Blitz thrived, becoming the hip place to hang out – it even had Boy George working in the cloakroom – and Strange became king of the London scene. After the original venue burned down, the Blitz moved to the upstairs of

The Venue in Victoria, before Strange hired out the Barracuda in Baker Street and started Club For Heroes in summer 1981.

By now other promoters were starting to join in and Gossips, a mini emporium, was a venue with enough space to have small separate clubs running on different floors. Promoters such as Gaz started the long-running Gaz's Rocking Blues, a sixties soul night called Soul Furnace opened and James Le Bon introduced London's first hip hop night, The Language Lab.

Night-club culture and warehouse parties emerged with lightening speed and by 1983 promoters were scouring London for suitable venues for legal and illegal parties.

In a period that emphasised designer goods and style, previously tacky late-night drinking clubs and venues were transformed, with projections and drapes, into trendy underground events. Alongside promoters a new breed of big-name DJs appeared as solo artists.

While in the early eighties DJs were generally faceless, hidden behind the name of the club or organisation running the event, by the late eighties the DJ had become the star of the show. Punters began going to nights because of the person behind the decks. By the nineties the much-vaunted economic miracle created by the Conservative government had given way to a depression. With long- and short-term employment prospects in the official job market looking extremely bleak, an alternative role model for young people appeared in the form of rave promoters, who were raking in ridiculous amounts of money. Much to the mortification of careers advisors, promoting had become the career to aspire to.

PSV An early alternative to the Haçienda in Manchester, and one of the few places that played acid house alongside hip hop, dub and all sorts, the PSV was based in the cultural centre, in the middle of Hulme housing estate. Far from being a salubrious environment, the PSV was constantly plagued by gangland violence and apparently random attacks.

Rumours about knife-point robbery and muggings in the cavernous ground floor dance area became stock-in-trade gossip among the clubbers, while the upstairs bar oscillated between being the cool place to chill and a gangland hangout. Despite this, the PSV maintained a loyal amicable crowd who would swear they weren't going back after each violent episode yet nonetheless returned to catch the grooves.

The PSV had a chequered history. More spliff and red stripe than an ecstasy culture, it drew in a predominantly black crowd, alongside local anarchist squatters and students too poor to afford the Hacienda's door prices.

Pubs With Gardens In the Warehouse days of the early eighties there would be at least one, if not two, major events every weekend. Hordes of teenagers would congregate in the scene pubs, which usually had gardens or landlords who weren't bothered about age restrictions, and await information and instructions about where the night's party would be.

The Churchill and The Gayety in west London, and The Freemasons and the Sir Richard Steel in north London, were regular hangouts for people from all corners of London.

In the nineties gardens gave way to decks and pubs became bars.

Punk While US artists such as Iggy Pop, Richard Hell and the New York Dolls are often cited as producing the first punk records, punk started as a movement in London in 1976, guided by the Sex Pistols and the fiery young singer Johnny Rotten.

The Pistols, who comprised of Rotten, Paul Cook, Steve Jones and Glen Matlock, played their first gig at St. Martin's College before securing a residency at the 100 club. It was here that punk culture developed. Fans such as Siouxie Sioux, Sid Vicious (who later replaced Matlock) and Billy Idol adapted bondage sex gear, torn clothing and anything that would shock, developing a do-it-yourself fashion movement.

Bands such as The Damned (whose 'New Rose' was the first punk single), The Clash and The Buzzcocks followed in the Pistols' wake, while they signed to EMI and released 'Anarchy' in the UK. After they broke into a swearing marathon on Thames Television's *Today* programme, EMI dropped them and they signed to A&M, who also dropped them – all of which was very lucrative for the band.

In 1977 they signed to Virgin and released 'God Save The Queen'. Despite the single being banned by a host of outraged radio stations, they reached number two in the UK charts in the week of the Queen's Silver Jubilee celebrations. By 1978 punk had started running out of steam and the band split up after a disastrous tour of the USA.

In the early nineties punk fashion re-emerged in the gay clubbing community and by the late nineties a new stylised punk look had been re-instituted in the club scene.

Thankfully the habit of hanging Watney's beer mats from your bum was left in the annals of history.

Pure Originating in 1986 as the Blue Monday club at the now-defunct Fire Island in Edinburgh, DJs Bill, Roxy and Bobby introduced a largely gay audience to Belgian nu-beat and hi-NRG. Coming from a punk background, the night also attracted Edinburgh's then cutting-edge goth population.

Mixing in industrial music alongside tacky disco, the DJs began dropping early garage music, gradually leading their crowd into house music. By 1988 the night had been renamed UFO, Steve

Miller and Keith McIvor had been brought into the club and it had moved to Murray House Student Union.

Gradually the goths such as Tiger, who was generally seen as the scene king, ditched their dark attire and sombre attitude in favour of baggy clothing, ecstasy and running around the club blowing whistles.

Opening at Venus in Edinburgh in 1990, the long-running Pure soon formed a reputation for playing Balearic music that mixed house with Hendrix, Beats International's 'Dub Be Good To Me' and Soup Dragons tracks.

Gradually becoming a dedicated underground house and techno night, notorious for its 'having it' crowd, the resident DJs adopted names such as Twitch, Brainstorm, Dribbler and The Bill. They attracted accolades from no-less a figure than the techno legend Derrick May, who once described Pure as the best club in Europe. Enough said.

Pushca Beginning in 1992 as a one-off event, organising irregular highly elaborate themed nights, Pushca formed part of the glam reaction to the increasingly violent or drab rave and hardcore scene.

Deliberately expensive and élitist, tickets for Pushca were available only in advance to those in the know – people who were already part of the family, and hence sent information sheets, or their friends. Their parties were cinematic in their extravagant décor and production qualities, and their mixed gay crowd was equally elaborate in dressing themselves up for the occasion.

Pushca became the flagship glam house night, and eventually moved to two monthly residencies, first at the Vapour Rooms in Leicester Square and then at The Ministry Of Sound. In 1998 they left the Ministry after a dispute about the kind of people the club's security were letting in, and took off for a joint venture in Ibiza with Trade.

Lest we forget:

Ce Ce Peniston
Shep Pettibone
Positiva
Pressure Drop
Public Enemy

Best we forget:

Pissing in your mate's wardrobe while sleepwalking
Prince Alberts and other eye-watering piercing
Pulling your best mate – being loved up does have limits

DJ Q-Bert Mainstay of the San Francisco hip hop DJ collective the Invisible Scratch Picklz, DJ Q and his crew members such as Mix Master Mike treat their turntables like bona fide instruments, creating original compositions through his own tunes and other people's records. Also an impressive showman, in 1992 Q-Bert and the Picklz entered the world DMC DJ mixing championships. They romped home to win, a trick they repeated until 1995, when DMC asked them to abstain since their presence was too intimidating for the other DJs. In response the Picklz set up the International Turntable Federation, running their own competitions.

Q-Bert has also run schools to tutor aspiring DJs. His scratch mastery can be heard on Dr Octagon's 'Dr Octagonecologyst'. Mix Master Mike released an album, *Anti-Theft Device*, in 1998.

Quadrant Park The legendary, and scary, Quadrant Park opened in Liverpool in 1991 to a seething mass of loved-up scallies – except unfortunately some of them weren't. In the era of hardcore and Italo house, Quadrant Park was the home of crashing piano house as DJs such as Andy Carroll and John Kelly kept the dance floor thrashing.

While the centre of the cavernous venue would be packed with loved-up punters, the many murky corners provided the perfect cover for dodgy dealings.

Finley Quaye Controversially the younger uncle of Bristol's downbeat trip hop master, Tricky, 23-year-old Finley Quaye appeared in the late nineties injecting commercial soulful reggae back into mainstream music. His first single, 'Sunday Shining', jumped into the UK top 20, while his second single, 'Even After All', made it into the top ten. Definitely on a blunt tip, Finley's soft vocals are accompanied by a diverse combination of reggae-, dub-, jazz- and soul-infused arrangements.

His background is equally varied. Coming from a Ghanaian family, he grew up in Edinburgh, London and Manchester. He was voted Next Best Newcomer in 1997's *Q* awards and 1998's Brit Awards. His debut album, *Maverick A Strike*, reached number three in the charts in 1998.

Queer Nation Started in London in 1991, Queer Nation opened its doors for its screaming Sunday session at the Gardening club in 1991. Patrick Lilley took the club's name from a radical US gay activist group.

Fine tuning the art of handbag and camp house, Queen Maxine and Luke Howard specialised in playing tacky-as-you-like disco and full vocal garage to a dance floor of sweating bodies of which even Larry Levan might have been proud.

By the late nineties Queer Nation had moved to Substation South, in Brixton – a good move considering Brixton at the time was experiencing a night life renaissance.

Queues Queues used to be the serious clubber's worst nightmare. They were feared by New Year revellers, who celebrated the chimes of the New Year outside the club they'd spent £35 to go to, and loathed by blaggers who'd sell their granny to queue-jump by getting their name on the guest list. Today, clubs such as The Blue Note in London, and Sundissential in Birmingham have made standing outside a status symbol. Unfortunate paying punters are waved straight through the doors while the guest-list queue stretches happily around the block.

Queuing is not simply a matter of standing in line. Having the advantage in winter months of being able to show off fashionable outer clothing that's too hot to wear in the club, the It-crowd, secure in hooded tops and hats pulled over their ears, display their de-rigueur winter clothing and buff their hands while expelling streams of steam through their nostrils. The queue shifts and swells, as jaywalkers pacing the line's periphery discover a vaguely familiar face near the door, greet them like a long-lost brother or sister and collect their mates from the back of the queue.

Banter about who's on which guest list passes up and down, while others negotiate over who's on the half price and who's on the free list.

Queuing may be cold, but it's also cool.

Rage Remembered for its pivotal role in the early jungle scene, Rage began life in the Balearic days at Heaven and was the first night at the club openly to encourage straight women through its doors. The idea of Heaven promoter Kevin Mullins, Rage catered for a harder sound and thereby ensured it survived other nights of the period.

By the early nineties up-tempo Belgium new beat had begun replacing the disco pace of the earlier house scene and the hardcore scene arrived. Two hardcore DJs, Fabio and Grooverider, were given a residency upstairs, where they blended the harder and faster beats with influences from black music.

Eventually being moved downstairs, they attracted a new crossover following from among the ragga and hip hop/break beat communities, who had previously been alienated by the rave scene. Soon-to-be Jungle stars such as Goldie became devotees, while lower-quality, speed-fuelled pills such as Snowballs picked up the crowd into a teeth-gnashing frenzy.

Raindance One of the first legal raves, Paul Nelson's Raindance began in late 1989 and managed to dodge legal licensing restrictions by staging its events in a sub-league football ground that had a small bar in a hut for club members. By obtaining a license extension for a private party in the hut from the council, they attracted crowds of 10,000 or more.

The Entertainments (Increased Penalties) Act came into force in July 1990 and the police used their new powers to come down heavily on illegal raves, yet Raindance managed to keep the vibe alive through 1990 to 1991. Located in east London, it brought a wave of new DJs on the scene, such as Slipmat, and acts such as the Prodigy played regularly.

Its reputation grew and soon limousines said to be carrying stars such as George Michael began to show up. Meanwhile Raindance regulars became the bedrock for Rage at Heaven.

Danny Rampling In the mid-eighties London-born Danny Rampling was regularly booked to play at Nicky Holloway's events in the Old Kent Road and central London. He gained DJ recognition playing a set alongside Gordon Mac, founder of the then pirate Kiss FM radio station. This led to Rampling being given a weekly soul music slot on Kiss.

It wasn't until he was invited to Ibiza by Holloway in 1987 that he came into his own. Here, in common with other DJs such as Paul Oakenfold, Trevor Fung and Johnny Walker, he discovered the intoxicating effect of Balearic beats, sunshine clubbing and ecstasy.

Bringing the sound back to London he and Jenni, his wife, started the legendary Sch-oom club in November 1987. Sch-oom, which went on to be called Shoom, set the pattern for Balearic and acid house clubs and opened the way for rave and the first Summer of Love in 1988.

In place of the mid-eighties uniform of black Levis 501s, waist-coats, sharp haircuts and hands-off dancing, Shoom generated a loved-up culture of floppy hair, hands in the air dance celebration. The Ramplings also adopted the smiley logo for Shoom flyers, thereby launching the symbol of acid house.

Rampling stayed with Kiss after it became a legal station, until Radio One recruited him in 1994 to save their flagging youth appeal.

R&S Records Founded by Renaat Vandepapeliere and Sabine Maes in Ghent in the early eighties, R&S aimed itself at underground and experimental dance. Originally releasing Belgian new beat material, in 1987 R&S released Code 61's Balearic anthem 'Drop The Deal', which established the label at the forefront of European dance music. Hard house classics followed, such as Spectrum's 'Brazil', which flooded into the UK's rave scene.

By the early nineties R&S had cornered the European techno market, releasing classics such as 'Energy Flash', by a then unknown young DJ called Joey Beltram. The roster of artists who have appeared on the label reads like a who's who of techno, with innovative names such as Kevin Saunderson, Derrick May, Dave Angel, CJ Bolland, Jam & Spoon, Pulsinger and Aphex Twin all making an appearance.

Soon sister labels emerged with Apollo dedicated to ambient, Global Cuts releasing uplifting house and the Diatomyc imprint pressing acid tunes. Its distinctive two-tone jacket sleeves and mimicked Ferrari Horse logo are now featured in every self-respecting DJs record bag. In the late nineties they released a downbeat series called Free the Funk.

Rare Groove The sound of London in the mid-eighties, rare groove essentially described the warehouse party vibe and up-tempo US seventies funk music, as epitomised by James Brown's 'Sex Machine' and Maceo Parker's 'Across The Tracks', mixed in with contemporary dance sounds such as hip hop and, later, house.

The term was coined by Norman Jay for his show on the pirate Kiss radio station, but it described a vast scene that ranged from club nights such as Black Market at The Wag to illegal parties held by Jay's Good Times Sound System/Shake and Finger Pop. In London rare groove was supreme for four years, until house elbowed it off the dance floor.

While the ubiquitous ripped Levis, Doc Martin shoes and decorated MA 1 jackets were the staple fashion of the period, rare groove also opened up a mix-and-match fashion, with large square-toed seventies shoes re-appearing along with Afro haircuts, flat funky caps and B-boy/hip hop fashions. Other cities joined the vibe, but it never quite sank as deeply into their culture.

By the late eighties a chasm had opened between rare groove freaks and the new house scene. Many failed to make the transition from rare groove's funky rhythm patterns to the straight disco four-four of house and instead moved towards rare grooves' natural descendent – acid jazz.

Raves Following the acid house explosion, which attracted the attention of the gutter press and the police, venues became harder to secure and, in the tradition of earlier warehouse parties that operated outside the legal licensing restrictions, raves began to be held in disused industrial spaces, fields, airstrips and farms.

One way of finding the party in the early days, when most of the venues were warehouses, was simply finding the area, turning up and then following the people who were running in one direction, desperately trying to get in before the place filled up or was busted.

The events happened all over the UK, but most notoriously took place in Blackburn, the south-east and London – centring around the M25 London orbital. The scene was almost exclusively fuelled by MDMA, although pills were increasingly just globs of amphetamine, and usually alcohol free. The events began to attract the attention of the police, who established the Pay Party Unit to monitor rave organisations.

Thus began a game of cat-and-mouse between the unit and the organisers, with rave promoters taking ever more elaborate precautions to keep the location of their parties secret. Flyers and word-of-mouth information would link ravers to meeting points, such as motorway garages, and mobile phone numbers, through which last-minute details would be released on the night – leading to police car chases and road blocks.

Organisations such as Sunrise, Genesis, Biology, Universe and Energy, among a million others, became legends in dance culture, although the scene became more and more seedy as organised crime began to recognise the huge profit potential of a captive audience in a country field.

In the early days the sudden arrival of thousands of teenagers in a sleepy corner of the south-east would perplex the police. On one occasion a convoy on its way to a Biology party found itself caught in a police roadblock in Meopham, Kent. A stand-off between the police and would-be ravers lasted for an hour. While the front cars negotiated the others, hearing the distant rumble of the bass and knowing they were near their destination, started necking pills and cranking up their car stereos. Unwisely the police turned their lights on, flashing waves of blue strobe along the convoy. Soon the panda cars were surrounded by grinning happy dancers, much to the confusion of the gob-smacked local constables who had unwittingly aided and abetted a rave.

Eventually the cat-and-mouse games came to a halt after the government introduced the Entertainments (Increased Penalties) Act 1990 and the Criminal Justice Act 1994. These enshrined the word 'rave' in statute, while making it illegal for a gathering of people to listen to repetitive beats in a field.

Reclaim The Streets Formed in London in autumn 1991 against the background of mass civil-disobedience campaigns against motorway and bypass building, Reclaim The Streets (RTS) aimed to bring the focus of the campaign against roads on to cars and to bring the struggle into the centre of cities.

From its outset RTS called for a campaign against cars and the automotive industry, cheap or free public transport, walking and cycling. Starting with small-scale disruptive events such as painting cycle lanes on London roads overnight, the network grew and by 1995 the organisation has been relaunched, after the campaign against the M11 had culminated in the police cracking down on what had essentially been a resistance street party.

Learning the lessons of the first incarnation, the new and larger organisation began holding street parties, the first of which turned Camden Town into an impromptu festival. RTS had hit a winning formula that combined dance music with a strong simple political message. Thanks to RTS, people were still raving despite the introduction of the Criminal Justice Act, but now they were united by more than just the music.

In July 1996 an event was organised on the West Way flyover – the dual carriageway that links central London to the M25 and M40. The planning followed RTS's standard formula. People were invited to a pre-arranged meeting point before being marched to the site of the protest, which only the key organisers knew in advance. The event went beyond everyone's expectations, with more than 8,000 people attending a party that lasted from Saturday morning until Sunday night.

While people danced to the sound systems or chilled over a spliff and a can of beer, huge figures on stilts covered by billowing skirts moved among the crowds. Beneath the skirts people drilled huge pits in the road. It was the perfect combination of politics and pop. Bakunin would have been break dancing in his grave.

Record Theft The cardinal deadliest sin of the DJ world, record theft is every self-respecting train spotter's nightmare and is a casualty of playing out, especially at parties where the area around the turntables usually resembles an alpine scene, as a cohort of DJs stash their bags waiting for their moment of glory. Records frequently wander into another DJs collections, but such incidents are invariably accidental.

Harder to explain is the disappearance of an entire record collection.

The most famous record theft story belongs to Gilles Peterson when he left his records in the caged impenetrable DJ booth after a Talkin' Loud night in The Fridge in 1992. Peterson returned to find his entire, extremely rare set had been lifted. Everything pointed to an inside job. The response from Peterson's fellow DJs at Kiss radio was deafening, as each jock repeatedly broadcast the story over the airwaves, pleading and guilt-tripping the thief to return the discs. It seemed a pointless exercise until Peterson returned to The Fridge the following week and found his records waiting for him in the DJ booth.

Reprazent and Roni Size In the Bristol tradition of band-as-collective, drum 'n' bass band Reprazent consists of a clutch of Bristol drum 'n' bass artists based around Full Cycle Records producer Roni Size. Included in the Reprazent tribe are artists such as DJ Krust, Suv, Die and Flynn and Flora. In an equally durable Bristol trend, the collective has taken the drum 'n' bass format and married it with the deep musical themes of their home town.

Size was born and raised in St. Andrews, Bristol. Kicked out of school when he was 15 years old, he started hanging around the Basement Project in Sefton Park youth centre where they had a Yahama RX17 drum machine. Soon he was playing with the club's midi systems and samplers – electronic gear that was well beyond his price range. This gave him a new lease of life and by 1992 Size had started releasing tracks on the V Recordings record label.

Teaming up with his friends DJ Krust and Chris Lewis, the trio formed Full Cycle Records, funding the new company with money they raised by playing local parties. Releasing their first record, 1992's 'Music Box', by Size and DJ Die, they earned £2,000 from the sales, enough to buy a new mixing desk and sampler for the label. A steady stream of releases followed and they soon attracted interest from the major record companies.

Opting for a distribution deal with Gilles Peterson's Talkin' Loud label in 1995, they released their first album as *Reprazent, New Forms*, in 1997 and immediately became the new ambassadors for drum 'n' bass by winning the prestigious Mercury award.

Rimini During the downturn of the Ibiza scene in the early nineties Rimini filled the gap, being tipped as the next big thing by the music press. Sadly for Rimini, or perhaps wisely, it failed to attract the mass exodus from Ibiza, possibly because Italian prices were considerably higher than those in the Balearic islands although the club prices – around £30 through the door and then an equal amount for a drink – were similar. Rimini's clubs even sounded like their Balearic counterparts, with names such as Paradiso, Ku, Ethos, Peter Pan, Pacha, White Elephant and Cocorico.

Despite being the home of pop-friendly Italo house, Rimini's DJs, which included Flavio, Ricky and Marco Trani, kicked the dance floor into a mad frenzy of Detroit techno and deep US house.

The Italian house scene continued to orbit around Rimini. Meanwhile a developing funky techno scene emerged around the Mafia organisation.

Justin Robertson Hailing from Amersham, near London, Robertson moved to Manchester in 1986. At the time he was listening to hip hop and reggae and a bit of indie music and started going to student nights at the Hacienda. His introduction to house came from Mike Pickering and Martin Prendergast's Nude at the Haçienda.

The Mancunian blend of house and hip hop blew him away and he lost interest in guitar music completely. When acid house took off in London he was originally suspicious, seeing house as an intrinsically northern form of music. 'House had been part of Manchester clubbing for a few years. It was seen as a bit of a northern soul thing. London liked hip hop. Manchester liked house.'

He began running his own clubs such as Jeopardy and Compulsion, which he describes self-deprecatingly as fairly unsuccessful, in the late eighties and started to experiment with his trademark eclectic style. Through reading *Boy's Own* he began to orbit around the Balearic scene.

Taking a job at Eastern Bloc Records, he met Greg Fenton, an Irish DJ who'd recently moved to Manchester. Both DJs were tired of the total dominance of house in the Manchester scene and together they hatched the idea for the seminal Spice club. Deliberately opposed to the rave culture taking over Blackburn at the time, it aimed to preserve the excitement of the early days, to create a small scene, playing all sorts of music and mixing stupid records into their sets – recreating the Larry Levan vibe of New York's Paradise Garage. Inviting DJs such as Rocky, Diesel, Ashley Beedle and Andrew Weatherall from the *Boy's Own* collective to guest, Robertson further attached himself to the Balearic network.

In 1989 he took up a residency at Konspiracy, often confusing the rave-driven punters with his eclectic beats. After briefly playing The Happy Medium, Fenton and Robertson's partnership ended, the former starting a new Friday night-club called Glitter Baby while Robertson began his legendary Saturday night-club, Most Excellent – re-introducing the smiley face logo of Rampling's Shoom. Both were held in a shabby basement venue, called the State, near Manchester's Piccadilly Station. By this time the Haçienda was experiencing one of its frequent closures due to violence and the State was heaving on its first night.

They stayed there for two-and-a-half years and attracted future pop stars such as the Chemical Brothers and Noel Gallagher. Musically, Most Excellent swung from pop house to warped techno, until Robertson killed the beats with a final hour of downbeat Balearic tunes.

After the nights reached overkill, Robertson moved to the Brick House to do a Monday night. His loyal following moved with him. The Spice trail finally ended at the Millionaires club (now the Wiggley Worm). By now the music policy had shifted to New York house.

In 1994 the Balearic scene fractured as a new interest in underground, anti-commercial techno emerged. Robertson followed the techno heads – a move he says lost him a lot of work. His sets began to feature anything that had a disturbing edge to it, such as Wildpitch and Felix Da Housecat records. Meanwhile Loved-Up started the Jolly Roger at Manchester's new gay venue, the Paradise Factory.

Robertson hooked up with John McCreadie and Richard Moonboots to start The Rebellious Beat Box, on the club's top floor, playing anything they wanted – from northern soul to MC5 – and laying the ground for latter-day eclectic DJing of Big Beat, pioneered in London by Heavenly Social.

In the mid-nineties Robertson began a techno night called Sleuth, promoted by Darren Hughes from Cream and returned to his roots in guitar music, charting with his crossover band, Lion Rock.

Rohypnol Rohypnol hit the headlines as the rape drug in the late nineties. A powerful prescription-only sleeping pill, rohypnol appeared on the club scene after the government began restricting other downers such as temazepam (a.k.a. jellies).

Usually taken as part of a cocktail of drugs, rohypnol was used as a downer after taking amphetamine-based drugs such as speed, ecstasy or cocaine at the end of a night. It soon found a more alarming use. Powerful enough to knock someone out, it would leave them conscious enough for physical movement but completely unaware of where they were or who they were with.

A similar pattern developed on both sides of the Atlantic. It would begin with the rapist chatting up a woman in a bar or club. He would then spike her drink. As she started to pass out, he would pretend she was drunk to the security people and kidnap her, knowing she would come to with no recollection of what had happened.

Roland 808, 909 and 303 The evergreen drum unit, the Roland 808 is used by hip hop artists for its distinctive snare sound and gives electro its sharp crisp drum beats. Its sub-bass kick drum sounds, which can be tuned to different frequencies, found a new home in varied-pitch jungle bass drum patterns.

The Roland 909 is responsible for the crisp hi-hat sound in house music. Its snare sound is heavier than the 808 and has been used on a plethora of house tunes.

The irony of the 808 and 909's appeal is that neither drum unit sounds like the instruments they're supposed to recreate. In fact, as attempts to mimic live sounds they're abysmal. Effects such as cowbells sound nothing like their namesake, but are fabulous for experimental electronic music.

The TB 303, a bass unit, was an equally pathetic and notoriously frustrating attempt to synthesise bass sounds, but its contribution to house and techno has been absolutely glorious, largely because of its self-willed determination to randomise data that's been stored in it. The 303 will quite literally write the music for you, one favourite trick being to remove its back-up batteries, wait an hour and turn it on. Presto! 64 random bass patterns at your disposal without so much as playing a note.

The machine behind the bleeps and squelches of acid house, Roland had deleted the model before it began to be used as the seminal sound of dance music. In the late nineties software versions for AppleMac and PCs began to appear. Usually coming in a package of two replica 303s and a replica 808 or 909 drum machine, the packages allowed users to create blinding dance anthems in seconds – the real joy being a random button that transformed whatever the user had programmed into an impossibly complex arrangement.

Without Roland dance music would have sounded completely different.

Run DMC Formed by NYC school chums Joe Simmons, Darryl 'DMC' McDaniels and DJ 'Jam Master' Jay, originally as Orange Crush, they became Run DMC in 1982 and signed to Profile Records. Their first release, 'It's Like That', with its b-side 'Sucker

MC's', scored an immediate underground hit and signposted the birth of modern hip hop. It featured stripped-down drum machine beats and scratching, but ditched the instrumentation of earlier rap releases.

They also promoted the B-boy street image, language and style, which later gained them the first sponsorship deal from Adidas to go to non-athletes. Their debut album, simply entitled *Run DMC* and released in 1984, was the first rap album to go gold.

Their success was further cemented in 1986 when they teamed up with Aerosmith to produce 'Walk This Way'. The rock-rap crossover introduced hip hop to new audiences on both sides of the Atlantic, dislodging the prejudices of guitar fanatics and producing a string of 'we can rap too' copycat guitar bands.

They made a somewhat sorry return to the charts in 1998 with Jason Nevin's hip house remix of 'It's Like That' – a reincarnation with which the band were so happy that they declined to shoot a video and constantly reminded journalists that the track did not represent where Run DMC was at. Still, they made some pocket-money.

Lest we forget:

Reinforced Records
Renaissance
Rezerection
Rising High
Ru Paul

Best we forget:

Raids by the boys in blue

S

Salsa An often under-rated contributor to the dance scene, Salsa and Latin vibes have infused funk and jazz through DJs such as Patrick Forge and informed a swath of house tunes. Salsa continued to exert its influence in pure form at clubs such as Salsa and La Finca, in London, and Jip and Chico's family of clubs in Leeds.

Its attraction and longevity are derived partly from the presence of a large Latin community in the UK and partly from the dancing, which offers intimate physicality in place of the stand-off posture of the house and hip hop scene. Latin venues such as the Mambo Inn in Brixton were legendary for their friendly vibe. The potentially off-putting complicated dance steps are overcome by most clubs offering free dancing lessons as part of the admission price.

Salsoul Created by three brothers, Joe, Ken and Stan Cayre, who had previously gained a reputation for their expertise in the Latin-American music market, the idea for Salsoul was inspired by Joe Bataan, who had crossed Latin rhythms with North American soul traditions in his reworking of Gil Scott Heron's 'The Bottle'.

Launching the label in the seventies, the Cayre brothers simultaneously founded one of the most important outlets for the developing dance market, introducing a new percussive Latin-driven dance sound to New York's gay club scene and to the world. But the label's influence didn't stop with the style of music it promoted.

In 1975 the label copied an idea from DJ and remixer Tom Moulton and released the first commercially available 12in record, the Walter Gibbons remix of Double Exposure's 'Ten Percent'. What had been a three-minute groove was now a twelve-minute dance marathon.

Samplers The arrival of the Akai S1000, the first 16-bit sampler, opened the way for a new breed of pinch-and-mix music. Samplers digitally copy a chunk of music and enable the producer to rearrange it – the type of machine used not being as crucial as it is with drum or bass units such as the Roland 303, 909 or 808.

As a generic technique, the arrival and improvement of samplers enabled producers and DJs to move dance music forward at lightening speed. Samplers revolutionised record production, allowing producers to turn out releasable records from their bedrooms.

As with most new technologies, samplers are getting cheaper and cheaper, enabling a nation of DIY dance producers to purchase bedroom studios for as little as £2,000.

Roger Sanchez A seminal New York-based house producer and DJ, Roger Sanchez's reputation rocketed in the early nineties as a result of his much-hyped DJ sets and record releases such as Logic's 'One Step Beyond', although he kept the world waiting until 1994 to release his first album under the alias of Roger S.

Having already made his mark with seminal soulful garage and house tunes, such as Juliet Roberts' 'Free Love' and 'Caught In The Middle', he set up his own label, One Records, with Eddie Colon and a UK management agency, Indeep, with Marts Andrups.

Sasha Born in Wales and based in Manchester, Alexander Coe a.k.a. Sasha was to become the most recognisable of the house DJ set, largely because he stood out as one of the few DJs that had a face anyone would want to look at. Fitting nicely with an inexplicable Manchester DJ tradition of working in the fish trade (also see Mike Pickering), Sasha was employed as a fish farm worker before becoming a star DJ.

A grade-eight pianist, he made his name pioneering cheesy piano-led Italian house before adopting a more soulful jazzy style on remixes such as Mr Fingers' 'Closer'. After the success of his 'BM:EX Appolonia' record – a reworking of an Italo house white label, he signed to DeConstruction and released 'Higher Ground', while also being signed to Polygram music on a publishing deal.

In 1998 he collaborated in the 2 Phat Cunts project.

Kevin Saunderson The legendary and original techno artists and musical talent behind Reese Project and Inner City, Kevin Saunderson was born in New York but relocated to Detroit in his early teens. Music was literally in his blood, with his mother being a former member of the soul band that would become the Marvlettes and one of his brothers being a member of Brass Connection.

After studying telecommunications at university, he developed a passion for music technology and became a studio doyen, composing and playing all the instrumentation on his songs. His debut release as Reese Project, 'Triangle Of Love' appeared on Juan Atkins' Metroplex label, but he found greater recognition with his next record, 'The Sound'. In 1987 he recorded 'Rock

To The Beat', which was to become hugely influential on the developing techno sound.

Teaming up with Paris Grey to form Inner City, their first single, 'Big Fun', remained unreleased for years until it was rediscovered by chance by a friend looking for material for a compilation album. It became an all-time dance classic.

Saunderson found commercial success through Inner City, with their first album selling more than six million worldwide. He runs his own label, KMS, through Neil Rushton's Network Records. In 1998 he released his long-awaited debut album *E-dancer*, on KMS.

Scandinavia Beyond its 'come on Barbie, let's go party' image, the dance music revolution launched Scandinavia into the vanguard of experimental techno and eclectic music in the mid- to late nineties. Record labels and acts such as April Records, Future 3 and Razmus picked up the UK's break beat culture and morphed it into northern Europe. In the early nineties Scandinavia had already begun to attract media interest, with magazines such as *Mixmag* tipping Nordic beat as the next big thing.

Swedish artists such as Leila K, Papa Dee and Titiyo and labels such as Telegram, Swemix and Sonet promoted a broad-based sound that took in hip hop, house and ragga – developing from an ancestry that went back to Stockholm's obsession with funk in the early eighties.

In the late eighties a wave of hip hop bands emerged and were snapped up by the major companies, ultimately smoothing out the scene and killing it. Acts such as MC Einar and Rockers By Choice produced Danish hip hop and dominated the market. By the end of the decade house emerged with artists such as Sweden's Terry Leigh and DJs such as Denmark's Kung and Tolstrup importing house and electronic music into Scandinavia.

In 1994 Kung established Multiplex to import house tracks and release them on 12in for the Danish market. By the end of the nineties DJs and artists such as Bjorn Svin, Tanea, Daniel, Klaus B and Lab began breaking the new school of techno, while Jet and 360 Degrees led the break beat scene and Opiate broke drum 'n' bass in Denmark. Daniel, Opiate and Svin all secured national radio shows.

Hip hop survives as a small community, hindered from securing venues because of its reputation for covering the walls in graffiti. Clubs such as 47 in Amagh and warehouse parties have succeeded in keeping the scene alive, and a new rougher hip hop sound is now breaking through with artists such MC Clemens, DJ Noise and Pelding turning heads.

Meanwhile downbeat techno has attracted international attention through artists such as Denmark's Future 3. April, Future 3's label, released their first record, 'Boredom', in June 1994. Their initial market was 95 per cent export. Today they're Denmark's most dominant electronic record label.

In October 1997 they started running the April club at Stengade 30 in Copenhagen. This three-floor affair played up-tempo house and drum 'n' bass on the main floor, downbeat on the second floor and freestyle in the cellar. The club acts as a showcase for the Scandinavian scene, breaking new DJs and bands. Since its early days, April has expanded and their club tours now take in London, Berlin and Sweden.

The Scandinavian dance scene is phenomenally segregated and Denmark is still dominated by a strong psychedelic trance scene, with organisations such as Rotunduno and Outpost throwing one-off events and warehouse parties.

Signs of change became evident in the late nineties. Mantra, in Copenhagen, which opened as a trance club in 1993, changed music policy under the direction of Tanea and Kung in 1997. It now plays host to weekly excursions into break beat, drum 'n' bass, deep house and Detroit techno. Meanwhile Organisations such as Deutsche organise gabber nights for a younger crowd.

In Norway DJ Abstract's Super Real club, in Oslo, play deep house and UK disco house while Jazid plays host to anything from Soma to Chemistry and Storm. Mars plays things on a conscious tip, inviting acts such as The Herbaliser to grace its stage.

Domestic media interest in Scandinavia's club scene is now growing and venues are trying to put on dance nights, escaping the more traditional rock fare. This has inspired a wave of promoters to emerge from the woodwork and established nights are having money chucked at them by opposing venues.

In 1995 the Stereo Bar opened in Copenhagen, sparking off a trend of DJ bars and inspiring a wave of new DJs to take up position behind the turntables.

Sch-oom and Shoom The seminal night-club started by Danny and Jenni Rampling in November 1987. Strawberry smoke machines would be on full blast, so seeing your hand let alone anyone else once you were on the dance floor was a chance occurrence. Dancers evaporated into their own world. Groups lost each other for the night, occasionally re-uniting in the smog. Friends would be found with their legs sticking out of the speaker bins, trying to merge with the music in an MDMA-induced frenzy. Punters took to checking the soles of each other's trainers before going in – hoping they would recognise one another at the end of the night should one of them end up head first in a speaker.

Despite its original relaxed atmosphere, the antithesis to mid-eighties élitist clubbing, the door policy became notorious as its popularity grew. The lighting was dominated by a strobe, which became a totem for the crowd: one time people claimed their night had been ruined when Coldcut turned off the strobe because one of them was epileptic.

Reflecting early Balearic eclecticism, the music policy roamed from pop classics, such as John Lennon's 'Imagine', to house. If it fitted it was played.

Permanent smiles decorated everyone's faces. Bumping into a stranger was more likely to result in a hug than the 'you spilt my pint' conflicts of earlier and later periods – not that anyone was interested in pints anyway.

Starting at The Fitness Centre, Southwark Bridge on Saturday nights, Shoom moved to RAW, Tottenham Court Road on Thursdays, the club became rammed beyond capacity with the original Shoomers complaining that acid teds had hijacked their scene.

This was the club that launched the smiley face of acid house in the age of big love. After moving to Busby's it came to an end at The Park, Kensington.

S-Express This was the early UK house project of long-time DJ Mark Moore, a half-Korean, London-club scene personality of the eighties, who had grown through the punk scene of the late seventies to become one of London's dance music champions in the early eighties. S-Express are mostly remembered for their 1988 release of 'Theme From S-Express'. While following releases such as 'Superfly Guy', 'Hey Music Lover' and 'Mantra For A State Of Mind' were successful, the advent of hardcore left S-Express' pop, funk house style behind and Moore moved on to establish Splish records with the backing of Rhythm King Records.

Sex The coy meeting of eyes, shared rhythmic experience on the dance floor and the possibility of going home with somebody new have always fulfilled the expectant attraction of night-clubbing. But sex in the full-on nineties went overground. Of course sex in night-clubs was not new, but it used to be confined to the back room. By the late nineties clubs such as Manumission in Ibiza offered a guaranteed live performance as the promoter and his girlfriend got down to it on the dance floor.

Fetish clubs became the fad for the late nineties, with clubs such as Submission, Skin Two and the Torture Garden pulling in scores of semi clad, fun-loving rubber merchants.

Not wanting to be outdone, regular punters began joining in the fun. Notorious frolics have become part of club-land legend. There's the couple who met at the Kraftwerk stage at Tribal Gathering. The attraction was strong, and after a brief kiss she proceeded to give him oral relief – thereby distracting half of Kraftwerk's audience. Then there's the women who stripped naked at the Time rave and randomly grabbed a partner off the dance floor before straddling him on the speaker stack; or the threesome who held up the toilet queue at the Vinyl Birthday bash . . . and what was that man doing with a camcorder in the next door cubicle? Safe? I don't think so.

Shadow Born and raised in the middle-class suburb of Hayward, San Francisco, California, Shadow became a devoted hip hop fan in the early eighties and started fiddling around with beats while he was at high school. His route to success came from across the Atlantic. Releasing his seminal 'In/Flux' 12in single on James Lavelle's Mo Wax label in 1992, DJ Shadow's symphonic, stripped-down, abstract approach to hip hop had instant impact. If one record alone kick-started the trip hop combination of downbeat hip hop and techno, then it was 'In/Flux'. His subsequent singles such as 'Lost And Found' and 'What Does Your Soul Look Like?' continued developing his eclectic, subtle and highly crafted style. His first album, *Entroducing*, was released in 1996 and *Pre-emptive Strike*, a retrospective, followed in 1998.

Shindig Newcastle's longest-running house club, Shindig's original promoters, Scott Bradford and Scooby, started running a club night in 1992 at Club Afrika. Getting the boot, they hooked up with Shindig's remaining promoters, Rob Cameron and Jim Mawdsley, and moved the night to an old indie venue, The Riverside. After closing for renovation, the venue re-opened in May 1994, with new bars, floors and a spanking new sound system. Starting small, as Shindig's reputation grew the club expanded over the venue's new floors, eventually reaching the full capacity of 1,100 punters.

Skint Records Formed by Damien Harris (a.k.a. the Midfield general) as a sister label to Brighton-based Loaded Records, Skint came about after Harris became frustrated with his attempts to produce house music. 'The Americans do it much better,' he quips.

He began producing dance music that reflected his own culture, combining hip hop, house, dub, rock and anything else that sounded weird. Meanwhile Fat Boy Slim (a.k.a. Norman Cook) had been producing similar material. Harris snapped him up, blagged backing from Loaded and released the first Skint 12in, 'Santa Cruz'.

Harris went on to sign an impressive roster of underground artists including Bentley Rhythm Ace and the Lo Fidelity Allstars. Skint signed a deal with Sony Music at the beginning of 1998, ensuring international distribution while still maintaining independence.

The Skint sound is united in diversity, although the label fits the big beat tag – a title Harris rejects while still running a club night in Brighton called the Big Beat Boutique.

Slam and Soma One of the longest-running and most influential house operations in Scotland, the Slam duo of Orde Meikle and Stuart McMillan ran a series of seminal clubs in Glasgow between 1988 and 1998, culminating in the four-roomed, 2,000-capacity Arches venue.

Starting in 1988 with Black Market, often cited as the club that introduced house to Scotland, they moved on to run the Joy and Atlantis at the Sub club, before settling for six years at the Arches.

Along the way Meikle and McMillan organised the first legal all-night rave in Scotland and started their own label Soma Records, along with other team members Dave Clark, Nigel Hurst, Jim Muotone and Glen Gibbons. As well as producing their own records, such as their classic 'Positive Education' single, the label has broken an impressive roster of artists including Daft Punk. In 1998 Meikle and McMillan withdrew from club promotion to concentrate on developing the label.

DJ Sneak One of Chicago's new school house DJs, Sneak moved to the motor city in 1983, as a 13-years-old Spanish-speaking Puerto Rican. Not understanding the American lingo, the only thing he related to was music.

Tuning into the radio he heard early disco, house, Kraftwerk and Larry Levan – an experience he describes as being the musical equivalent to going to school. He became a graffiti writer and for seven years worked in record stores.

At first he was too young to go to clubs, so he went to underground cellars, such as the Bass Ring, warehouse parties and raves, where DJs such as Derrick Carter cut their teeth. Sneak started playing clubs such as Red Dog and the hugely influential Shelter (where most of the second wave of Chicago DJs played) largely thanks to its open-deck policy, which allowed anyone to have a go on the turntables.

Starting with banging Chicago ghetto tracks, he heard Carter playing new groove and began digging up old disco breaks and sampling them. Instead of using an analogue keyboard Sneak cut up disco samples as if they were analogue.

In the late nineties Sneak moved to Toronto, Canada, where he's been creating a new club scene around the Industry venue.

Solaris The baby of Nick Coleman, Dave Manders and Roscoe had parties in venues such as Westway Studios, London, in 1988, before starting their legendary Sunday night session.

Booking Mike Pickering to play their first night, they established a reputation for playing host to the scene's most respected DJs. Paul 'Trouble' Anderson, Andrew Weatherall, Judge Jules, Graeme Park, Noel Watson, Pete Heller and Harvey all made regular appearances. Going on to promote one-off events under the Kimeta banner, Solaris finally closed in November 1990.

Finding a regular slot on Gray's Inn Road, Solaris became a central London magnet on the Sabbath, despite being located in the then dead City of London and at a time when Sunday night-clubbing wasn't on the calendar.

Soul II Soul Growing out of the two-step scene, where promoters such as Mistri would organise events at Night Groves in Shoreditch, Soul II Soul went on to become one of the late eighties' most successful dance collectives. While the rare groove and then house scenes were pumping out up-tempo dance tunes, two-step music seldom went above 90 b.p.m., but it swung. Soul II Soul's core membership consisted of north Londoner Jazzie B,

Nellee Hooper (a former member of Bristol's The Wild Bunch) and Philip 'Daddae' Harvey.

Working as a collective with collaborations coming from a huge variety of other artists, the band grew out of Jazzie B and Harvey's DJ and PA agency. The Soul II Soul sound system ran a series of warehouse parties, such as The Paddington Dome near King's Cross, before setting up their own venue, where they ran into Hooper. Together they started their seminal residency at the Africa Centre and signed on to Ten Records. Their reputation grew rapidly, aided by Jazzie B's tireless self-promotion on Kiss FM, via T-shirts and two Soul II Soul shops.

Their third single 'Keep On Moving', with Caron Wheeler on vocals, hit the Number five slot in the UK charts, while their debut album, 1989's *Club Classics*, became, as its title suggests, a classic. Via the collaboration of Nellee Hooper, Soul II Soul had married the London and Bristol downbeat scenes.

Over the Atlantic the band had begun to take off in the USA, and their business empire was expanding with breathtaking speed. In 1990 their second album, *Club Classics Volume II*, entered the UK charts at number one, but it failed to impress the critics.

Hooper left the outfit to work with Bristol-act Massive Attack and, despite several other hit singles, the powerhouse of ideas behind Soul II Soul slowly began to grind to a halt as their output became increasingly dominated by soul influences and lost its eclectic crossover appeal.

Soulboys Versus West Enders Dance music has always inspired division as well as unity. Today the divisions are marked by musical taste. In the early eighties it was a question of style and class, as soulboys lined up against West End trendies.

In truth, style magazines such as *i-D* exaggerated the differences. In the early days, at least, black music clubs and warehouses brought previously alien cultures together, football bootboys, dance heads and ragamuffins started hanging out together, united by the quest for the next party and the next high. The unity was short-lived, as dance heads found the frequency of fights among their new mates hard to tolerate.

Spain Alongside the popularity of the Balearic islands, mainland Spain has a formidable reputation for clubbing excess. Having risen in notoriety at the end of the eighties, largely for its bars as well as its clubs, Barcelona and Madrid dropped from popularity in the mid-nineties.

In the late nineties the scene began to rekindle. Friendly, music-loving and up -or-it crowds pack clubs such as the Apollo, in Barcelona, a vast space containing 1,000 screaming ravers and with an open-music policy.

In Madrid Kathmandu caters for leftfield dance music, inviting DJs such as Gilles Peterson, Simon Lee, James Lavelle and Patrick Forge to grace its decks. Further south in Valencia's Route De Baccalau, which translates as the cod-fish road, is in an infamous stretch of clubs that runs down one road outside Valencia.

Clubs such as Chocolate (which is Spanish slang for hashish) and Spook open one after the other, so that punters can keep going for 24 hours – infamously indulging in three day benders, driving from club to club as one closes and another opens around the clock.

Needless to say road safety is not at the forefront of the revellers' minds and by the end of the nineties car accidents reached such high proportions that the Spanish authorities began to clamp down on the partying.

Special Branch Taking their inheritance from the Soul Mafia suburban dance heads of the late seventies and early eighties, Special Branch operated from pubs such as The Royal Oak, and The Swan and Sugar Loaf pub in Tooley Street, where Nicky Holloway would book DJs such as Gilles Peterson, Danny Rampling, Trevor Fung and Pete Tong.

In the mid-eighties Special Branch held an infamous party at the Natural History museum. Brilliant in its inception, the night was dampened by the DJs having to keep the volume down so they didn't disturb the dinosaur bones.

Later parties included the legendary Do At The Zoo bashes, where rare groove, soul and jazz funk gave way to acid jazz and acid house – the former initially being played to an empty dance floor, while Gilles Peterson packed them into the jazz room. The wooden podiums, put there for acid house heads to dance on, got absolutely trashed.

Spectrum and Land Of Oz The first of Paul Oakenfold's legendary Monday nights, Spectrum opened on 11 April 1988 at the 1,500-capacity Heaven. It was dubbed the Theatre Of Madness. The idea of promoter Ian St. Paul, the venue was no stranger to the gay house scene and so was perfect for bringing in the first Summer of Love, although it failed to attract more than a couple of hundred Ibiza veterans for the first month.

On the point of closure, with the two partners close to bankruptcy, the venue exploded, with queues stretching around the block. While Oakenfold and Johnny Walker spun Balearic dance tracks, incredible visuals such as spaceships and snow storms swept across the dance floor.

Upstairs Terry Farley dropped downbeat sounds in the original chill-out area. The arrival of a mass audience fractured the close-knit acid scene and the original crowd grew resentful of the new recruits copying their dance moves, clothing and phrases and necking their drugs. It also brought unwanted media attention.

In August *The Sun* ran an expose on the drug culture at Spectrum and a week later Richard Branson, then owner of Heaven, visited the club to observe for himself. Rather than closing it down, he asked Oakenfold to rename it and take a break for a month.

Given the prevalence of drugs on the gay scene, Heaven could have been no stranger to the antics of this new loved-up straight crowd. Land Of Oz, the renamed Spectrum, ran from autumn 1988 until the end of 1990 and became the location for the first sound clash between the two giants of the north and south house scenes – Heaven and the Hacienda.

Oakenfold, Walker, Mike Pickering and Graeme Park lined up behind the decks, playing one-on-one, each trying to outdo the other with a more choice cut. The night stayed religiously Balearic. When guest DJ Alex Paterson, of the Orb, played 'Telephone Man' by Meri Wilson one night, a confused journalist, Kirk Field, stumbled to the booth to ask him what the fuck he thought he was playing. Paterson replied 'what the fuck I want.'

Land Of Oz became infamous for its queues, where people would meet and swap stories about the illegal parties they'd been to over the weekend. Gossip would revolve around pulling one over the police, getting chased or arrested and the pills people had dropped – while they inevitably necked more in the queue. A fine start to the week.

Speed Properly called amphetamines, speed was the drug of the Northern soul scene and is still one of the most widely used club drugs. In street form it is usually sold as powder crystals and is snorted or injected. The tooth-gnashing effects provide the user with an energy boost and an insatiable appetite for alcohol. Conversely its other effects include a loss of appetite for food, leading the drug to be used as an aid to crash-course diets. Amphetamines, like adrenaline, not only effect the brain but also the heart, lungs and other organs. Deaths from amphetamines have occurred from burst blood vessels in the brain and from heart failure.

Spice Run by Justin Robertson and Greg Fenton as a members-only club on Sunday nights, Spice attracted criticism for élitism, which the club pursued in a conscious effort to deter the rising violence among lads in Manchester clubs. In fact the membership was a ruse to get around the UK's archaic laws, which prohibit dance venues on Sunday nights.

Spice was populated by an extended family, who would congregate early at the Cavern, in Piccadilly. Growing out of its original venue, it moved to Richfield's, off Deansgate, where the membership expanded.

Despite the night achieving legendary status, Robertson and Fenton were forced to close after a year and a half. An attempt to produce a fanzine, following the example of *Boy's Own*, failed dismally after two editions. Robertson binned it after seeing the third draft, which he describes as abysmal.

By this time the music policy had started to adopt an attitude that Robertson simply describes as silly. It was certainly eclectic, spinning Herbie Hancock and The Cure amidst Chicago house tunes.

Spice also initiated inviting guest DJs to play – an unheard of occurrence at the time yet one that has now become as common as muck.

Spiral Tribe Growing out of the London squat and free party scene and based around six key members, the Spiral Tribe shot to prominence as the main force at the Longstock summer solstice festival in 1991 – the biggest free festival in seven years. Working as a loose collective, dressed in black combat gear, with shaven heads and playing harder sounds than other sound systems, they dominated the event.

It was an experience that was to change all their lives, as they set out on the road, from then on living the lifestyle seven days a week and picking up new members such as MC Scallywag on the way.

A trail of festivals were left in their wake, such as Stoney Cross and the White Goddess at Camelford, as they developed an alternative lifestyle, based around psychedelic drugs, tribal techno music and new age belief systems. They adopted the number 23 as their symbol because the world is angled at 23 degrees and there are 23 chromosomes in the human body, and they described themselves as 24 hour 23 people.

In April 1992 they had their first run-in with the authorities, which raided a Spiral Tribe warehouse party in Acton Lane, London. Storming the building by bulldozing the wall of the building, officers rigged up in full riot gear wielded long batons at a peaceful partying mass of 1,000 people. Satisfied with the harm they'd inflicted, the police officers disappeared as suddenly as they'd arrived.

The signs of change were writ large on the wall. Later that year a more wary Spiral Tribe made their way to Avon Free Festival at Castlemorton to join a host of other sound systems. The four-day party that followed became legendary, but in the aftermath the police focused on the Spiral Tribe convoy, tracking their movements and eventually arresting the group at the centre of the collective and impounding the Tribe's vehicles.

The Tribe hit back adventurously by striking at the heart of authority. The Spiral Tribe were convinced Castlemorton had been staged by the authorities. They had been heading for Salisbury and had been diverted to Castlemorton, a green belt area. The police then announced on national TV that a fuse party was happening and was unstoppable, attracting ravers from across the UK. Organising a free party to celebrate the summer solstice at Canary Wharf, the architectural emblem of Thatcher's Britain, 1,000 people made it to the venue before the police had swung into action and sealed the area.

The police were now coming down hard on the techno festival scene and the government was preparing to clamp down on raves through the Criminal Justice Act. Meanwhile the core figures in Spiral Tribe were tried for being a public nuisance and breaching the peace. After a two month trial they were acquitted by an eleven to one majority.

Among the traveller convoys, unity was fracturing and some were blaming Spiral Tribe's confrontational attitude for the backlash. Feeling the pressure, Spiral Tribe moved to Paris in late 1992 to establish themselves in the European free festival movement. By 1993 they were running Teknivals across Europe and moved to Berlin, where they hooked up with the long-running Mutoid Waste Company and squatted a wasteland at the former site of the Berlin Wall on Potsdamer Platz. While some of the tribe moved back to the UK in the late 90s, others took the sound system across the world starting a year long tour of the USA in 1997. The party had started and would not finish.

Star DJs The centrality of DJs to the rave scene, and club culture in general, elevated their status to that of rock stars.

Punters followed big name DJs around the country and it was no longer a question of whether a club was playing the right tunes but who was playing the tunes that mattered – in some cases even if they were playing them badly.

Soon promoters cottoned on to the fact that they could pack their venue, and thereby make a killing, by booking the right name. Naturally DJs also cottoned on to the fact that their name was worth a considerable amount of cash and the big names began charging serious salaries for a two-hour set.

The bean feast really gets going on New Year's Eve, when star DJs tour a number of clubs, taking in as many as five or six bookings and charging £8,000 a session. Promoters have also been known to operate scams, by putting a DJ's names on flyers knowing that it is at least unlikely they'll turn up (sometimes agreeing a £1,000 cut for the DJ).

Even less scrupulous promoters put DJs on their flyers without even attempting to book them. Not that most punters mind. The chances are they won't even notice.

The State A seedy central Manchester venue that rose to prominence as a late-night, post-club venue in the early nineties, The State's heyday began after Justin Robertson's Most Excellent and Greg Fenton's Glitter Baby opened there during one of the Hacienda's frequent closures.

A drab club, spread over two rooms with two bars, Fenton disguised the stained, once-red flock wallpaper in the upper floor with streams of glitter. The downstairs room, an undecorated black hole of a dance floor, dripped with sweat and stunk of poppers. Punters slipped and writhed to the music, while being careful to avoid head-butting the deceptively thin black metal support columns, which inconveniently dotted the dance floor.

The State later played host to FEVA, Manchester's first breakbeat club to break into the mainstream of clubbing – mapping the path that Electric Chair would later follow. Despite its good points, The State was a pit run by dodgy landlords who thought it was a good idea to run only hot water through the taps in the toilets. The punters sucked ice cubes.

Strictly Rhythm Formed by Mark Finkelstein and Gladys Pizarro, who had worked together at Spring Records in 1988, Strictly Rhythm had scored its first underground hit with Logic's anthem, 'The Warning', within six months.

Further releases, such as Scram's 'I Believe' and Raw Power's 'Strings' soon established the label's credibility and they began signing more commercial releases such as 'My Family Depends On Me' by Simone as well as Latin-edged releases such as Rare Arts' 'Boriqua Posse' and hip house forays with Tech Nine's 'Slam Jam'. Revered artists such as Todd Terry and Louie Vegas were by now making regular appearances on the label and George Morel was brought in to provide a more vocal, pop ingredient.

In July 1991 Strictly Rhythm released its first album, *This Is Strictly Rhythm*. Pop success was further ensured when the label signed Reel 2 Real's 'The New Anthem', which they followed with 'Move It'. By 1993 the label had brought DJ Pierre into the fold as a producer to develop the label's output further by adding some of his acidic touch. By 1994 the label had opened subsidiary branches in the UK, Argentina and Holland, while sister imprints Groove On, Groovilicious and the pop-orientated Grand Slam Records were set up.

Claiming awards such as Billboard's number one promotion label in 1995, five times voted independent label of the year by the National Dance Music Awards in the USA and winning Best

International Label in 1996, the label was responsible for yet another club anthem in 1997 when Ultra Nate released 'Free'.

Studio 54 Opened on 26 April 1977 by Steve Rubell and Ian Schrager, who met while dating the same girl, Studio 54 was to become the essential hedonistic and glamorous disco club, setting the standard that others would copy around the globe for decades to come. The venue lived and breathed night-club legends, although its meteoric rise can be partially put down to luck, after Bianca Jagger held a party there. During the evening a couple appeared naked on a white horse. Not one to miss a photo opportunity, Jagger leaped on to the horse and the image was duly captured and reprinted the world over. Within a week of opening, the club was internationally famous.

One of the club's less welcome contributions to club culture was the introduction of fierce door policies, which set the standard for the eighties. The scrum at the door, vying for the attention of doorkeeper Mark Benke or Rubell himself, became more renowned than the club.

Gaining entry was made even more difficult by the whimsical way Benke and Rubell applied the rules: dressing up (or turning up naked) was as likely to get you turned away as let in. One couple who turned up naked on a horse were told their steed could come in but they couldn't. Nonetheless the brutality of the admissions' procedure was effective. Having gained entry, the punters would be driven by a mad euphoria into wild reckless behaviour.

In 1980 Rubell and Schrager were sentenced to three-and-a-half years for tax evasion. Studio 54 struggled on until 1983 when it finally shut and Rubell died in 1989. Although the club closed, the venue remained unchanged and various attempts to re-open it looked like they would come to fruition in 1998, when the London-based club Café de Paris put in a bid to buy the venue.

The Summers of Love 1988-9 Eighty-eight, the first Summer of Love, was the year everyone ditched the confining sharp-suited dress codes of the eighties, let their hair grow and discovered ecstasy. In fact by 1988 Jamie Principle and Farley Jackmaster Funk had been producing Chicago house music for four years, Marshall Jefferson had been using Roland 303s (the distinctive acid house sound) since 1985 and DJ Pierre and Phuture had been producing acid house tunes for 12 months. Farley Jackmaster Funk's 'Love Can't Turn Around' entered the UK charts in August 1986 and Steve 'Silk' Hurley's 'Jack Your Body' followed in January 1987. Graeme Park and Mike Pickering had been dropping house tunes in northern clubs since 1986. Paul Oakenfold had been spinning a 70 per cent house set at his Project club since early 1987 and Derek Boland had been playing a pure Chicago house set at the Blackmarket club night since 1986.

The sharp early eighties look had been replaced by ragamuffin styles and baggy slogan T-shirts by the mid-eighties. In Manchester, lads adopted sports clothes and floppy hairstyles, which *i-D* magazine called Baldricks after the Tony Robinson's *Blackadder* character, in 1986. Also by summer 1988 Oakenfold's Project club and Ibiza reunion parties had been and gone and Danny and Jenni Rampling's Shoom nights were firmly established.

So what did happen in the Summer of 1988? For a start, ecstasy became widely available and acid house clubs exploded. Oakenfold opened Spectrum at the Haçienda, Richard West (Mr C) and Paul Rip's Rip night in Clink Street started on a Saturday night, before overflowing into a Friday and then a Sunday night, to accommodate the house-hungry punters. The Ramplings introduced the smiley face logo on Shoom flyers and London records began marketing acid house as a genre. Nicky Holloway's Trip saw punters sprinting down Charing Cross

Road to try and beat the queues and inevitable lock-out, while warehouse raves sprung up all over the city.

The northern scene kicked off in Manchester, where the Friday Nude night had been mixing house with hip hop beats for some time. On Wednesday 13 July a young DJ called John Dasilva started a new night at the Haçienda called Hot. Soon Laurent Garnier and Steve Williams were playing Virtigo at Legends on Monday nights and the city had three nights spread over the week catering for the ecstasy generation. It became a magnet for clubbers from all over the UK.

While London continued along a more eclectic path, the north became a dedicated house zone. Until now clubbers had usually been content to stay on their own turf. Suddenly people were flying up and down the country to sample the flavour in different cities. The house nation was born.

Parallel to this, and often attracting the same audience, the acid jazz scene sprang up, trying to mix the jazz heritage of DJs such as Paul Murphy with the new energy of acid house. Gilles Peterson's Sunday night sessions at The Belvedere pub, his collaboration with Patrick Forge and Eddie Pillar at Talking Loud And Saying Something at Dingwalls and The Fez, beneath the Great Western Hotel, all packed in punters.

In the Summer of 1988 UK music exploded out of its rare groove and hip hop past, but, as John Dasilva says, the vast majority of people really experienced their first Summer of Love in 1989. By then the media were already calling it the Second Summer – and who were the punters to argue?

If 1988 was the first Summer of Love, then 1989 was when everyone found out about it. E-culture and house music became the national pastime for the UK's youth and everyone went mental, mental – radio rental. The summer of 1989 was a scorcher, the sun-drenched days extending into long balmy evenings. It was the year that raves replaced acid house parties, with seminal events such as Sunrise's White Waltham rave and Energy attracting 11,000 and 20,000 loved-up people.

The recently completed M25 London orbital became an arterial link via which ravers from London and the south-east accessed raves in remote countryside locations. And it was the year of press vilification and hysteria, with *The Sun* announcing that Britain's youth had gone drug crazy – ensuring Britain's youth would do their damnedest to fulfil the prophecy. Ravers loved the attention, scanning the press for reports of their weekend activity, while it inevitably drew howls of condemnation in Westminster, with Douglas Hurd calling for a crackdown and Graham Bright MP laying the ground for his Entertainments (Increased Penalties) Bill.

The police established a national network to monitor raves around Superintendent Ken Tappenden's Pay Party Unit. A series of cat-and-mouse games followed, as the police attempted to intercept convoys of cars heading for industrial spaces, airstrips and farms to dance under the stars. Mobile phones and BT voice banks became tools of subterfuge, as promoters used new information technology to outfox the police – only announcing the address of a party on a dedicated phone number at the last minute. The police responded by spreading confusion among the scene and releasing bogus information about non-existent raves to pirate radio DJs.

Musically the rave scene began to raise the tempo, laying the bed for hardcore as the legion of DJs, booked to play short sets, only spun their most dance floor friendly tracks. Piano-led Italian house burst on to the scene and Clapham Common, London became a spontaneous Sunday meeting point where ravers from all over the south-east would congregate and swap stories about the weekend's parties around ghettoblasters and sound systems.

Meanwhile the Balearic faith was kept alive by the *Boy's Own* fanzine. Run by Steve Mayse, Terry Farley, Andrew Weatherall, and Cymon Eckel, *Boy's Own* became the spokesperson for the non-rave dance scene and the defining viewpoint on music, politics, humour and drugs. It brought together a lasting loose collective of DJs and promoters, while running seminal parties – the first of which was held in spring 1988 in a barn near Guildford, ironically paving the way for later outdoor raves.

In Manchester the opening of the Thunderdome had extended the scene to harder-edged techno and Belgian new beat, while bringing a harder, north Manchester crowd into E-culture. Madchester was born, with dance releases by A Guy Called Gerald and 808 State becoming national club anthems and baggy bands such as the Happy Mondays, the Stone Roses and Inspiral Carpets ushering in an era of flares, floppy hair and tent-sized tops. Meanwhile the infamous Blackburn raves drew in post-club crowds from all over the north.

The third Summer of Love should have come in 1990. By now the acid house scene had given way to mammoth raves and constant media exposure. Dance music had exploded to hitherto unimagined popularity. Acid teds, late arrivals who adopted the clothes and language of the early scene, had invaded. The original Balearic scene reverted to high fashion, black Jonathan Richmond shirts and sharp trousers, while the newly initiated bounced around in purple T-shirts and hooded tops. Ecstasy tablets were everywhere, although they were by now mostly big blobs of speed.

While the raves got bigger and bigger, the house scene witnessed its first of many divides, as the original punters from clubs such as Shoom, Future, Nude, Hot and Land Of Oz drew a sharp line between themselves and mass culture. In Manchester the unity of the first Summer of Love had given way to an increasingly violent and fractured community. The drug gangs had moved in to reap profits from thc ecstasy generation, and the police began clamping down on the clubs, attempting to remove their licenses.

The Haçienda responded by increasing their own policing of events, introducing door searches, turning away undesirable (and some desirable) punters and leading patrols of uniformed police officers across the dance floor. In the end their efforts only succeeded in killing the party atmosphere and the Hacienda was forced to make the first of many closures after a gun was pulled on a doorman.

In the meantime the Jam MC's Konspiracy, based under the Corn Exchange on the northern end of Manchester city centre, had opened. Alongside the original Haçienda crowd, it attracted a harder clientele from the north Manchester estates. Soon the club was being run by gangs who operated the security, controlled the dealing or simply turned up to steal the door takings. In reaction DJs Justin Robertson and Greg Fenton opened Spice, a private members' club that deliberately contrived to keep the 'scally' element out and protect the old scene.

It was a World Cup summer and New Order's 'E For England' had the England team singing a none-too-subtle testimony to ecstasy on the terraces. It spawned a stream of E references in pop tunes. Meanwhile cocaine made a re-entry as the drug of choice. Guitar bands such as Primal Scream, Flowered Up and the Stone Roses, who had little to do with the electronic/disco origins of house, became associated with the scene. Reacting against rave, Balearic-influenced DJs began taking the beats down tempo and ambient nights played whale songs and Brian Eno effects.

In London clubs such as Nicky Holloway's Milk Bar and Sean McClusky's The Brain led the way to promoter-owned venues. Shoom, the original acid house club, closed down.

By this time the authorities had started to take a carrot-and-stick approach to illegal parties. The parliamentary rage against rave had geared up to full swing and in July the Bright Bill became law. Promoters now faced up to £20,000 or six months in jail for organising parties. Meanwhile the first batch of London clubs were granted licenses that allowed people to carry on dancing after 3 a.m. The scene was becoming institutionalised and corporate clubbing was around the corner.

Sundissential Starting in 1996 in Birmingham, Sundissential, a members-only club, immediately attracted attention across the nation for capturing the energy, hedonism and nuttiness usually associated with the early rave years and London's Sunday gay extravaganza, Trade. The latter is no surprise, given that the club would invite Trade DJs, such as Tony De Vit, to play. Not only nutty in attitude, the promoters encouraged punters to turn up in glam, outrageous, fetish and fancy-dress clothing. Building on their reputation, the club spread their mad message by opening nights in Leeds, Plymouth, London and Brighton in 1998.

Sunrise Organised by Tony Colston-Hayter (a flamboyant son of a university lecturer and entrepreneur) and David Roberts, Sunrise became the most celebrated rave organisation of the late eighties. Adopting themes from mid-eighties warehouse parties, such as laying on bouncy castles, Sunrise events were big-production affairs with full-on lighting displays, dry ice and lasers.

Originally calling the nights Apocalypse Now, the first events took place in August 1988. While the Balearic scene were doing their best to protect the scene and keep it out of the by now hysterical media, Colston-Hayter courted publicity and invited ITN cameras down to film his parties.

Renaming the organisation, the first Sunrise party was organised for October, but Colston-Hayter soon felt the backlash of the publicity he'd generated when the police prevented the event from going ahead. Undeterred he calculated that organising parties in London had become impractical. Booking an equestrian centre in Iver Heath, Buckinghamshire, he called the event the Mystery Trip and displayed his considerable organisational skills, arranging for coaches to transport thousands of people to the undisclosed site.

So began a long-running game of cat-and-mouse with the police. The next event, the Guy Fawkes Edition, held on a gasworks wasteground in Greenwich, sold 3,000 tickets but was besieged by police in full riot gear. After attempting to blockade people out of the venue, the police eventually capitulated to the swarm of ravers and allowed the event to start at 5 a.m. DJ Steve Proctor, who until then has been stopped from playing music, turned on the decks and dropped Kraze's 'Let's Get This Party Started'. High on their victory and of course pills, the crowd exploded.

As time went on, increased pressure from the authorities meant that Colston-Hayter had to become increasingly inventive with his organisational skills. Using tricks exploited by warehouse party promotes, he organised nights as members-only events – hiring a lawyer to present the police with a full list of those present when they tried to raid it. Exploiting British Telecom's new voice bank system, he started a messaging service, withholding the address of the venue until the last minute, ensuring that a large enough convoy of cars had gathered to make it impossible for the police to close down the event.

Meanwhile the organisation expanded, with Roberts starting a sister party machine called Back To The Future. By the time of Sunrise 5,000, the organisation had a mailing list of 6,000 people.

The demise of Sunrise followed considerable tabloid press attention and subsequent public and political outcry – something the punters at the time luxuriated in, not realising they were in effect digging the rave scene's grave.

Sunrise's Midsummer Night's Dream party in 1989 attracted 11,000 people to an airstrip in White Waltham, Berkshire. Slipping in among the ravers, tabloid reporters had a field day describing 12-year-old children falling victim to sinister drug dealers. A political backlash was now certain and Colston-Hayter enlisted an old friend, Paul Staines, to organise a response. A right-wing anarcho-capitalist, Staines set about establishing the Freedom To Party campaign, claiming that Sunrise, in the best traditions of capitalism, was merely recognising that there was a demand for its product and was simply satisfying that demand. Prime Minister Margaret Thatcher was clearly not convinced.

Under continual pressure, Sunrise's last event, on New Year's Eve 1990, ended in disaster as the landlord of the venue pulled out at the last minute and Colston-Hayter was forced to send his ticket holders to Biology and Genesis's party.

Swingbeat Emerging in the early nineties, when it inspired the usual plethora of compilation albums, swingbeat has its origins in the late eighties and the innovative work of Harlem-based DJ Teddy Riley. The music combines Riley's hip hop past with modern soul, producing melodic, up-beat dance music. It quickly became known as swingbeat, although it also attracted the New Jack Swing moniker. While the sound failed to catch on with the hip hop, house or underground soul communities, it had strong commercial appeal and Riley found his services being used on all manner of remixes.

Artists such as TLC, SWV, Mary J. Blige and Jodeci took the sound into the charts, while swingbeat clubs attracted young audiences to tacky venues. Ultimately swingbeat suffered the same fate as P-Funk in the early eighties and has been smoothed out and consumed into mainstream pop music – informing the bland soul of boy and girl bands. Needless to say this has little in common with the original sound.

Lest we forget:
Shut Up and Dance
Smith and Mighty
Smoke Machines
Sol Y Sombre
Stereo Mcs

Best we forget:
Sandal trainers
Sesame's Treet
Smiley T-shirts
Sports Wear and Sporty Spice
Stage diving

Taboo Infamous for its up-for-it, flamboyantly dressed punters, Leigh Bowery and Tony Gordon's mid-eighties London club, Taboo at Maximus, Leicester Square, took gay clubbing themes out to the straight community. Glammed-up gays and transvestites mingled with dolled-up babes, high-fashion Japanese girls and sharp-looking dudes. The music policy slipped from hi-NRG to mid-eighties disco, breaking cultural boundaries and paving the way for the house explosion of the late eighties and glam clubbing of the early nineties. Plastered in thick make-up to the point of being unrecognisable, Bowery's costumes alone were enough to ensure media interest. Equally notorious was the club's door policy. Mark, its famous doorkeeper, would happily keep celebrities such as Jean-Paul Gaultier waiting in the rain.

Bowery died in 1994 but not before his fame and fashion sense had made him an international star. Copycat dressers in New York, known as Club Kids, adopted Bowery's style and by 1988 were being paid as much as $1,000 by promoters just to turn up and be seen at their clubs.

Infamous NYC club glitterati such as Michael Alig, Julie Jewels, Michael Tronn, Mathu, Zaldy and Keoki all paid homage to Bowery as the original.

Tackhead Although Tackhead officially formed in 1987, the band had existed in a previous incarnation in the USA as the backing band for the seminal early hip hop releases of the Sugar Hill record label. Keyboard and percussionist Keith LeBlanc, bass player Doug Wimbush and guitarist Skip MacDonald were responsible for flare-shaking music on anthems such as 'Rapper's Delight', 'The Message' and 'White Lines'.

In 1984 they were invited to London by Adrian Sherwood and Mark Stewart and became an essential part of the On U Sound record label. Stewart introduced them to his fellow Bristolian Gary Clail and brought a dub element into their work, while the emerging popularity of hip hop in London and Bristol conferred star status on the trio.

Teaming up with Clail on vocals they released 'Tackhead Tape Time' in 1987, followed by 'Friendly As a Hand Grenade' in 1989. Returning to the USA they released a dance/rock crossover album, *Strange Things*. The project failed, but the band had already achieved the accomplishment of being part of both the early days of hip hop and the emerging Bristol sound.

Talkin' Loud And Saying Something Gilles Peterson, Patrick Forge and Eddie Pillar began their legendary acid jazz Sunday sessions at the original Dingwalls in Camden Lock, London in 1986. Live bands such as the Brand New Heavies, Galliano and the Jazz Renegades played sets between DJ sessions. Packed with hot, sweaty, spinning bodies, the sessions captured the energy of the house scene and set it to jazz beats.

The Sunday session finally came to a close when the venue

was closed for redevelopment, with the last record to spin on its decks, Sly And The Family Stone, 'It's A Family Affair', being thrown into the crowd. The record was caught by a young aspiring DJ, Simon Lee, who was later to form a nu-disco outfit called FAZE Action. Peterson went on to form his own record label, Talkin' Loud, while Pillar formed Acid Jazz Records and in the mid-nineties opened The Blue Note night-club. Forge went on to become one of London's most ubiquitous DJs.

Tech House Tech house is an abstract, minimalist and funky derivative of house and techno. Some people credit the name to Mr C, although he vehemently denies this despite making mix tapes called techno house and tech house as early as 1991, and The End certainly hasn't held back from promoting the term. The music combines psychedelic and techno sounds with house grooves, electro and break beat and classically is pitched at 120-140 b.p.m.

It's eclecticism means the term can be applied to a broad range of music, and it is perhaps better defined by its adherents and the clubs that play the music rather than by artists or record labels. Tracks such as 'Someone' and 'The Blue Hour' by Killer Loop (a.k.a. Mr C and Layo Paskin), 'Flash' by Stacey Pullen, 'The Drop' by Hot Lizard and 'Agoraphobia' by Kenny Larken are classics. Nights devoted to tech house are few and far between, but Sub-terrain at The End and the more reclusive Wiggle and Heart and Soul are dedicated to the sound.

Technics Versus Vestax The seminal DJ turntable, often copied but never repeated, the Technics SL1200 is perfect for DJ tricks such as mixing, scratching and rewinds, largely because of the unfussy functionalism of its design. Developed in the early seventies, Technics designed the SL1200 for home use as a hi-fi turntable.

Towards the end of the decade they tweaked the motor and made some minor design changes to the casing, and released the more common SL1200 mark II and SL1210 mark II, which is the same model except in black rather then silver. As a design it has proved to be unsurpassable, the only close challenge coming from the Vestax turntable in the late nineties. Created specifically as a DJ turntable, the Vestax built DJ tricks into the design, so that most of the operations carried out by manually spinning the record on a Technics could be operated by flicking a switch on the Vestax. The design was intended to revolutionise DJ culture, but the jump was too great for many DJs, who were used to getting their hands dirty and making direct contact with the record.

Techno Inspired by the mid- to late eighties house and garage club scenes of New York and, more directly, Chicago, techno has its roots in the motor city of Detroit. Artists such as Kevin Saunderson, Derrick May and Juan Atkins took the developing dance sound and married it with influences such as Kraftwerk, The Human League, Gary Numan and electro.

Developing the Detroit sound through record labels such as Transmat, Metroplex, Planet E and Red Planet, the music is said to have first attracted the name techno in an article in *The Face* in 1988. Detroit's automotive industry was by this time in a downward spiral of decline and while house provided hedonistic escape, techno reflected a backdrop of urban decay. Detroit also lacked the club scenes of the Big Apple and Chicago.

Techno was at once darker, more industrial and more cerebral than house. Obsessed with automation and the mutation of sounds, the formula they developed is capable of producing storming four-four dance anthems, dark electronic hip hop and emotional, post-club ambient landscapes.

As with house, techno has found its ideological home in Europe, where record labels such as Warp and R&S built a support base among young clubbers who weren't satisfied with formulaic house music. Its fascination with pushing the limits of technology to create new and weirder noises means techno has a breathless capacity to reinvent itself.

Danny Tenaglia An Italian-American and native New Yorker, Danny Tenaglia entered dance music through the early disco boom, playing his first gig at the age of 13 at a local club in Bayside, in the Queens area of the Big Apple. He was drawn into house and techno music through the work of artists such as David Morales and Kevin Saunderson. In the early nineties, his profile grew alongside a batch of New York DJs such as Junior Vasquez (with whom he was to develop an acrimonious relationship) – although Tenaglia isn't slow to point out he's been doing it for longer than most.

Resident at New York's legendary Twilo club, he moved to the equally legendary Tunnel in the late nineties after the promoter Phil Smith booked Vasquez to play the Twilo.

His popularity in the UK and Europe remained huge, although his last-minute cancellation of a night at The End in London prompted the venue to hold a free-entry night, which they dubbed Who Needs Danny Tenaglia?

Todd Terry Occasionally referred to as God, Todd Terry, a formative house DJ and producer, earned his stripes playing hip hop and house at parties in New York. Notching up classics such the Todd Terry Project's 'Bongo (To The Bat Mobile)', which prefigured acid house, his many aliases such as Giggles, Fascination, LA Girls and Black Riot obscured him from view on a string of early releases that were to inform the development of house.

For someone who played a crucial part in dance music's history he has remained resolutely humble.

Thunderdome An early and short-lived house club in Miles Platting, Manchester, the Thunderdome opened its doors in 1989. Attracting a more local, white working-class crowd than Nude and Hot at the Hacienda, it did a great deal to break house music in the rainy city.

Ultimately the club suffered from the violent tendencies of its punters, and closed after a mere six months. While the rest of the city basked in the Summer of Love, the Thunderdome revealed a more sinister future that awaited the city's dance culture.

Titanic Set in a two-floored, flock-wallpapered underground dining/conference centre, between 1982 and 1984 the Titanic, alongside The Language Lab and White Heat and The Wag, provided early eighties London with its first rap/hip hop experiences. In fact the music policy was eclectic, with soul and disco also making it on to the dance floor.

DJs such as Cyberman span grooves ranging from The System's 'In My System', the Valentine Brothers' 'Money's Too Tight To Mention', Herbie Hancock's 'Rocket', 'Grandmaster on the wheels of Steel', Melle Mel and the Furious Five's 'White Lines', Prince Charles' 'Who's Taking All The Money?' to Indeep's 'Last Night A DJ Saved My Life', while the crowd sweated, span and body popped. Meanwhile house and guest rappers and toasters such as Man Friday practised early lyrical licks such as 'everybody on the floor, it's what you paid your money for' and 'titanic, don't panic, go-a-go-a-go frantic'. On-stage entertainment came in the form of arc-welding, sound clashes with rival systems and freaky fashion shows. One of the more bizarre side-shows came from the resident croissant stall, operated by a white-suited chef. As an added bonus punters were given a free cheese croissant on entry – these were indeed the days of innocence.

Other early hip hop clubs included The Rock Box in Old Street. One of London's original hip hop nights, this was where Dizzy Heights, Nutriment, Sir Drew and The Untouchable Crew did the honours, rapping and scratching their way through early US releases. Meanwhile Shady Grove, an old skool jam in Tottenham, saw Cutmaster Swift, DJ Pogo and Cosmic Jam honing their skills.

Pete Tong Born in Dartford, Kent in 1960, Pete Tong's first DJ booking was at a friend's wedding when he was 15 years old. Around the same time he started running gigs, booking local bands and clearing profits of £300 a time.

Hearing soul music through Robbie Vincent's Radio London show, his musical tastes veered towards black music and he started playing out as part of the Kent soul Mafia, buying himself a mobile disco after leaving school.

Between 1979 and 1983 he secured his first steady job working with *Blues and Soul* magazine as the features editor, until he joined the newly formed London Records as A&R manager.

By 1988 he had set up his own dance label, FFRR, under the umbrella of London, signing dance acts such as Salt 'n' Pepa, the Cookie Crew, Steve 'Silk' Hurley, Lil' Louis and D Mob.

Meanwhile he had embarked on a career as a radio DJ, initially appearing in his youth on Radio Medway, he moved on to do occasional shows on Radio London during the early eighties. In 1984 he joined Radio Invicta in Kent, presenting his own soul show and in 1987 he moved back to Radio London and then on to Capital.

In January 1991 he went to BBC Radio One to present the Friday night dance show, securing a residency that would last throughout the decade.

Tonka Originating from Cambridge, the members of the Tonka sound system had a heritage that spread back to the late sixties and early seventies. Tonka were there, from parties at Grantchester Meadows in 1969 through hip hop warehouse jams to acid clubs, Glastonbury and their infamous free parties on Brighton beach, where punters would thrash to the music until dawn broke over the waves.

Trade The most important all-night after-club in London, Trade famously attracts hordes of muscle-bound, stripped-to-the-waist party people, who sweat and stagger to relentless nu-NRG and techno. The brainchild of long-time promoter Laurence Malice, the club based itself on European lifestyles, where venues such as Space in Ibiza opened and closed later. Starting at four on Sunday morning and closing at one in the afternoon, Trade caters for the mostly gay, up-all-weekend and having-it-large club scene. The punters pour into Turnmills, in Farringdon, having already worked their bodies into a suitably groovy mood at other venues such as Heaven.

A particular favourite with muscle Marys, the way to stand out in Trade is to keep your clothes on, if you can stand the heat. Otherwise get your nipples, and any other body parts that grab your fancy, pierced and get your tits out while your muscles ripple to the nu-NRG. A legion of DJs including Paul Newman, Trevor Rockliffe, Smokin' Jo and Sister Bliss cut their teeth there. Sadly Trades' most legendary DJ, Tony De Vit, died in 1998.

Train Spotters Ever-present night-club creatures, train spotters live a vampire-like existence, crawling out of their vinyl-strewn dwellings shortly after sun down and only ever seen by day harassing the staff in a suitably unfriendly record shop.

Congregating in small packs around DJ booths in night-clubs, their necks strained over the top of the booth's walls, eyes squinting through thick spectacles (the result of too many nights straining at tiny print on rotating record labels), they nod to themselves knowingly as they fake instant recognition of the first beat of the DJ's latest selection.

If only train spotters were like this. Unfortunately their social habits are far more oppressive, as they chew your ear on the dance floor all night, rhetorically asking you what a tune is before telling you the answer and smugly leaning back, arms folded, with a 'you see, I was right' grin on their face. Frankly we couldn't give a toss – we're trying to dance here mate.

Trance Developing out of the psychedelic culture in Goa, the roots of trance go back to the early electronic experimentalism at the infamous beach parties of Anjuna and Vagator. Here DJs such as William Orbit cut, looped and added drum machine patterns to eighties electronic music, pillaging sources from anything appropriate – from Bronski Beat to the Psychedelic Furs, The Pet Shop Boys and Cabaret Voltaire.

The DJ most credited with developing the Goan sound of psychedelic trance in the late eighties was Goa Gill. The music has evolved into a furious techno-influenced, four-four, ambient, chemical-induced throb. It has its own fiercely independent culture, infused with spirituality drawn from India and the psychotic effects of their chosen drug.

Of all dance cultures, the Goan-inspired trance movement has most faithfully stuck to its anti-establishment roots. For them it's about the music, vibe and culture – and not about money. This doesn't mean that trance nights have not flourished and made money. Escape From Samsara and Otherworld, at The Fridge, and record labels/party organisations such as Return To The

Source, Blue Room, Dragon Fly and Kundalini have managed to thrive. Famously Return To The Source have held nights where they've attempted to take their audience on a journey through their Chakras, and have invited in shaman to cleanse venues before events. Star DJs have emerged from the scene, such as Yazz, Lol, Tsuyoshi Suzuki, Sid Shanti, Dino Psaris and Mark Allen.

Education, globalism and spiritualism run deep in the trance scene – themes that notoriously came together with 1987's Party for Tibet in the Brixton Academy. The event united clubbers around the world by having DJs play the same song at the same time across the globe.

Trax Records The original Chicago house record label, Larry Sherman's Trax had a roster of artists that reads like the roll-call of the heroes of house. Releasing early classics such as Jamie Principle's 'Baby Wants To Ride', Mr Fingers' 'Beyond The Clouds' and Mr Lee's 'Pump Up Chicago', the record label's stature became huge, despite it being based in a disused warehouse.

The Trip, Made on Earth and Sin Nicky Holloway's legendary night in the Astoria on London's Charing Cross Road, The Trip opened its doors on 4 June 1988. It extended acid house to an inner city, more socially and racially mixed crowd. Naturally it also made room for the media to move in.

Ecstasy and Trips were everywhere and when the club turfed the still-up-for-it crowd out at 3 a.m., spontaneous street parties would erupt, blocking the streets of central London.

After a brief incarnation as Made on Earth, Sin, the heir to Trip, began at the same venue in autumn 1989. Promising to be a rave within a club, at a time when raves were frequently being busted, it immediately attracted mile-long queues, desperate to gain entry but frequently finding themselves turned away to seek out more dubious entertainment in one of Charing Cross Road's less salubrious drinking haunts.

On nights when Energy or Sunrise weren't happening, Sin would turn away literally thousands of punters. Despite heavy security searches, the club attracted a loyal following by promising guest DJs such as Todd Terry, Frankie Bones, Fast Eddie and Lil' Louis Vega.

Trip Hop A general term for downbeat music that rebelled against the ever-faster increase of beats per minute of the house and rave market of the early nineties. Used to describe the use of hip hop beats, dub bass lines and ambient chords and samples, the trip hop moniker began being used in the music press and style magazines after it had been coined by *Mixmag* journalist Andrew Pemberton.

While it gained popularity, the pioneers who produced, recorded and collected the music despised the term. James Lavelle, whose Mo Wax record label and That's How It Is club night were instrumental in developing the music, sneered at the term. Moonshine Records produced a series of albums called *This Ain't Trip Hop*, which complied trip hop classics while sticking two fingers up at industry attempts to pigeon-hole the sound.

Record labels such as Ninja Tune, Pork Productions and Dorado and artists such as Fila Brazilia and Howie B developed the UK sound. The music also found unlikely collaborators such as Kruger and Dorfmeister from Austria. Trip hop had a natural affinity with the Bristol sound of artists such as Massive Attack, Tricky, Neneh Cherry and Portishead.

Despite its unpopularity, trip hop has continued to be used as a term for describing a broad area of music that is otherwise unclassifiable.

Lest we forget:
Table Dancing
Ten City
Torsos (naked)
Trans Global Underground
Tummy Touch Records

Best we forget:
2 Unlimited
2 Unlimited
2 Unlimited
2 Unlimited
2 Unlimited

UK Disco House The UK tradition in producing disco house goes back to the late eighties and artists such as Dave Lee (a.k.a. Joey Negro), although it experienced its largest revival in the late nineties, with acts such as FAZE Action, Basement Jaxx and the Tummy Touch record label pushing a new Balearic attitude and chilling the dance floor to thudding disco beats.

Meanwhile an influx of French disco-orientated house flooded on to the market, launching acts such as Bob Sinclar, Daft Punk and DJ Dimitris from Paris, who regularly appeared at the Scaramanga parties in Brixton, south London. Meanwhile Nuphonic Records launched their night, Gumbo, in summer 1998, attracting the cream of London's club scene to sweat it out to FAZE Action's long slow-building and groove-ridden sets.

UK Garage This is the least objectionable title bestowed on London-based garage music, other names for the genre including the media-hyped speed garage, gangsta garage and plus eight.

UK Garage takes the soul, funk and disco four-four beats of US musicians such as Todd Terry, Todd Edwards, Armand Van Heldon and Masters At Work and adds London influences.

Ragga-inspired MC chants and deep sub-bass lines, borrowed from drum 'n' bass, are thrown in the mix, and the tempo is pitched up. Names on the UK garage scene include Matt Jam Lamont, Karl Tuff Enuff Brown, Grant Nelson, 187 Lockdown and the Dreem Teem.

According to the 'official' version, UK garage grew out of Timmy Ram's 1991 Sunday after-club in the Elephant and Castle, where DJs such as Matt Jam Lamont spun deep New York grooves – in the process pulling in converts from the house and drum 'n' bass scenes. Meanwhile Rhythm Doctor's Feel Real at the Gardening club, which took over from Moist, introduced the concept of MCs chanting over the top of garage grooves. UK record labels, such as Nice 'n' Ripe, picked up on the New York signatures of stripped-down funky bass loops and steady drum patterns, and developed a UK version.

By summer 1997 speed garage was slipping off everyone's tongues as if they'd invented the term. Nigel Benn swapped his gloves for a pair of turntables and released a compilation album, and nights such as Twice As Nice were packed with smartly dressed punters, who attracted attention with flashy displays of wealth, giving the music yet another name – champagne garage. The more the merrier, I suppose.

Underground This ubiquitous term used to describe any type of music is especially popular among DJs who play the same tunes as everyone else but opt for the obscure dub-plate white label remix.

Underground garage, underground house, underground jungle and underground hip hop DJs are as common as breathing. After a while you yearn for someone to describe themselves as a crap pop tune and handbag disc jockey. Which begs the question – if underground is so underground, how come so many people play it?

Underworld Consisting of Karl Hyde (lyrics, vocals and guitar), Rick Smith (programmer) and DJ Darren Emerson, and linked to the Tomato multimedia project (which was founded by Hyde in 1991), Underworld merit a mention on the strength of their 'Rez' and 'Born Slippy' single releases alone. Ironically neither single features on the band's two albums, 1994's *Dudnobasswithmyheadman* and 1996's *Second Toughest In The Infants*.

The band became influential not only through their recorded releases but also their significant contributions to the direction UK dance music would take with their seminal live performances.

Clocking up remixes for artists such as St Etienne, Björk, Simply Red and Sven Vath, the band will be remembered for summing up the mood of 1996 with the 'lager, lager, lager' refrain of 'Born Slippy'. The single had in fact been released a year earlier, but on its re-release sold more than 500,000 copies in the UK while reaching the top ten in Italy, Australia and Belgium.

Alongside Tomato Underworld have also been prolific creators of advert sound tracks – perhaps a less worthy but more profitable occupation. Their third album is scheduled for release in 1999.

Universe The original organisers of Tribal Gathering, Universe found themselves locked in a legal wrangle in the late nineties and therefore the subject of much media gossip.

Paul Shurey, Roger Spurrell and Rob Vega began organising raves in the West Country in 1989. Gaining their reputation through word of mouth (they had a strict 'no-press' policy), by 1992 their one-off parties were attracting crowds of 11,000.

In April 1993 they organised the first Tribal Gathering in Warminster, Wiltshire (25,000 attended) followed by the first Big Love party in August. By the end of the year the team separated. Shurey teamed up with Ian Jenkinson and opened Final Frontier, a regular club night at the now-defunct Club UK.

The Criminal Justice Act made raves unviable in the UK, so Tribal was moved to the old Munich airport in Germany for 1994. Universe however were determined to find a way of holding legal events in the UK. This they did by joining with the Mean Fiddler organisation (promoters of Reading and Phoenix festivals) in 1995.

After three successful years of organising Tribal Gathering and club nights, Universe pulled out of the partnership. A disappointed Mean Fiddler immediately issued an injunction stopping Universe from using the Tribal Gathering name.

In 1998 Tribal Gathering was renamed Universe 98 – billed as a weekend long rave at Knebworth. Beck was booked to headline and, in the Universe tradition of luring reclusive acts on stage, they've persuaded Atkins' Model 500 to play. Their only previous gig was in front of 75 people in Detroit, making the 60,000 at Knebworth a considerable leap.

Meanwhile Mean Fiddler hooked up with the super-club Cream to present their own mega event, the Creamfields, two weeks earlier. In the end Creamfields squeezed Universe out of the market.

While most of the dance community sympathised with the Universe camp, they proved not to be strong enough to take on Mean Fiddler. By mid-1998 Paul Shurey had distanced himself from the Universe to concentrate on Tribal Gathering.

Lest we forget:
Underground Resistance and Mad Mike Banks
United Future Organisation
Urban Records
UV lighting
u-Ziq

Vapour 98 The fruit of the loins of Marcus Weedon and the Riki Tik Productions team, Vapour is a celebration of the cream of the UK's independent dance record labels. Conceived as a fluid touring showcase, the music outlook is eclectic, reflecting the diversity and energy of dance culture. Labels involved include Nuphonic, Concrete, Wall Of Sound, Warp, Grand Central and Athletico. Their first event in London was a storming success.

Junior Vasquez Beginning his career in dance music as a reluctant hired dancer at Larry Levan's Paradise Garage in New York, Junior Vasquez (a.k.a. Donald Matern, born in 1946) was soon attracted to DJing and started working in record shops such as Downstairs Records, where he first met Shep Pettibone. Building his status as a DJ through playing house parties and clubs, he started organising his own club nights, such as Heartthrob, at the Funhouse, the Bass Line club, before starting the legendary Sound Factory in 1991.

Adding plenty of gimmicks to his sets, such as throwing in live samples on to his tribal house music and appearing from behind his decks to give people flowers, a mythology soon developed around his sets, attracting stars such as Madonna to his nights.

An army of faithful black and Latino, mostly gay followers would dance their pants off to his idiosyncratic style, which would drop the volume of a song down to zero or chuck 'The Stripper' in the mix without warning.

The Sound Factory suddenly closed, Vasquez moved briefly to The Tunnel and the Palladium, before settling at the Twilo in late 1997. Releasing records such as 'X', 'Get Your Hands Off My Man' and 'Nervaas' through Tribal Records, his reputation in Europe began to explode, despite his reluctance to play any clubs apart from his own, which barred him from playing to his European fan base.

By the time Vasquez finally made it to the UK, a by now cynical audience greeted him with a lukewarm reception.

Sven Vath The best known of Germany's techno DJs, Sven Vath started to DJ at his father's bar, The Queen's Pub, playing old disco tunes. His early influences included electronic music by artists such as Tangerine Dream, Holger Czukay and Jean Michel Jarrre and he played his first gig at the Dorian Gray club in Frankfurt when he was 18 years old.

In the eighties he became front-man for Euro dance pop band The Off and had a hit with 'Electric Salsa (Baba Baba)'. Splitting from the rest of the band, who went on to become Snap!, his former tastes were blown away by the house explosion in 1988.

Opening the Omen club later that year, he gained his reputation playing ambient house and releasing tracks such as 'Barbarella', which used Jane Fonda samples from the cult film of the same name.

In 1991 he set up three record labels under the umbrella of Eye Q Records (Harthouse, the Eye Q imprint and Recycle Or Die), but the project was to fail after the company moved to Berlin in 1997 and went bankrupt, eventually being sold off as separate parts. Vath signed to Virgin and released his *Fusion* album.

V Festivals Bestowing the unlikely venue of Chelmsford, in rural Essex, with rock credibility, the V Festivals are run by a collaboration of some of the UK's largest gig promoters: SJM Concerts, Metropolis Music, DF Concerts and MCD. Uniting north and south, the V festivals offer easy accessibility by running a parallel event in Leeds, with exactly the same line-up playing both venues: Chelmsford's Saturday line-up plays Leeds on Sunday, and vice versa.

V started organising indie-based events during a period when other festivals were becoming more dance orientated. The result was a deliberately civilised festival that resembled a relaxed family occasion compared with the now familiar lunacy of other events such as Tribal Gathering and Glastonbury. In 1997 V introduced a dance tent to reflect the now mainstream position of dance music. The Chemical Brothers, Propellerheads, Daft Punk and Bentley Rhythm Ace ensured the mayhem commenced.

Vicks Alongside the more ridiculous antics of the early nineties rave scene, such as wearing sanding masks, white gloves and sucking dummies, the toytown and happy-hardcore set adopted a new pharmaceutical treat to accompany the buzz of their, by this time dodgy, ecstasy tablets. Vicks VapoRub and nasal sticks, rammed deep into nostrils like tusks, became dance floor necessities, supposedly having a heightening effect on the drugs.

In a period when club culture wasn't exactly loved up, Vicks introduced the touching spectacle of mutual body-rubbing, as stripped-to-the-waist geezers dabbed the decongestant on each other's backs, necks and chests – not an easy or pleasant job when the recipient was drenched with sweat.

Lest we forget:
V Recordings
Venus
Venus Rising
Vinyl being replaced by CDs

Best we forget:
Velcro trainers
Visible pants and beltless baggy jeans

The Wag Destined to become the last refuge of mods and indie kids in the nineties, The Wag was pivotal in developing dance music in the UK. Based in Chinatown and formerly called Whiskey A Go Go, it had been responsible for ruining many a punter's night.

It was re-launched as The Wag in the early 1980s, when a new breed of DJs such as DJ Hector were installed to transform the venue from being a sad drinking joint to one of London's hippest clubs.

Becoming home to the seminal Blackmarket nights, which led the club scene through hip hop, rare groove and into house, The Wag became the venue of the eighties. The door policy, reflecting the club élitism of the period, was notoriously fickle, as Winston the doorman turned people away at a whim. By 1988 The Wag was playing host to Love, the first legal night in London to gain a late-night license, until 4 am, rather than 3 am.

In variance to the norms of the acid house scene, and in contradiction to its name, Love maintained the strict door policies of earlier Wag nights.

Wall Of Sound Mark Jones and Marc Lessner first met in the mid-eighties at the Special Branch functions in Tooley Street,

London, where Lessner sold records and Jones projected visuals. Following Nicky Holloway and co. to the legendary soul weekenders, through which they came into contact with the early acid house and Balearic scene, by 1988 Jones found himself projecting visuals at Danny Rampling's Shoom nights.

Jones and Lessner reunited in the early nineties when Lessner employed Jones to work for him at his Soul Trader distribution company. Finding common musical interests – they shared a love of dance music as well as rock acts such as Led Zeppelin, the Monkees and Phil Spector – they used their contacts in the music industry to compile an early trip hop compilation album, *Give 'Em Enough Dope*.

Taking their name from Spector's production style, they established Wall Of Sound Records, aiming to revive and update the eclectic Balearic spirit and jazz influences of Special Branch scene. Signing their own acts such as Mekon and the Wiseguys, the label came to represent the blueprint for trip hop and big beat and launched artists such as Jon Carter and Derek Dahlarge into the limelight.

Further signings such as the Propellerheads, who gave the label their first top 40 UK chart hit with 'Spybreak', have secured Wall Of Sound as a cutting-edge, experimental, independent dance label. Meanwhile their excursions into club land through the Back 2 Mono nights acted as showcases for the label's musical diversity.

Warehouse Parties While official venues such as Camden Palace, The Venue, The Wag and the Hippodrome opened up to the developing dance scene in early eighties London, punters and promoters were frustrated by license restrictions and the pop orientation of much of the music.

Sound systems such as Norman Jay's Shake and Finger Pop, Mastermind, Dirtbox, Nicky Holloway's Special Branch, the Grey

Organisation and Graham Ball's Westworld, began organising warehouse parties in weird and wonderful venues. Industrial spaces such as a huge hangar in Battlebridge Road, disused hospitals (the most central being in Golden Square, Soho), defunct department stores (such as a two-storey affair in King Street and Whitley's in Queensway) and even London Zoo were dressed up and put to new uses. Bizarre venues such as a vast space-age complex under the Little Venice roundabout on Westway, used by Giles Cherry and Grant Haley for one memorable party, were transformed into drive-in clubs.

In the absence of sound systems large enough to fill the cavernous spaces, punters whacked up their car stereos, transforming the events into a thousand small parties. People flitted between cars, sharing spliffs, speed and poppers and re-stocking with cans of beer from the illegal bar.

Themes such as Johnny Davis' tongue-in-cheek roller disco in King Street were the order of the day. Cadir Gery's Drive In Demolition Derby, in Lotts Road, Chelsea had spot-welder Tom Dixon transforming a Renault 4 car into a forklift truck.

By the mid-eighties, One Nation were pumping out the funk in Goswell Road, Westworld were erecting fairground attractions at their raves and Mutoid Waste were pushing the boundaries of sensibility with their squatter-mentality DIY affairs. Decorating their venue in futuristic themescapes such as Mad Max parties, they introduced London to all-night raves long before ecstasy culture kicked in.

Warp Formed in Sheffield by Rob Mitchell and Steve Beckett, who had previously played together in an indie band, Warp Records was soon caught in the whirlwind of acid house and rave music of the late eighties. The first release, The Forgemasters'

'Track With No Name', featured DJ Parrot, whose DJ sets at the Jive Turkey had been influential on the duos conversion to house. The record was limited to a release of 500.

The next release, 'Nightmare on Wax's Dextrous', found greater circulation through a deal with King Street Records and by the advent of their sixth release, LFO's 'LFO', the label had notched up a top 20 hit while Tricky Disco established the label by reaching Number 14 in the UK charts.

However the defining sound of Warp wasn't to emerge until the release of their *Artificial Intelligence* compilation album in 1992. Here acts such as Autechre and Alex Paterson developed downbeat techno-fused tracks that were designed to be listened to rather than just danced to. The project continued with collaborations coming from Aphex Twin, Richie Hawtin, Plaid, Joey Beltram and Speedy J, while the label licensed Red Snappers' first three EPs from Flaw and signed the band.

Water and Energy Drinks The cure and cause of ecstasy-related deaths, the availability of water rather than alcohol from club bars became the (ahem) hot issue in post-acid house club culture. Clubs soon found they could make up for lost beer revenue by charging a fortune for bottled water. Irresponsible club owners sought to increase their profits by turning off cold taps in the toilets or, in some clubs in Ibiza, supplying the toilet sinks with seawater.

Club magazines such as *Mixmag* responded by listing water price and availability in their club listings, while some local councils set up a complaint service for clubbers to dob-in unscrupulous venues.

Drinks companies also sought to cash in on the soft drink phenomenon, introducing a new range of energy drinks and alcopops, which disguised booze in soft drink flavours and successfully wooed club kids back on to beer.

Andrew Weatherall Beginning the eighties working on building sites and film sets, Andrew Weatherall started DJing towards the end of the decade when he secured residencies at Shoom and Spectrum clubs during the acid house years. Hooking up with Terry Farley and Steve Mayes, Weatherall founded the *Boy's Own* fanzine, which went on to become the bible of the Balearic scene and later the *Boy's Own* record label.

Making his name as a DJ by fearlessly throwing tunes into the mix, he built his reputation for being the DJ who would have the records that no one else thought of playing – dropping 'Rising High' rave anthem in the middle of a progressive house set, or suddenly killing the beats to 90 b.p.m.

After remixing Primal Scream's 'Loaded', he became much sought-after and worked on records by artists from Galliano to Flowered Up and Björk. His status was secured by his supervision of the recording of Primal Scream's seminal *Screamadelica* album.

Setting up his own record label-cum-remix operation, Sabres Of Paradise, in 1993, he also signed a publishing deal with MCA music.

Weekend Clubbers A derogatory description for the exodus of out-of-town club-goers into city centre clubs on Friday and Saturday night, the term drips with élitism.

Ending up in a club full of weekenders is the serious clubber's worst nightmare. Naturally the targets of abuse make up the largest body of club clientele, without whom the clubs frequented by serious clubbers wouldn't exist.

Suburban DJs and clubs have often played a vital part in club history and nights such as Sound Of The Suburbs, in Kingston-upon-Thames, are frequently cited as seminal nights. In truth many who use the term have unspoken suburban roots.

Welsh Dance Culture During the late eighties Wales was still benefiting from the recent launch of S4C and the injection of funds it brought into Welsh culture. Not slow to spot a gift horse, a wave of aspiring musicians turned their attention to producing contemporary music in Welsh. Among the first Welsh language dance acts was Llwybr Llaethog, a Peckham/Wales-based rave band. Other acts such Ty Gwydr and Dat Blygu, who attracted a follower in John Peel, grew out of the Welsh language festival circuit (the Eisteddfod) and universities. In-jokes abounded, such as Ty Gwydr organising Reuf (pronounced raves) – Reu being Welsh slang for hash.

Meanwhile clubs such as Strictly Groovy in Swansea, run by DJ Lynsey and Chris, imported the rising stars of house music and introduced dance culture to the land of the leek. Always adaptable, Club Ifor Bach in Cardiff, a traditional Welsh club, became a hangout for bands such as the Super Furry Animals and Catatonia. Known as 'The Welsh Club' by English-speaking residents, it was set up for Welsh-speaking people. Ironically it became home to imported dance cultures such as hip hop nights run by the Hustler Allstars, drum 'n' bass and mod nights.

Meanwhile areas around Wales began to develop their own brand of club culture. Up For It, run by DJ Danny Slade at Chequers blew the roof off Tenby, hardcore and drum 'n' bass exploded in Newport and Bass FM, a pirate radio station in Cardiff, broadcast the good news.

Urban mythology also has it that the Super Furry Animals used to run raves in the hills. More reliable information says they were once involved in a band called Coffi Pawb, a drug reference that translates as Coffee For Everybody – you can still hear the cries of 'Cafeeeeeeen' on the dance floor.

World Music Invented as a marketing ploy by a group of record labels in the mid-eighties, world music sought to describe the eclectic scene playing anything from African and Latin dance rhythms to ethnic shindigs. Record companies such as Ben Mandelson's Globestyle, Joe Boyd's Hannibal, World Circuit, Earthworks, Discafrique and Cooking conspired to create a new form of dance by introducing roots music to Western ears and re-inventing indiginous sounds.

Labels sought to mix-and-match musicians from wildly different backgrounds, one of the more unlikely combinations being Cooking's Edward II, which married English folk instruments such as accordions with a jazz horn section. It had the Mad Professor on production and secured remixes from Mix Master Morris.

Meanwhile Akin Nawaz's Nation Records saw the possibilities of taking world music in a different direction. Spotting the potential of artists such as Talvin Singh long before the mainstream, Nation had a huge influence on clubs such as the Whirly Gig, transforming them from hippie affairs into full-on club experiences.

In the early nineties a new generation of promoters picked up on these mix-and-match themes and began pushing the boundaries of world music beyond its original marketing intention.

DJ Guy Gondwanna's club, Gondwanna, opened at the Road House in Manchester in 1993 and began playing traditional world music from Africa and Latin America. Moving to The Fitzcoraldo, a boat moored in Salford quays, Gondwanna renamed his club One Tree Island and argued that, to be worthy of the title, world music should reflect global music trends.

Teaming up with Mr Scruff and Stephano, they began playing a cut-up mix of break beats, hip hop and deep house – proclaiming them all to be valid components of world music. Meanwhile Pete Lawrence's Big Chill, at The Union Chapel in Islington, London, pursued similar themes. Pushing musical boundaries, fusion ran riot as ethnic sounds collided into contemporary production techniques.

Lest we forget:
Wagon Christ
West World
The Wild Bunch
Wildpitch
World Dance

Best we forget:
Waking up in a stranger's bed
Walking home because the cabs won't take you
Throwing a whitey

XFM Billed as London's alternative station, XFM started life in 1991 when Sammy Jacob secured a Restricted Service License (RSL) to broadcast to Reading Festival. It went on to secure an RSL in London between April and May 1992 and soon attracted the attention of Chris Parry, who joined Jacob at the station's helm. Together they secured a further RSL at the end of the year.

Focusing on alternative rock music during a period when bands such as Suede and Blur were building the UK's Brit pop reputation, the station soon attracted a considerable following as well as media attention. In June 1993 XFM, still only operating on RSLs, organised Great Xpectations in London's Finsbury Park, drawing a crowd of 27,000 people.

After two further RSLs and releasing two albums, the station went quiet while it applied for a full-on license. Broadcasting in earnest began in September 1997. In the meantime club culture had moved on from the strict four-four music policies of the early nineties.

Still committed to alternative rock, the station broadened its horizons and became a spokesperson for alternative dance beats – a trend that had been signposted by the inclusion of acts such as Transglobal Underground on XFM's second album.

Daytime DJs slipped between guitar tunes, Balearic, hip hop and underground house music (the only criteria being some sense of 'alternativeness') and specialist evening shows covered anything from rock to eclectic dance.

Meanwhile the comic twittering of Ricky Gervais, who specialised in interrupting DJs and turning their shows into a shambles, attracted cult status. Gervais' mission statement, to be the worst broadcaster on radio, was pursued admirably.

In summer 1998 XFM was bought by the major commercial radio station Capital Radio. The station dropped all its dance shows.

XL Formed as the harder wing of Citybeat Records, itself a collaboration between Groove and Beggars Banquet record shops, XL picked up on the early nineties hardcore scene. Initially importing Belgian and Dutch new beat artists, XL scored its first top 40 hit with T99's 'Anathasia'. Chart success was also found by the experimental signing of SL2, whose combination of break beat, sub bass and ragga samples laid the blueprint for jungle music and also found chart success with the release of 'On A Ragga Tip'.

Proving an ability to diversify, in 1993 XL signed Irish-American hip hop outfit House Of Pain. Their single, 'Jump Around', became a club anthem as well as a chart hit. The label's fortune was made by the arrival of Liam Howlett and the Prodigy. Gaining their reputation through live performances, they released 'Charly' which shot straight to number three in the charts. The subsequent release of *Music For The Jilted Generation* saw the album enter the charts at number one in July 1994.

In 1996 the band returned, having re-invented themselves as a brash big beat outfit, and stormed into the charts, as well as controversy, with 'Firestarter'. The Prodigy have now sold in excess of five million records worldwide – not bad for an independent dance label.

X Press 2 Originally formed by Rocky and Diesel, two collaborators hanging around the *Boy's Own* fanzine scene in the late eighties, X Press 2 soon picked up a third member. Ashley Beedle, a young north London DJ, had been working alongside Phil Perry at his Queen's club and was introduced to X Press 2 by Perry while they were recording their first single, 'Muzik X-press'.

Further club classics followed with the release of 'Rock 2 House', 'Tranz Europe X-press', 'Say What' and 'London X-press'. Having played together as DJs at the legendary *Boy's Own* parties, they teamed up as a house DJ outfit, pinching a hip hop sound system trick and playing their sets over four decks and two mixers.

Exhibiting their broad roots, the three joined with Dave Hill to form an eclectic, jazz-inspired, experimental offshoot, the Ballistic Brothers, to compliment X Press 2's house output. Meanwhile they continued to pursue joint and separate DJ careers, opening their own night, London Express, in Rathbone Place, in 1993 and gaining a residency at Cream in 1997.

Beedle finally split from both X Press 2 and the Ballistic Brothers in April 1998 to develop his solo career.

Lest we forget:
Club X, the nightmare TV club programme

Best we forget:
Club X

Y

Yello Switzerland's answer to Kraftwerk, Yello formed in 1977 when Boris Blank and Carlos Peron met at an automobile test lab. Constructing music using tape recorders as samplers, they linked up with vocalist-cum-millionaire and gambler, Dieter Meier (at the time singing with The Assholes), who came up with the name.

After releasing a single on the Periphery Perfume label in 1979, they landed a contract with San Francisco-label Ralph and released their first album, *Solid Pleasure*, in 1980.

'Bostisch', the second single release from the album, broke in the USA as an underground dance anthem, having found favour with Afrika Bambaataa and NYC black music station WBLS.

In the UK 'Bostisch' found a home in the electronic hearts of the New Romantic movement, although chart success alluded them until 1983 when they released two singles and an EP on Stiff. After their third album, *You Gotta Say Yes To Another Excess*, Peron left the band.

By the release of 'The Race' as a remix, in 1988, Yello had established themselves as avant-garde, international hit-makers and Yello records found their way into emerging acid house DJ sets.

Alongside their musical output, the band maintained a strong visual element, producing their own videos and writing film scores. They also run the Solid Pleasure Swiss dance label.

Yellow Productions Despite the popularity of Parisian clubs such as Les Bain Douche among UK clubbers in the 1980s, French music had remained singularly despised or ridiculed – even by the French.

In the early nineties the Sylvie Vartan image of French music was kicked into touch by a new wave of Parisian hip hop, which, led by MC Solaar and Yellow Productions, appeared to explode from nowhere.

Yellow Productions, an experimental French dance label, was set up by Christopher 'The French Kiss' LeFriant and DJ Yellow in 1993 – inspired by their frustration at not being able to record, DJ or even buy quality French dance music.

Drawing influences from hip hop, jazz, downbeat and house, the label pulled together the cream of Parisian artists such as Dimitris, DJ Cam, Mighty Bop, Kid Loco, Bob Sinclar and Etienne de Crecy. Releases such as 'Yellow 357', 'Sacre Bleu' and 'Super Discount' have drawn consistent critical acclaim.

Yellowman Born an albino, Yellowman rose to fame as a Jamaican dancehall toaster in the early eighties. Subverting his light skin colour, which was usually derided in Jamaica, he played on his unusual looks, using explicit lyrics to brag about his sexual prowess and general ability to bed women.

He was soon dubbed 'Mr Sexy' by adoring female fans, while his lyrics inspired controversy for their apparent sexism and homophobia. Despite this, his vocal style and lyrical content proved to be hugely influential, shaping the ragga music that was later popularised by artists such as Shabba Ranks.

At his height, Yellowman was a prolific, if somewhat inconsistent artist. In 1982 he had 40 records on release in Jamaica. By the nineties he had been eclipsed by younger, and equally controversial, artists.

Young Disciples A London trio who shot to fame with their sublime *Road To Freedom* album in 1991, the Young Disciples comprised Marco, Femi and guest vocalist Carleen Anderson. Their music combined hip hop with jazz inflections in the traditions of US artists such as Gang Star and the band rapidly became Talkin' Loud's flagship act. Anderson wrote most of the lyrics and much of the music. She came from an awesome musical heritage: her mother Vicki Anderson was a backing vocalist with James Brown; her stepfather, Bobby Byrd, was a jazz-funk trumpet legend; while her cousin was Jehlisa Anderson.

After Anderson left to pursue her solo career, in which she pointedly continued to play many of the songs she had written with the Young Disciples, the group ceased to function, although Marco and in particular Femi continued to play out as DJs using the Young Disciples banner for several years.

Lest we forget:
Yellow Magic Orchestra
Sydney Youngblood's 'If Only I Could'

Best we forget:
Yazoo
Yazz

Z

ZE Formed by Mike Zilkha in New York, ZE Records produced a string of the early eighties dance hits, breaking acts such as Was Not Was, Kid Creole And The Coconuts, Coati Mundi and Bill Laswell's Material through compilation albums such as 1980's *Dance Ze Dance* and 1981's *A Christmas Record* – featuring 'The Waitresses' Christmas Wrapping'.

The label's output, which was licensed to and popularised by Island in the UK, introduced UK clubbers to funk, Latin and rap themes that were later to spawn the UK's hip hop, Latin and rare groove communities.

Meanwhile Kid Creole took their funky, Latin, calypso crossover music to a wider audience, scoring UK hits in 1982 with tracks such as 'Stool Pigeon' and 'I'm A Wonderful Thing (Baby)'.

Zion Train Formed in 1990 and centred around Colin C, who once had connections with the Spiral Tribe, Zion Train were a north London collective who blurred the distinction between dub music and house music with releases such as 'Follow Like Wolves'.

Their first releases, a batch of limited-edition 7in dub records such as 'Power One', 'Power Two' and Jah Hold's 'The Key' were released on their own Zion imprint and were immediate sell-outs, becoming sound system favourites in the early nineties. Their first album, *Passage To India*, was a mellow dub plate but it succeeded in finding the band a wider audience.

Hooking up with the Tassilli Players, a broad alliance of musicians from Africa, India, Japan, the Caribbean and Europe, they produced an album, *Great Sporting Moments In Dub*, and entered the world of remixing, finding clients in Gary Clail, Knights Of The Occasional Table, The Shaman, Loop Guru and many others.

Their next releases displayed a new set of influences from the rave scene and the acid house explosion, prefiguring other artists who were to match dub sounds with up-beat tempos. On the strength of their crossover success, they established a new imprint, Universal Egg.

Surprisingly their next album, *Natural Wonders Of The World In Dub*, returned to their mellow dub roots, initiating a consistent pattern of releasing up-beat 12in singles and downbeat albums. Moving to China Records in 1995, they built their reputation playing live sets across Europe in the late nineties, combining roots dub music with up-beat techno.

Zippies The term and culture of Zippy was promoted by Frazer Clark, a long-serving, unreformed hippie and veteran of Stonehenge festivals who saw acid house and rave culture as recruiting ground for hippie ideals. It combined the shamanist paganism of new age travellers with the hi-tech culture of raves.

The zippy name stands for 'Zen-inspired professional pagans'. Ditching hippie Luddite mistrust of technology, zippies sought to harness modern communication tools such as the Internet to create an alternative, self-governing culture.

In 1993 Clark, who edits the *Encyclopedia Psychedelia*, got together with Brighton-based rave organisers and opened the

Megatripolis club. The night strove to form a new consciousness through the collective experience of clubbing and, alongside psychedelic trance and ambient music, featured a Parallel University, where speakers such as Timothy Leary and Terence McKenna would give lectures.

Although Megatripolis eventually came to a sticky end after the promoters fell out, the psychedelic torch continues to burn in clubs such as Escape From Samsara, at The Fridge, and Mega Dog, at the Rocket, in London.

Zippies are fiercely international, organising live Internet links between club nights across the world. In 1994 Clark attempted to unite the US hippie Rainbow Family with the UK scene, holding a World Unity festival in the Grand Canyon. The event attracted huge media coverage, resulting in it being swamped by journalists and avoided by hippies and zippies.

In common with earlier psychedelic movements, zippies are passionate about mind-bending drugs and love LSD, MDMA, DMT, Goa, Thailand, Amsterdam and north Wales during mushroom season.

Zoom Records Set in the site of the former Soul II Soul shop in Camden, Zoom Records shop and label were run by DJ Billy Nasty and Dave Wesson. Releasing an unpredictable output that was as at home with the jazzy hip hop of 3:6 Philly as it was with the hard techno of Ubik, the label came to prominence with 1989's Red Ninja UK hip hop release. The shop's reputation should have assured it a long life, but it closed, being turned into a Tower Records branch, in 1996.

ZTT Market leaders in the UK's remix culture, which dominates today's dance, pop and indie releases, ZTT Records was formed in 1983 by Trevor Horn, Jill Sinclair and Paul Morley. The title is taken from Zang Tuum Tumb, an obscure phrase from the turn-of-the-century, Italian, Futurist book *The Art Of Noise*. Zang Tuum Tumb is said to describe the sound of Russian guns in the Crimean War.

ZTT's first hit came almost immediately with Frankie Goes To Hollywood's 'Relax', which rocketed through the club scene into the charts. The label's association with remix culture was established with the release of no less than 14 different versions of 'Relax', much to the perplexity of an untrained, record-buying public. Assumed to be a cynical marketing ploy, Horn maintains the remix-mania started by accident after he included a 'Sex Mix' on the original 12in release of 'Relax'. Complaints that the track was too offensive spawned another shorter remix, with the offensive parts removed. This in turn led to complaints that people couldn't find the original – and so on.

Horn had discovered the power of 12in mixes while clubbing in New York in 1983 and immediately rushed back to the studio and laid down the 'New York Mix' of 'Relax', which alone sold over a million copies.

ZZT went on to form an eight-year partnership with the Warner Group, before heading off on their own again.

Goodnight

Disco Biscuits

EDITED BY SARAH CHAMPION

DISCO BISCUITS is an anthology of new stories capturing the hedonistic spirit of the nineties – from illegal raves to corporate club culture. It includes nineteen anarchic, out-there tales of drug, sex, dancefloors, dealers, police and DJs.

At a warehouse party, rival football hooligans are united by Ecstasy. In the sweltering heat of a Mediterranean Island, things get very strange when a hypnotist is employed to brainwash clubbers. In a future Manchester, sinful dancing and natural-born DJs are outlawed by the authorities. Riots erupt when an outdoor party is busted by police, the sound being sampled and amplified through the speakers. A chill-out club goes disastrously wrong, with the arrival of a psychotic ex-con, fresh out of jail. A drunken night-out becomes surreal with the discovery of a mystery suitcase.

In Thailand a 'beach guru' makes preparations for a Full Moon Party. And chaos descends on a holiday jet to Alicante when a jungle sound-system begins broadcasting through the cabin PA . . .

SCEPTRE